iPad 2

the missing manual®

The book that should have been in the box®

J.D. Biersdorfer

Beijing | Cambridge | Farnham | Köln | Sebastopol | Tokyo

iPad 2: The Missing Manual, Second Edition

BY J.D. BIERSDORFER

Published by O'Reilly Media, Inc., 1005 Gravenstein Highway North, Sebastopol, CA 95472.

O'Reilly books may be purchased for educational, business, or sales promotional use. Online editions are also available for most titles (*safari.oreilly.com*). For more information, contact our corporate/institutional sales department: 800.998.9938 or corporate@*oreilly.com*.

Editor: Peter McKie

Production Editor: Dan Fauxsmith

Illustrations: Rob Romano, Katherine Ippoliti, and J.D. Biersdorfer

Indexer: Julie Hawks

Proofreader: Marcia Simmons

Cover Designer: Karen Montgomery

Interior Designers: Ron Bilodeau and J.D. Biersdorfer

Print History:

May 2010	First Edition.
April 2011	Second Edition.

ISBN: 978-1-449-30173-6

[TM]   [2011-06-10]

Contents

Chapter 4

Chapter 5

Chapter 6

Chapter 9

Chapter 10

Chapter 11

The Missing Credits

About the Author

J.D. Biersdorfer (author) is the author of several O'Reilly books, including *iPod: The Missing Manual, Best iPhone Apps, Second Edition*, and *Netbooks: The Missing Manual*. She's been writing the weekly computer Q&A column for *The New York Times* since 1998 and has covered everything from 17th-century Indian art to the world of female hackers for the newspaper. She's also written articles for the *AIGA Journal of Graphic Design, Budget Travel, The New York Times Book Review*, and *Rolling Stone*. She studied in the Theater & Drama program at Indiana University and now spends her limited spare moments playing the banjo badly, drinking copious amounts of tea, and watching BBC World News. Email: *jd.biersdorfer@gmail.com*.

About the Creative Team

Peter McKie (editor) learned the ins and outs of his iPad 2 by editing this book. He has a master's degree in journalism from Boston University and every once in a while sneaks into abandoned buildings to take photos. Email: *pmckie@oreilly.com*.

Dan Fauxsmith (production editor) lives in Belmont, Mass. From time to time he adds photographs of plants to his website (*www.theplantbase.com*). Email: *dfauxsmith@oreilly.com*.

Julie Hawks (indexer) is an indexer for the Missing Manual series. She is currently pursuing a masters degree in Religious Studies while discovering the joys of warm winters in the Carolinas. Email: *juliehawks@gmail.com*.

Marcia Simmons (proofreader) is a writer and editor living in the San Francisco Bay Area. She's author of the book DIY Cocktails. Blog: *www.marciaisms.com*.

Acknowledgements

I would like to thank David Pogue for getting me into the book business back in 2002 and for being a terrific editor on our mutual projects over the years. Also thanks to editor Peter McKie for making sense of things during the mad scramble, and to all the Missing Manual folks at O'Reilly Media—especially Monica Kamsvaag, Cheryl Deras, and Frank Deras for the custom iPad photography gracing these pages.

Big thanks to Mac guru Alan Yacavone for sharing his knowledge and to Matthew Silver for the valiant loan of his brand-new iPad 2 for a photo shoot. Katherine Ippoliti's graphics work in this edition also deserves a shout-out.

And thanks to the friends who don't get offended when I go into the Deadline Zone, and to family (especially and most importantly, Betsy Book) for putting up with me during the long hours with the show tunes and bluegrass blasting forth from the writing corner.

—J.D. Biersdorfer

The Missing Manual Series

Missing Manuals are witty, superbly written guides to computer products that don't come with printed manuals (which is just about all of them). Each book features a handcrafted index.

Recent and upcoming titles include:

Access 2007: The Missing Manual by Matthew MacDonald

Access 2010: The Missing Manual by Matthew MacDonald

Buying a Home: The Missing Manual by Nancy Conner

CSS: The Missing Manual, Second Edition, by David Sawyer McFarland

Creating a Web Site: The Missing Manual, Second Edition, by Matthew MacDonald

David Pogue's Digital Photography: The Missing Manual by David Pogue

Droid X: The Missing Manual by Preston Gralla

Dreamweaver CS4: The Missing Manual by David Sawyer McFarland

Dreamweaver CS5: The Missing Manual by David Sawyer McFarland

Excel 2007: The Missing Manual by Matthew MacDonald

Excel 2010: The Missing Manual by Matthew MacDonald

Facebook: The Missing Manual, Second Edition, by E.A. Vander Veer

FileMaker Pro 10: The Missing Manual by Susan Prosser and Geoff Coffey

FileMaker Pro 11: The Missing Manual by Susan Prosser and Stuart Gripman

Flash CS4: The Missing Manual by Chris Grover with E.A. Vander Veer

Flash CS5: The Missing Manual by Chris Grover

Google Apps: The Missing Manual by Nancy Conner

The Internet: The Missing Manual by David Pogue and J.D. Biersdorfer

iMovie '11 & iDVD: The Missing Manual by David Pogue and Aaron Miller

iPad: The Missing Manual by J.D. Biersdorfer

iPhone: The Missing Manual, Second Edition, by David Pogue

iPhone App Development: The Missing Manual by Craig Hockenberry

iPod: The Missing Manual, Ninth Edition, by J.D. Biersdorfer and David Pogue

JavaScript: The Missing Manual by David Sawyer McFarland

Living Green: The Missing Manual by Nancy Conner

Mac OS X: The Missing Manual, Leopard Edition by David Pogue

Mac OS X Snow Leopard: The Missing Manual by David Pogue

Microsoft Project 2007: The Missing Manual by Bonnie Biafore

Microsoft Project 2010: The Missing Manual by Bonnie Biafore

Netbooks: The Missing Manual by J.D. Biersdorfer

Office 2007: The Missing Manual by Chris Grover, Matthew MacDonald, and E.A. Vander Veer

Office 2010: The Missing Manual by Nancy Connor, Chris Grover, and Matthew MacDonald

Office 2010 for Macintosh: The Missing Manual by Chris Grover

Palm Pre: The Missing Manual by Ed Baig

PCs: The Missing Manual by Andy Rathbone

Personal Investing: The Missing Manual by Bonnie Biafore

Photoshop CS4: The Missing Manual by Lesa Snider

Photoshop CS5: The Missing Manual by Lesa Snider

Photoshop Elements 8 for Mac: The Missing Manual by Barbara Brundage

Photoshop Elements 8 for Windows: The Missing Manual by Barbara Brundage

Photoshop Elements 9: The Missing Manual by Barbara Brundage

PowerPoint 2007: The Missing Manual by E.A. Vander Veer

Premiere Elements 8: The Missing Manual by Chris Grover

Introduction

Steve Jobs revealed the original iPad on January 27, 2010, finally confirming rumors that had been swirling for years: Apple was making a tablet computer! And when that first iPad model hit stores a few months later, the public snapped up 300,000 the day it went on sale.

Less than a year later after the first one arrived, Apple put out an even better iPad in March 2011. Thinner, lighter, faster, and equipped with a pair of cameras, the iPad 2 created its own huge lines around the country when it went on sale. Apple's inventory pretty much sold out the first weekend.

So what's the big deal? Tablet computers are nothing new. Tech companies have tried the concept since the 1990s. But those flat slabs never caught on for a variety of reasons. Some required input with an easy-to-lose stylus; some had slow, unresponsive touchscreens; and some were so heavy it felt like you were hauling around a patio flagstone that happened to run Windows XP. Most of the public took one look and went: "Nah."

So why has the iPad proven so popular, even as competitors rush to put their own clunkier imitations out there, lurching for Apple's thunder? One theory: combine a growing desire for Internet access and a shift to digital music, books, and video with a sophisticated, fast, lightweight touchscreen device and you have a gadget perfectly suited to the emerging world of personal media devices. Sure, the iPhone does all that, but you don't have to squint on the iPad. The iPad is both an evolution and a solution.

And thanks to the thousands of third-party apps already available, the iPad can move beyond being just a platter that serves up media and Internet content. In fact, it can pretty much be whatever you want it to be.

And come to think of it, that's probably why it's so popular.

How to Use This Book

The small card that Apple includes in each iPad box is enough to get your tablet up and running, charged, and ready to play on the Internet. But you probably want to know more about how the iPad works, all the great things it can do, and where to find its coolest features. This book gives you more iPad info than that wee card. It's pre-printed for your convenience, neatly organized by task and topic, *and* it has nice big color pictures.

About→These→Arrows

Throughout this book, and throughout the Missing Manual series, you'll find sentences like this one: "Open the View→Column Browser→On Top" menu. That's shorthand for a longer series of instructions that go something like this: "Go to the menu bar in iTunes, click the View menu, select the Column Browser submenu, and then slide over to the On Top entry." Our shorthand system keep things more snappy than these long, drawn-out instructions.

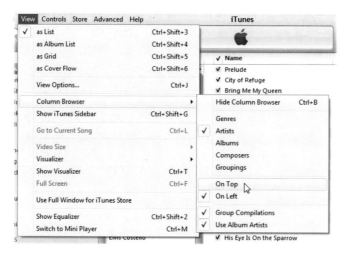

The Very Basics

To use this book, and indeed to use a computer, you need to know a few basics. This book assumes that you're familiar with a few terms and concepts:

- **Clicking.** To *click* means to point the arrow cursor at something on the screen and then to press and release the clicker button on the mouse (or laptop trackpad). To *double-click*, of course, means to click twice in rapid succession, again without moving the cursor at all. To *drag* means to move the cursor *while* pressing the button.

When you're told to *Ctrl+click* something on a PC, or *c-click* something on the Mac, you click while pressing the Ctrl or c key (both of which are near the Space Bar). But this is an iPad book. You'll tap more than click.

- **Menus.** The *menus* are the words at the top of your screen or window: File, Edit, and so on. Click one to make a list of commands appear, as though they're written on a window shade you just pulled down.

- **Keyboard shortcuts.** Jumping up to menus in iTunes takes time. That's why you'll find keyboard quickies that perform the same menu functions sprinkled throughout the book—Windows shortcuts first, followed by Mac shortcuts in parentheses, like this: "To quickly summon the Preferences box, press Ctrl+comma (c-comma)."

If you've mastered this much information, you have all the technical background you need to enjoy *iPad 2: The Missing Manual.*

About MissingManuals.com

This book helps you get the most out of your iPad. As you read through it, you'll find references to websites that offer additional resources. Each reference includes the site's URL, but you can save yourself some typing by going to this book's Missing CD page at *http://missingmanuals.com/cds/ipad2mm/*.

There, you'll find clickable links to the sites mentioned in this book.

The Missing CD page also offers corrections and updates to the book. To see them, click the View Errata link. You're invited to submit corrections and updates yourself by clicking "Submit your own errata" on the same page. To keep this book as up to date and accurate as possible, each time we print more copies, we'll make any confirmed corrections you've suggested.

While you're online, you can register this book at *http://tinyurl.com/yo82k3*. Registering means we can send you updates about the book, and you'll be eligible for special offers like discounts on future editions of *iPad 2: The Missing Manual.*

Safari® Books Online

 Safari® Books Online is an on-demand digital library that lets you search over 7,500 technology books and videos.

With a subscription, you can read any page and watch any video from our library. Access new titles before they're available in print. Copy and paste code samples, organize your favorites, download chapters, bookmark key sections, create notes, print out pages, and benefit from tons of other time-saving features.

O'Reilly Media has uploaded this book to the Safari Books Online service. To have full digital access to this book and others on similar topics from O'Reilly and other publishers, sign up for free at *http://my.safaribooksonline.com*.

Get to Know Your iPad

Sure, you've seen the concept of the iPad before. It's a popular prop on futuristic science-fiction shows like *Star Trek: The Next Generation*: a flat slab of a computer, wirelessly connected to a network that instantly pulls down any information you need, right then and there. (In fact, in the *Star Trek* universe, that device was called a PADD, short for Personal Access Display Device.)

But one thing those movie and TV gadgets never seemed to have is a manual so you could find out things like, say, how to turn down the sound when someone asks you a question during a heated game of Angry Birds, or how to get back to the screen where your photos live.

Here on 21st-century Earth, these things may not be obvious for new iPad owners, but that's where this book comes in. In this chapter, you'll learn how to navigate your iPad so you can find the programs you want, jack it into your computer to load it up with movies and photos, and make sure you get it charged up for a full day of fun.

The science fiction is no longer fiction; the future is now.

Turn the iPad On and Off

Think of Apple's iPod, iMac, and iPhone. In addition to starting with "i," all these products are sleek gadgets with a minimum of buttons to disrupt their smooth skin. The iPad is no exception.

Run your finger along the iPad's top edge and you'll find a small black button on the right (circled). It's got a long name: On/Off, Sleep/Wake.

Here's what it does:

- **It turns the iPad off and on.** To turn your iPad off completely, so that it gobbles no power at all, press and hold this button down until you see an on-screen arrow confirming your request. Touch the arrow with your finger and slide it along the screen from left to right. If you're not going to use your 'Pad for a few days, a total shutdown is the way to conserve as much battery life as possible.

  To turn the iPad back on, press the On/Off button again for a second or two, until you see the Apple logo. After a minute or so of  boot-up gyrations, you're back in business.

- **It puts the iPad to sleep and wakes it up.** Tap the button briefly to turn off the iPad's screen and put it in power-saving Sleep (standby) mode. To wake the iPad from its power nap, quickly press the button again. (You may also need to wake your iPad if you leave it untended for more than a few minutes, because it goes to sleep all by itself to save power. To change its nod-off settings, see page 281.)

Whenever you turn on the iPad or wake it up from its electronic slumber, you end up on a locked Home screen (unless you have one of Apple's Smart Covers; see page 296). To get to the iPad's goodies, swipe your finger along the slider in the direction of the arrow. Why does the Home screen lock itself? Because on a touchscreen device, one unintended tap when the 'Pad's in your

pocket or bag can turn on a program without you knowing it, and *poof*, there goes *that* battery charge.

Use the Mute/Lock and Volume Buttons

The buttons on the right edge of the iPad control the audio for movies, music, and other apps that make noise. Here they are, from top to bottom:

❶ **Side Switch**. The small black nub on the iPad's right edge does one of two things, and it's your call. Out of the box, the switch is a Mute button that silences the iPad's audio alerts when you slide it down until you see an orange dot. (Slide the button up to restore your alerts.)

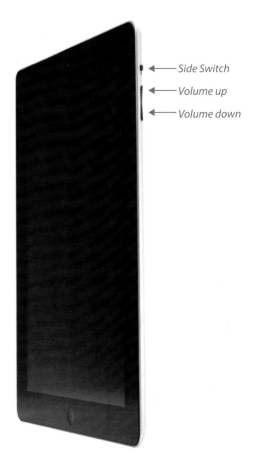

Side Switch

Volume up

Volume down

If you don't need a Mute button, you can turn the switch into a screen-orientation lock that keeps the iPad's display in either the vertical or horizontal orientation so the screen doesn't spin around as you move about. To lock the screen, press the Home button and tap Settings→General→"Use Side Switch to" and choose Lock Rotation. Choose Mute to go back to the way things were.

If you use the side switch to mute your iPad, you lock the screen by double-clicking the Home button, swiping right-to-left in the panel of apps that appears, and tapping the Screen Orientation Lock (🔒). If you use the switch to lock the display, you mute the iPad by turning the volume all the way down, as described next.

❷ **Volume.** Press the top half of this rocker-style switch to increase the volume of the iPad's speaker or your earbuds, if you're wearing them (see page 5). Press the bottom half of the switch to lower the volume. The iPad displays a little volume graphic onscreen so you can see where you are on the Relative Scale of Loudness.

Connect Through iPad Jacks and Ports

While the iPad's innards are full of state-of-the-art electronics, the outside isn't very complex at all—just four buttons (On/Off-Sleep/Wake, Volume, Side Switch, and, discussed on page 6, the Home button). The outside of the iPad sports two jacks where you plug in cords. Here's what you do with 'em.

❶ **Headphone Jack.** Although it doesn't come with its own set of headphones, as iPods and iPhones do, the iPad does offer a headphone jack on its top-left edge. You can plug in any pair of earbuds or headphones that come with the standard 3.5-millimeter stereo miniplug. Page 5 has more on that.

❷ **Dock Connector.** The flat port on the iPad's bottom edge is called the Dock Connector. You plug the provided USB cable in here to connect your iPad to your computer for battery-charging, as well as for music, iBook, and video fill-ups from your iTunes library. This thin port has been a fixture on iPods since 2003, which means that certain accessories, like stereo-audio docks meant for an iPod, may work with your iPad—so check the tech specs before you buy anything new. The Dock Connector snaps right into the tablet's optional external keyboard, too (page 31).

 Note You may notice two other features on the iPad's outer edges (no, sadly, neither is a USB port or an SD card slot). The small hole in the center of the top edge is the iPad's microphone for Voice Memos, FaceTime, and other "listening" apps. And the perforated patch on the back near the Dock Connector hides the iPad's external speaker (which many say sounds better than the original iPad's).

Add Earbuds and Earphones

Want to listen privately on your iPad? Back in the old days, the only headphones you could get came with a cord attached, and those still work just fine. But if you want to free yourself from wires while you lay back, relax, and listen to a Bach cello suite, get a pair of Bluetooth stereo headphones that connect wirelessly to the Bluetooth chip inside your iPad. Then, your only entanglement will be mind with music.

Here's how you get either type of headphone to work on the iPad:

- **Wired.** Pretty much any pair of headphones or earbuds with the ubiquitous 3.5mm stereo plug fits the iPad's headphone jack. (Why, yes, you *can* use the familiar white earbuds from your iPod if you want.) Just be sure to push the plug firmly into the jack so it fully connects.

- **Bluetooth.** When you shop for stereo Bluetooth headphones, look for those advertised as *A2DP*; they're designed to play back music in stereo. To get them to work, you need to pair your headphones with the iPad. (*Pairing* means introducing two Bluetooth devices so they can communicate with each other; you only have to do this the first time you use the two devices together.)

The 'phone manual tells you which button to push on the headphones to pair the two. As for the iPad, start on the Home screen and tap Settings→General→Bluetooth. Turn Bluetooth on. The iPad looks around and once it finds the 'phones, it lists them by name. If the headphones require a passkey (listed in the manual), the iPad keyboard appears so you can type it in. Once paired, the iPad screen says *Connected* next to a headphones icon, and the sound now plays over your wireless connection.

Tip On some Bluetooth headsets, a small transceiver plugs into the iPad jack and communicates with the 'phones. If you have one of these, you don't need to turn on the iPad's Bluetooth chip; the transceiver does the communicating for you.

Find the Home Button

There's only one switch on the front of the iPad: the Home button (circled below). This round, gently indented switch sits in the bottom-center of the iPad's black or white picture frame (known as a bezel in geek-speak). You'll probably use this button more than any other in your iPad adventures.

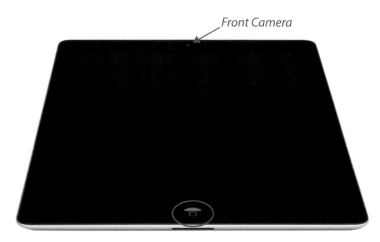

Front Camera

The Home button handles a few tasks. For one, it *always* takes you Home—back to the iPad's main screen—where you'll find all your apps. Since the iPad displays only one program at a time, you also use the Home button to switch from one app to another. You could be waist-deep in a Keynote presentation, for example (page 170), and want to watch an episode of *Glee*. Press the Home button to close Keynote (and automatically save your file) and go back to the main iPad screen, where you can tap the Videos icon to get to your shows.

While your iPad *displays* only one program at a time, it can *run* several apps at once, a process known as *multitasking*. The Home button is your ticket to switching among these *active* apps, too (flip to page 9 for more).

Finally, second-generation iPads come with two tiny cameras built into the tablet's front and back. The camera on the front, which looks like a small pin-hole, is smack dab in the middle of the bezel's top edge. This is the camera you use for FaceTime chats and wacky Photo Booth self-portraits (Chapter 6). You use the rear camera, the small round lens below the Sleep/Wake switch, to snap still pictures and shoot videos. See Chapter 6 for more on that as well.

 Note The iPad 2 also has a built-in *gyroscope*, an orientation sensor that tells the tablet which way you're holding and moving it. Games (Chapter 9) that incorporate the gyroscope functions can be even more thrilling to play since they move with you.

Tour the Home Screen Icons

Even if you don't add a single app to your iPad, it comes with a whole bunch of programs ready to use. These include personal-organization tools like Calendar, Contacts, and Notes; a Maps app so you can find your way around; FaceTime for video chat; YouTube for web videos; Camera and Photo Booth for picture fun; Game Center for games; and a Videos app to play movies you store on the iPad.

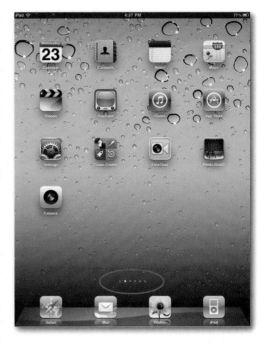

The iTunes and App Store icons take you to Apple's online stores, while the Settings icon lets you adjust the way the iPad and its programs behave. Along the bottom of the screen, you'll find icons for Safari (the iPad's web browser), Mail, Photos, and iPod—the latter is where all your iTunes music hangs out. Don't worry, you'll learn about all these apps in Chapter 6.

More Home-Screen Tricks

Once you start adding programs to your iPad, you may find the Home screen getting a little crowded. Fortunately, the iPad lets you have more than one Home screen—in fact, you can have 11 of 'em.

To navigate among them, flick your finger across the iPad's surface. The small white dots at the bottom of the screen (circled above) indicate how many Home screens you have and which one you're on.

Want to rearrange your icons? Press and hold one for a few seconds until all the icons start wiggling. As shown at the right, use your finger to drag them around to new locations—or off the edge of one screen and onto the next. Press the Home button to stop the Dance of the Icons.

Make Home Screen App Folders

Even with a generous 11 Home screens, some app-loving folk can quickly fill them all with icons. In addition, some people might prefer a tidier way to group their apps, rather than dragging them around to different pages.

That's where Home-screen *folders* can make everything better. You can group up to 20 apps in a single folder—which looks like an icon with little icons nestled inside it (right). Putting apps in folders saves screen space and keeps common ones corralled.

To create a folder, press and hold an icon until it wiggles, and then drag it on top of an icon that you want in the same folder. A box appears with a generic name for the folder, like "Games" (see below). You can keep this name or replace it with one of your own, like "1980s Arcade Games." Once you set up a folder, you can drag up to 10 more apps into it. Tap the screen to close the folder.

To get to an app inside a folder, tap the folder to open it, and then tap the app. (Later forget where you stashed an app? Swipe left to right as far as you can go—that brings you to the iPad's uber search box, the Spotlight screen. Type in an app name to search for it, and then tap the app open from the list of search results.)

If you change your mind and want to pull an app out of a folder, press and hold its icon to start the Wiggle Dance. Now you can drag it out of the folder and back to its place on the Home screen proper.

To get rid of a *folder*, press an icon to get them all wiggling. Drag all the apps out of the folder and back to the Home screen. When you take out the last app, the folder disappears.

Use the Home Button to Switch Apps

Putting apps in folders helps you organize your iPad. But it doesn't save you a lot of time when you're in the middle of one thing and want to switch over to another app real quick—like if you're reading email and want to nip out and turn on your Pandora radio app so you can be entertained while you shovel out your Inbox. Who wants to go all the way out to the Home screen for that?

Fortunately, the iPad (iOS 4.2 and later) has a shortcut: Click the Home button twice. When you do, a row of icons sprouts from the bottom of the screen (below).

This row represents the apps you've recently used. Tap one to quickly switch to it. Turn on Pandora, check your sports scores, or do whatever you wanted to do. When you finish, double-click the Home button again. When the row of icons appears, tap the one for the app you were initially using to get back to it.

If the app you want isn't in this initial row, flick the icons from right to left until you find it—all your recently used apps should be here.

To weed out apps that you haven't used in forever from the row, press down on an icon until the ● symbol appears. Tap it to remove the app from the recently used list—but not from the iPad itself. Press the Home button when you finish.

In addition to displaying your most recent apps, the Home button double-click offers another time-saver. Instead of flicking right to left to see the recent apps, flick left to right to find the music playback controls. This saves you the trouble of going all the way out to the music app's Now Playing screen to skip a track in a playlist. And if you opted to make the iPad's side switch a Mute button (page 3) but get agitated when the iPad screen reorients itself as you try to read an eBook in bed, swipe left and tap the first icon, the circular arrow in the left corner (at right). That locks the iPad into portrait mode no matter which way you hold it—until you tap this icon again to unlock the screen.

Install iTunes on Your Computer

To set up your iPad—and copy over music, videos, and other stuff from your Windows PC or Mac—you need to install Apple's iTunes multimedia, multi-function jukebox program on your desktop computer (you'll set up your iPad in just a second). With iTunes, you also get Apple's QuickTime software—a video helper for iTunes. Don't worry, it's all free and just a web download away:

❶ **Fire up your computer's web browser and point it to** *www.itunes.com/downloads*.

❷ **Click the "Download Now" button.** (Turn off the "Email me…" and "Keep me up to date…" checkboxes to spare yourself future marketing missives.) Wait for the file to download.

❸ **When the file lands on your hard drive, double-click the** *iTunesSetup.exe* **file.** If you use a Mac, double-click the *Install iTunes.pkg* file to start the installation. If your Mac's younger than six years old, you probably already have iTunes installed. Go to ❖→Software Update and ask your Mac to see if there's a newer version of iTunes, just in case.

❹ **Follow the screens until the software installer says it's done.**

You may need to restart your computer after you install iTunes. Once that's done, you're ready to connect your new iPad to your computer.

 The hardware and operating-system requirements needed to run iTunes are listed below the Download Now button. If you have an older computer, it's worth a glance just to make sure your rig can handle the program.

Connect to Your Computer

Odds are you had that iPad out of its box about 5 seconds after you got it, running your hands over its smooth edges, admiring its tapered thinness and high-gloss screen. In addition to that sleek tablet, you'll find the following in the box:

❶ A white USB cable with Apple's flat 30-pin Dock Connector plug on one end and a standard flat USB plug on the other.

❷ A square-shaped10-watt USB power adapter.

❸ A little card of basic quick-start information that's not nearly as fun or as colorful as this book.

What you want right now is the USB cable. Connect the small, narrow end to your computer's USB port and the wide, flat end to the iPad. The first time you connect, the iTunes Setup Assistant launches and walks you through a few steps to get your iPad ready to go.

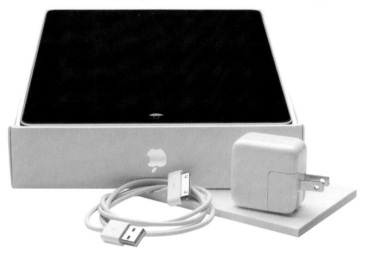

 If you have an iPad with 3G service from AT&T, you'll find a tiny piece of wire that looks like a paperclip stuck to the iPad's pamphlet folder. This highly technical piece of gear serves one purpose: to open the SIM card tray on an AT&T iPad (Verizon iPads don't use SIM cards). You insert the pin into a tiny hole on the left edge of the iPad and pop open the tray. SIM cards (short for Subscriber Identity Module) store information about your AT&T cellular account. The card is so tiny, it's technically a *micro-SIM* card, but you may wonder why you need to eject the card in the first place. Most of the time, you don't need to bother with it at all—unless the iPad has 3G troubles and you need to replace the card, or if you travel internationally and want to pop in a card from a local carrier for data service.

Set Up Your iPad in iTunes

Unless you had a kind soul in a bright t-shirt set up your iPad at the Apple Store, you'll be using iTunes to activate, register, and set up your brand new tablet. The first time you plug in your iPad (after you install iTunes, of course), the Setup Assistant leaps into action, asking you to name your slab and if you'd like to sync all the content on your computer to the tablet.

If you use iTunes already to manage an iPod or iPhone, odds are you already have a healthy media library on your computer. And if you've had an iPad before, iTunes offers to put the content from your old iPad onto your new one.

Depending on the size of your new iPad's drive, you may be able to fit all your stuff on it—or maybe not, if you have more than 16, 32, or 64 gigabytes of digital treasures on your computer. If you have less than that and want to take it all with you, just click the Done button in the Setup box. iTunes loads a copy of everything in its library onto your iPad. If you have more media than your iPad has storage, iTunes loads up your 'Pad until it's full.

The iPad also includes a VoiceOver feature, which is part of Apple's accessibility software (described at *www.apple.com/accessibility/voiceover*). VoiceOver is a screen reader for the visually impaired that announces menu names, icons, and titles out loud. If you're not prompted to turn it on during the setup process, click Configure Universal Access in the Summary screen with your iPad connected to iTunes (page 15). On the iPad, you can turn VoiceOver on by choosing Settings→General→ Accessibility→VoiceOver→On.

Disconnect from Your Computer

When it comes time to disconnect your iPad from your computer, you don't really have to do anything special: Just unplug the cable and take off, iPad in hand. The only time you *don't* want to unplug the cable is when the iPad screen says *Sync in Progress*. That means the iPad and computer are exchanging info, and if you disconnect the USB cable, one of those devices *won't* get all the files you're trying to copy between the two.

Tip You can cancel a current sync session by dragging the Cancel Sync slider on the iPad's screen.

Now, the simplicity of this disconnection process may sound scary to longtime iPod owners who remember ominous error messages and sometimes scrambled iPods if they forgot to first eject their gadget before pulling the plug on it. If you want to go old-school with an Eject button, iTunes gives you a couple of options:

❶ Click the little Eject icon next to the name of your iPad in the iTunes Source list (circled)—that's the left-most column in iTunes.

❷ If your iPad's already selected in the Source list, choose Controls→Eject iPad or press Ctrl+E (⌘-E).

Now you can unplug your iPad without fear (if you had that fear to begin with).

Tired of plugging your iPad into the computer with a quaint old USB cable to sync, activate, or update your slab? That should be a thing of the past when iOS 5, the next version of the iPad's operating system, arrives in the Fall of 2011. The new OS promises wireless iTunes syncing, data backups, and software updates over the air (and a WiFi connection).

Work with iTunes

iTunes not only lets you decide which songs, books, and videos end up on your iPad, it also helps you keep your iPad's internal software up to date, shows you how much space you have left on your tablet, and lets you change your music, video, and podcast syncing options.

When you connect your 'Pad to your computer, it shows up in the iTunes Source list. In the Devices section, click the iPad icon to see your options, represented by a series of tabs at the top of the screen. Each tab lets you control a different kind of content, like music, photos, or books.

Here, on the Summary screen, iTunes tells you:

❶ Your iPad's storage capacity and its serial number.

❷ Whether your 'Pad has the latest software on it (and if you're having problems with your iPad, you get the chance to reinstall the software).

❸ Whether you set iTunes to automatically synchronize your iPad and computer or whether you need to update its contents manually. (Automatic means everything in iTunes ends up on your iPad—space permitting, of course; manual means you get to pick and choose what gets transferred.) Other boxes iTunes offers in the Options area let you encrypt your iPad backup files, convert large song files to smaller ones so they don't hog space, choose standard-definition videos over their heftier HD counterparts, and configure the Universal Access features for visually and hearing-impaired users.

❹ The different media types filling up your iPad. This info comes in the form of a bar at the bottom of the screen. iTunes color-codes your media types (blue for Audio, orange for Photos, and so on) and shows you how much space each takes up using the appropriate color in the bar. For even more detail, click the bar to see your media stats in terms of number of items, the amount of drive space they use, or the number of days' worth of a particular type of media you have.

❺ Your iPad's contents and playlists. Click the flippy triangle next to the iPad (circled right).

So that's what you can learn about your iPad and its contents from looking at iTunes. Later in this book, you'll learn how to transfer different types of media to the iPad and how to use them on the tablet.

For example, Chapter 13 is all about playing your favorite music on the iPad, Chapter 14 covers syncing and playing videos, while Chapter 15 explains copying your photos from computer to iPad—which makes a great handheld picture frame to show off your shots.

To learn more about iTunes and how it works, take a trip to Chapter 11 for a detailed tour through the program. And if you want to explore the virtual shelves of the iTunes App Store so you can load up your iPad, skip to Chapter 7.

Charge the iPad Battery

Many Apple devices ship with enough power to run for a short while. But as you poke and prod your new gadget, that charge won't last long, so you'll want to get the iPad connected to a power source to refill its battery properly. You can charge your 'Pad in one, or maybe two, ways:

- **Charge by AC adapter.** Look! Another charger for your collection! Your iPad comes with a square little 10-watt AC adapter ready to keep your tablet charged. It has a USB port on one side and a plug on the other. To boost your battery, plug the flat end of the iPad's USB cable into the cube's USB port. Then plug the cube's pronged end into an electrical outlet. Hitch up the Dock Connector side of the USB cable to the bottom of your iPad and charge away. (Older, smaller adapters from iPhones and older iPods may work if you turn the iPad screen off to direct the full stream of juice to the iPad's battery, but their low flow will likely charge the iPad much more slowly than its native adapter.)

- **Charge by computer.** Unlike iPods and iPhones, charging the iPad over your computer's USB port isn't a sure thing anymore. While USB ports on some newer computers—like late-model iMacs—have enough juice, many older ones don't. To see for sure, grab the USB cable and plug your iPad into your PC or Mac's USB port. If you see a "Not Charging" message in the top corner of your iPad, you know your port is underpowered. (The USB port will probably "trickle charge" if the iPad screen is off, but very slowly.)

It takes only a few hours to fully gas up your iPad's battery. The iPad displays a translucent battery that fills up with green power as you recharge. A smaller, black-and-white battery icon up in the iPad's status bar (circled) displays a lightning bolt, along with a percentage of the battery's current charge.

The iPad is fully charged when the battery icon in the menu bar shows 100%. Apple says a full iPad battery charge lasts up to 10 hours for web browsing, videos, and listening to music. Your results may vary.

Extend Battery Life

Apple posts various recommendations on its iPad website to ensure long battery life:

- Don't expose your iPad to extreme hot or cold temperatures—keep it between 32 and 95 degrees Fahrenheit. (In other words, don't leave it in a hot, parked car, and don't expect it to operate on Mt. Everest.)

- Use your iPad regularly (not that you wouldn't). And be sure to charge it at least once a month to keep that battery chemistry peppy.

- Put the iPad to sleep to conserve power (press the Sleep/Wake button on top).

- Take the iPad out of any heat-trapping cases before you charge it up.

- Dim the screen when you don't need it at total brightness (see page 288).

- When you see the Low Battery icon or message, plug your iPad into an electrical outlet using the AC adapter. The iPad battery indicator shows roughly how much charge the battery has left.

- Features like the music equalizer—or jumping around within your media library—can drain your battery faster, as can using big, uncompressed file formats, like AIFF (see page 204). (To cut back on the equalizer, see page 208. Some streaming apps can take their toll on the battery's power, too.)

- That wireless chip inside the iPad saps power even if you're not trawl- ing the Web. Save energy by turning it off when you don't need it; go to Settings→Wi-Fi and tap Off. Lower the frequency with which you check email or have data pushed to the iPad to save some energy as well—make those adjustments at Settings→Mail, Contacts, Calendars. Bluetooth and Location Services also take their toll, and you can turn them off by visiting the Settings icon.

Keep the iPad Screen Clean

Like the iPhone and iPod Touch, the iPad's glass touchscreen is the main way you communicate with the device. Each time you surf the Web or send some email, your fingers tap, slide, and flick across the smooth surface. Do this sort of thing on a normal piece of glass and you end up with a smudged and sticky window or mirror, gunked up from finger grease, moisturizer, and whatever else you may have on your hands.

Thanks to a special coating (explained in the Note on the opposite page), the iPad's screen tries to repel fingerprints. But with enough use, even that has its limits; your screen begins to look like a small child has been eating glazed doughnuts and touching your iPad repeatedly—with both hands. If this happens, wipe the screen gently with a soft, lint-free cloth—the kind you use to clean a flat-panel TV screen, camera lens, or pair of glasses.

Whatever you do, *don't* use products like Windex, Formula 409, stuff from spray cans, ammonia- or alcohol-based cleansers, solvents, or a scratchy cleaning pad. These types of products compromise the screen's special coating, and you don't want that.

If the rest of the iPad gets schmutzed up, a quick cleaning session can return its shine. To buff it up, turn it off (page 2) and unplug it from any connected docks or USB cables. Then take a lightly water-dampened lint-free cloth and

 Tip Smears and screen glare got you down? A thin sheet of plastic screen-protector film from your favorite accessory dealer could be your ticket to iPad happiness—and extra protection as well. For example, there's Zagg's $40 military-grade InvisibleShield at *www.zagg.com*.

wipe down the iPad's back and sides. Be careful not to slop water into openings like the headphone jack, Dock Connector port, or speaker grills. Then wipe your slab down with a *dry* lint-free cloth.

The iPad screen is scratch-resistant, but it could break if you accidentally bounce the tablet off a concrete floor or have some other gravity-related mishap. If disaster strikes and you crack or chip the screen, don't use the iPad or try to pry out the broken glass. Put it in a box or wrap it up to prevent glass shards from falling out, then take it to your nearest Apple Store or authorized Apple service provider for repair. Appendix B has more on iPad care and repair.

To protect your iPad as much as possible, both from accidental drops or even bouncing around in your shoulder bag alongside house keys, sunglass cases, and loose credit cards, consider a case for it. Accessory makers have already come up with a huge selection, from stately leather portfolio models to neon-colored rubber shells meant to jazz up your iPad while helping you keep a firm grip on the thing.

When considering a case, think about how you plan to carry and use your iPad. If it's going to ride along in a backpack, a sturdy padded pouch may be more protective that a thin leather binder-type cover. Page 296 has some tips on the type of cases available and where to buy them.

 Note Apple describes the iPad's screen as having a "fingerprint-resistant *oleophobic* coating," which makes it sound like the device has some sort of psychiatric condition or a fear of butter substitutes (known as oleomargarine back in the day). Not to worry! *Oleo*, from the Latin *oleum*, just means "oil"—like the natural oils from your fingertips when you slide them around the iPad's glossy screen. The oleophobic coating is just a plastic polymer applied to the iPad's glass that's supposed to cut down on smeary paw prints.

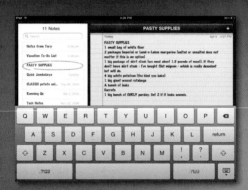

Interact with Your iPad

These days, touchscreens are nothing new; you find them everywhere. They've been on automatic teller machines for years, and dispensing New York City subway fare cards for more than a decade. Some delis let you order up a turkey-and-swiss by pressing a touch-sensitive menu. So, in the grand scheme of things, the iPad's touchscreen isn't unfamiliar.

But *using* the iPad takes more than touch. You tap, you flick, you swipe, you double-tap, you drag, you press-and-hold. *Which* motion you make and *when* you make it depends on *what* you're trying to do at the time. And that's *where* this chapter comes in.

Over the next few pages, you'll learn how to do the digit dance so your iPad responds to your every command. You'll also pick up a few keyboard shortcuts and learn how to use your fingers to find stuff on your 'Pad. So get those hands limbered up by turning the page.

Finger Moves for the iPad

The "brain" behind the iPad—its operating system—is smart enough to respond to a series of very different touches. The ones you make depend on what you want to do. Here are the moves:

- **Tap.** Take the tip of your finger and lightly press an icon, thumbnail image, song title, or control you see on-screen. The iPad isn't a crusty old calculator, so you don't have to push hard; a gentle touch does the trick.

- **Drag.** Keep your fingertip pressed down on the glass and slide it around to scroll to different parts of the screen. That's how you adjust volume sliders and pan around a photo. A *two-finger drag* scrolls a window within a window (like the floating window that pops up over your Facebook screen when you call up your friends list).

- **Slide.** A slide is like a drag, except that you use it almost exclusively with one special control—the iPad's Unlock/ Confirm button, which sits in a "track" that guides your slide as you wake your iPad from sleep or confirm a total shut-down.

- **Flick.** Lightly and quickly whip your finger up or down your screen and watch a web page or song list whiz by in the direction of your flick. The faster you flick, the faster the screen scrolls by. In a photo album, flick side-to-side to see your images parade triumphantly across your screen.

- **Finger Spread and Pinch.** To zoom in on part of a photo, document, or web page, put your thumb and index finger together, place them on-screen, and make a spreading motion across the glass. To zoom out, put your spread fingers on-screen and pinch them together.

- **Double-Tap.** This two-steppin' tap comes into play in a few situations. First, it serves as a quick way to zoom in on a photo or web page. Second, if you're watching a video, it lets you toggle between aspect ratios—the full-screen view (top right), where the edges of the frame get cropped off, and the widescreen, letterboxed view (bottom right), which movie lovers favor because that's what the director intended the scene to look like.

Use the iPad Keyboard

The iPad has no physical keys—unless you buy the optional keyboard (see page 31). A virtual keyboard, therefore, is the standard way to enter text.

The iPad's keyboard pops up whenever you tap an area of the screen that accepts input, like the address bar of a browser, a search box, or the text area of a new email message.

To use it, just tap the key you want. As your finger hits the glass, the light-gray target key confirms your choice by flickering to a darker gray.

The keyboard works in portrait (vertical) mode, but it's roomier when you go for the landscape (horizontal) view. The button with the keyboard icon in the bottom right (circled above) makes the keyboard go away. The keyboard has a few other special keys. They are:

❶ **Shift (⇧).** When you tap this key, the normally clear arrow turns blue (⇧) to show you it's activated. When you see the blue arrow, the next letter you tap appears capitalized. Once you type that letter, the ⇧ key returns to normal, signalling that the following letter will show up in lowercase.

❷ **Backspace (⌫).** This key deletes in all kinds of ways: Tap it once to delete the letter just to the left of the blinking cursor. Hold it down to delete in reverse, zapping each letter as you go. Finally, hold it down a bit longer and it deletes entire *words* instead of just individual letters.

❸ **.?123 .** Tap this button to insert punctuation or numbers. The keyboard switches from alphabet mode to serve up a grid of numerical and grammatical symbols. Tap the same key—which has now become **ABC**—to return to the alphabet. (Happily, there's a much faster way to get a number or symbol—touch and hold the **.?123** key, and then drag your finger to the number or character you want.)

When you're using the numbers/symbols keyboard, a new **#+=** button appears. Tap it to invoke a *third* keyboard layout, which offers more obscure characters, like the # and % symbols, bullets, and brackets.

When you type letters into a web form (or anyplace that's not a web address), the iPad adds a return key to the keyboard so you can move from one line to the next. This key morphs to say "Join" when you type in a WiFi password, "Go" when you enter a URL, and "Search" when you query the search box.

iPad Keyboard Shortcuts

As you've probably discovered by now, the iPad keyboard has to get a bit creative to fit all the keys you need on a small patch of glass. But let's face it, when you're trying to finish an email message, jumping around between keyboard layers to find an ampersand or apostrophe gets old fast. To help balance economy and efficiency, Apple built in a number of keyboard shortcuts and tricks to help you out.

- **Web addresses.**
  When you type a web address into Safari, the iPad's web browser, the keyboard helpfully includes keys for commonly used

  characters. For example, you get a slash, underscore, hyphen, and, best of all, a *.com* button (circled). Not going to a *.com* address? Press and hold the *.com* button to get your choice of *.edu*, *.org*, or *.net*, and slide your finger over to the one you want. When you finish, tap the Go button.

- **Instant apostrophes.** The iPad fills in the apostrophe of many contractions for you, so if you type *cant*, the tablet corrects it to *can't*.

- **Bad aim.** Finger on the wrong key? If you haven't lifted your digit off the screen yet, slide it over to the correct one and let go.

- **Punctuation.** Apple's bad-aim press-and-slide trick works in a couple of other places as well. Need an apostrophe instead of that comma key on the main keyboard? Press the comma key and slide. Need an ampersand but don't want to tap all the way into the .?123 keyboard? Press the .?123 key and slide over to it without taking your finger off the keyboard—or having to switch back to the ABC keyboard.

- **Accented characters.** Need an accented letter, say, an *é* instead of a plain old *e*? Press and hold the *e* character to reveal a whole bunch of accented choices. Slide your finger to select the one you need. This trick works on most letters that take accent marks.

> **Tip** If you don't look at text as you type—and don't notice the iPad's auto-corrections until after it makes them—you can have the tablet pipe up and verbally announce its word suggestions. Just tap through to Settings→General→Accessibility→ "Speak Auto-text." You can turn the feature off here, too.

- **Auto-correction.** The iPad's dictionary tries to automatically correct typos and spelling errors as you tap along. If you want to accept the suggested correction for a word you just typed, hit the space bar and keep going. Don't agree with the iPad? Tap the word to reject the suggestion. Proper nouns often make the iPad's dictionary overeager to help, but if you reject its suggestions enough times, it eventually learns what you want. In some programs, words the iPad is still suspicious about get underlined in red; tap them to see alternate spelling suggestions. (If the constant corrections bug you, turn them off at Settings→General→Keyboard→Auto-Correction.)

Speaking of the Settings area, the iPad tucks away several helpful shortcuts there. Go to Settings→General→Keyboard to see them.

- **Auto-Capitalization.** When you turn this setting on, the iPad automatically capitalizes the first letter after a period.

- **Check Spelling.** The iPad flags misspelled words in Mail and text apps with a red underline. Tap the flagged word to see replacement options.

- **Enable Caps Lock.** If you NEED TO TYPE LIKE THIS FOR A WHILE, flip on this setting. Now, when you double-tap the Shift (⇧) key, it turns blue and keeps capitalizing until you tap it again to turn it off.

- **"." Shortcut.** With this setting turned on, you just double-tap the space bar at the end of a sentence to end it with a period and move one space to the right to start your next sentence with a capital letter.

When you tap the International Keyboards option, you can add foreign-language keyboards. Turn the page to find out more.

Use an International Keyboard

If American English is your only language, you can skip these next two pages. But if, over the course of your iPadding day, you find yourself communicating in French, Spanish, German, Russian, Chinese, Japanese, Cherokee, Dutch, Flemish, Italian, Canadian French, or British English, you can add a keyboard layout that reflects the standards of those languages.

To give your iPad some global input:

❶ Tap Settings→General→Keyboard→International Keyboard and tap Add New Keyboard.

❷ On the Add New Keyboard screen, peruse the list of languages and tap the one you want. "German," for example, adds a German-character keyboard. The iPad includes the keyboard in your list of personal 'boards at Settings→General→Keyboard→International Keyboard→Keyboards.

❸ You get your choice of keyboard layout, too. To pick one, tap the language name in your list of keyboards. Here, you can pick the keyboard layout (QWERTY, AZERTY, QWERTZ, and so on) for the iPad screen. If you plan to use an external keyboard as well (or instead), you can select a hardware layout, too, like the one for a Bluetooth keyboard that uses the standard German character map or the Dvorak layout.

Once you add and configure your new keyboards, call them up when you need to leap into a memo in Dutch or Japanese.

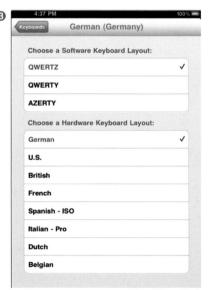

You switch keyboards two ways:

❶ First, you can tap the key that has the globe icon (circled), just to the left of the space bar. With each tap, you cycle through your personal keyboards as their names flash on the space bar. Stop when you see the keyboard you want.

❷ Alternatively, you can press down on the globe key for a minute to pop up a list of all your keyboards, then slide your finger up to the one you want.

Type away. When you want to switch back to English or to another keyboard language, go to the globe.

Delete a Keyboard

To delete an international keyboard you no longer want, choose Settings→General→Keyboard→ International Keyboard. Tap the Edit button above the Keyboards list, then tap the ⊖ next to the one you want to lose, and then tap the Delete button that appears. To rearrange the order in which your keyboards appear in the globe menu, use the grip strip icons (☰) to drag them into the desired new world order. Then tap Done.

 Note The iPad offers several languages that use non-Western character sets, including Japanese, Chinese (Simplified) Pinyin, and Chinese (Simplified) Handwriting. "Handwriting on a keyboard?" you wonder. No problem for the iPad: When you select Chinese (Simplified) Handwriting as your keyboard option, your screen becomes a virtual touchpad where you can enter Chinese character strokes with the tip of your finger. The iPad sees what you're doing and offers a list of matching characters you can choose from.

Cut, Copy, Paste, and Replace

The iPad's ability to move text and images around within a document (or between documents) is useful, but it's not the tablet's most intuitive feature. And no, you can't use Ctrl-C to copy something because the keyboard *has* no Control key. But never fear, here's how you move text and images from place to place—or program to program:

❶ To cut or copy text that you can edit (like an outgoing email message or a note), double-tap a word to high-

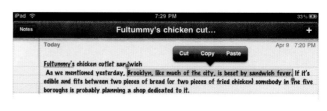

light it. A Cut | Copy | Paste | Replace box pops up. To select more words, drag the blue dots on either end of the selected word. Then tap the Cut or Copy command. (If you select more than one word, you don't see the Replace option; the next page has more on that.)

❷ For pages you *can't* edit (like incoming emails), hold your finger down until you see a magnifying glass and insertion-point cursor. Drag it to the text you want to copy. When you lift your finger, a Select or Select All box appears. Select high-lights the underlying word and displays the blue dots so you can include more text or photos. Select All highlights everything

on-screen. Either way, lift your finger to get a Copy button. Web pages work a little differently: When you lift your finger there, you skip the "Select" options and go right to the Copy button, as shown above.

❸ Tap the spot where you want to paste the text or photo to call up the Paste button. You can even jump to a different program; tap within it to paste.

❹ Tap Paste to copy the text or pic into the new location, file, or program.

Make a mistake and wish you could undo what you just did? Give the iPad a quick shake and tap the Undo Paste or Undo Typing button that appears.

Tip Need to select a whole paragraph at once? Tap it quickly four times.

Just be careful when you shake that iPad—you don't want to send your $500 high-tech tablet flying across the room because you pasted the word "celery" on the wrong line of a recipe.

In addition to the Cut, Copy, and Paste options in files where you can edit text (like Notes), you can also replace a misspelled word with one that's spelled correctly. Or you can replace one word with a different word altogether. To get the Replace option, double-tap or select a word on-screen. When the Cut | Copy | Paste | Replace box appears, tap Replace. The iPad offers up a few alternate words for you. If you see the word you *meant* to type, tap it to replace the text.

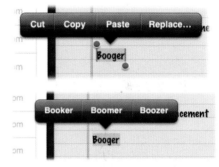

But enough about text—want to copy a photo or video into a message-in-progress or some other program? Hold your finger down on the screen until the Copy button pops up, as shown in the screenshot below. Tap the Copy button, create an email, and tap the message body to get a Paste button. Tap it to insert your image or video.

If you want to copy multiple items, like pictures out of a photo album, tap the ✉ icon in the top-right corner. Next, tap the photos you want to copy; blue checkmarks appear in the corners to indicate your selection. Tap the Copy button on the top-left side of the toolbar, switch to the program where you want to deposit your pics (like a mail message under construction), and press the glass until the Paste button appears.

> **Tip** The Notes program on the iPad is a handy place to stash text when you find something from a web page or email message you want to keep. If you use Outlook 2007 or 2003 for Windows or the Mail program that comes with Mac OS X 10.5.7 or later, you can sync your notes back and forth between your iPad and desktop computer. Just connect the iPad to the computer, click its icon in the iTunes Source list, and click the Info tab. Scroll down and turn on the Sync Notes checkbox, then click Apply.

Search the iPad

Once you get your iPad fully loaded, you may actually want to find something on it—a certain song in your music library, a calendar appointment you need to reference, or someone's address. If you have 64 gigabytes of stuff on a bulging iPad, you may not want to wade around looking for a nugget of information. You can, however, shine the *Spotlight* on it.

Spotlight is the iPad's built-in tool for introspection and self-searching. It lets you scan your iPad for words, apps, phrases, names, titles, and more. You can call up songs, appointments, email messages with directions to a house party, and all sorts of other things. You can get to Spotlight a few ways:

- If you're on your first Home screen, press the Home button to call up Spotlight.

- If you're a few Home screens deep, flick backwards from left to right until you *pass* your first Home screen and arrive at the Spotlight screen, where you can flick no further.

Once you're on the Spotlight screen, type the name or words you're looking for ("Doctor Lee" or "Harrigan" or "Gettysburg"). Spotlight begins to search even before you finish typing, and narrows the list as you continue. On the search results screen, tap any item to open it. In iOS 4.2 and later, you even get the option to search for your topic on the Web and Wikipedia with Safari. You can even launch an app from the list of results—which is a great way to fire up programs after you fill up your 11 Home screens with icons and don't have any place to display app icons anymore.

 Tip Tired of songs by The Smiths popping up when you search for messages from your cousins—also named Smith? You can fine-tune your Spotlight search results to weed out certain types of files. Just tap Home→Settings→General→Spotlight Search and turn off the checkmarks next to items like Music or Videos.

Add an External Keyboard

It's okay, you can admit it. You tried and tried and tried, but you just can't deal with that flat-glass typing surface. Your fingers long for the tactile feel of softly clicking Chiclet keys, especially when you're working on huge documents or programs that require lots of text entry.

If this describes you, fear not. You can get the comfort of a physical keyboard, and you even have a couple of options.

Bluetooth Keyboard

The iPad conveniently has a Bluetooth chip tucked inside it, so you can use the slab with a Bluetooth-enabled wireless keyboard, like the stylish $69 model Apple makes (shown here). To get the iPad ready for the wireless keyboard, choose  Settings→General→Bluetooth→On. Then follow the instructions that came with your particular keyboard to put it into Bluetooth pairing mode—this usually means holding down a button until something blinks.

The iPad looks around for nearby devices, and should find the keyboard singing its Bluetooth siren song. When you see the keyboard in the Devices list, select it and type in any passkey numbers it requests (check your keyboard manual for them) to complete the connection. The Bluetooth icon (✻) and keyboard name appear on-screen to announce their pairing. To go back to the virtual keyboard, choose Settings→General→Bluetooth→Off or press the Eject key on the Bluetooth keyboard.

iPad Keyboard Dock

If you want to power your 'Pad as you type, consider Apple's combination iPad Keyboard Dock. It's a full-size keyboard sitting atop a charging dock. You plug the power cord into the wall, stick the iPad in its charger booster seat, and peck away with the screen tilted at a comfortable viewing angle.

You can also connect the $69 iPad Keyboard Dock USB cable to your computer to do some syncing. With even more optional cables, you can connect the dock to your TV, stereo, or video projector. Visit *store.apple.com* to see the iPad Keyboard Dock and other accessories, like the plain iPad Dock, the Component and Composite AV cables, and the Digital AV Adapter.

Print With Your iPad

You pretty much have two ways to print messages, photos, and other documents from your iPad: apps or AirPrint.

The App Store (Chapter 7) offers dozens of utility programs for your iPad that make it possible to print files from your iPad to your home printer. Some may be more elegant than others, but odds are you can find something in the Store that'll let you print for less than $10.

If you've never searched for an app before, page 122 shows you how; just type *print* into the App Store's search box and go to town. When you find an app that appeals to you from its description and reviews, buy it, install it, and follow the app's directions for printing.

The other way to print uses Apple's *AirPrint* technology. This approach can be more expensive, but ultimately easier to use because the technology is built into your iPad—you're not at the mercy of a third-party app.

The AirPrint option can be pricier is because it currently works with only about a dozen printer models—all of them made by HP. So if you don't already have an AirPrint printer in the house, you have to buy one, which can cost at least $90. You can see the full list of AirPrint-compatible HP printer models at *http://support.apple.com/kb/ht4356*.

AirPrint will hopefully become more widespread soon, But if you do have a printer that works with it, here's how AirPrint *itself* works:

❶ Find an AirPrint-ready printer. If you just bought one to use with your iPad, follow the printer's setup instructions for adding it to your wireless network. (You may have to upgrade certain models, like the HP Photosmart D110a, with a firmware update from the manufacturer; check the printer's manual for specific steps.)

❷ Pick a file on your iPad you want to print. AirPrint works with Mail, Safari, iBooks, and pictures from Photos and Photo Booth. Other apps from the App Store, like iWork (Chapter 10) and the note-organizing Evernote, also offer the Print option. With the file open, tap the ✉ icon and choose Print. (In Mail, tap the ↩ icon; in iWork, the Print command lives under the Tools menu.)

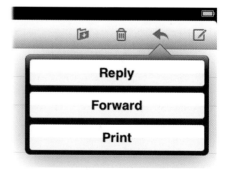

❸ Tap Select Printer. The iPad searches the network for all the AirPrint machines it can locate and presents a list of the ones it finds. Tap the name of your printer in the list to select it.

❹ With your printer now selected, tap the Printer Options arrow to go back to the main Print box. Tap Range to choose the pages you want to print. By default, you get All Pages, but if it's a long web page or file, you can change that. Tap the - and + buttons to decrease or increase the number of copies you print.

❺ Tap the Print button and listen for the sound of your printer whirring into action.

After you configure AirPrint the first time, the iPad remembers your printer and offers it as the default choice the next time you need to make paper.

Managing Print Jobs

Like other computers, the iPad shows you how many print jobs you have lined up to go through the printer. It also gives you the chance to cancel a particular print job if you change your mind—or realize you just told the iPad to print 12 copies instead of two.

To see what jobs you have in the print queue, double-click the Home button and swipe through the app panel until you see the Print Center icon (circled). Tap it to see a summary of the print job (or jobs). Tap the Cancel Printing button to stop a job and save that ink and paper for another time.

3

Select a Wireless Network

ChateauNet	🔒 📶
eagles	🔒 📶
Kin	🔒 📶

Cancel

 slide to unlock

Get Online

You can get content onto your iPad two ways: by pulling it down from the sky—or rather, the Internet—and by synchronizing it with your computer to copy over music, videos, books, and other media through iTunes. This chapter tells you how to get your iPad set up for that first option. (If you just can't wait to read up on syncing, jump ahead to Chapter 11.)

Every iPad can connect to the Internet over a WiFi connection. You can get online from your home wireless network or from a WiFi hotspot at a local tech-friendly coffee shop. But some iPads don't need to be anchored to a stationary WiFi network to get to the ether. Wi-Fi + 3G iPads can reach out and connect to the Web through the same network you use to make cellphone calls—the 3G network. Whether that's AT&T or Verizon's network depends on which 3G iPad you bought.

This chapter explains the difference between WiFi and 3G, the difference between AT&T and Verizon's offerings, how to set up each type of connection, and how to stay safe online while using either. So if you're ready to fire up that wireless chip and get your iPad out on the Internet, read on.

Should You Use WiFi or 3G?

If you bought a WiFi iPad, you don't have much of a decision to make here— you get to the Internet by jumping onto your nearest wireless network (like a home network) or onto a *hotspot* (which is a wireless network, but usually in a public place, like an airport or coffee shop; it's sometimes free, but more likely you have to pay to use it, as page 36 explains).

If you bought a WiFi iPad and have your own WiFi network, say at home, you can loop in your tablet with just a couple of taps—see the next page for instructions. If you don't have your own network, you need to set one up or find a nearby WiFi hotspot you can legally use if you want to download email, web pages, and iTunes Store content out of thin air. (The iPad doesn't have an Ethernet jack for those old-fashioned wired network connections, by the way.)

But if you bought a 3G-enabled iPad, you have a choice of connections— you're not limited to WiFi networks because you can use AT&T or Verizon's nationwide 3G network—the same one that smartphones use for email, web surfing, and telephone calls.

You need to decide which company to use—AT&T or Verizon—*before* you buy your iPad. That's because the two companies use different network tech- nologies—AT&T's is called *GSM*, and it's popular around the world. Verizon uses a *CDMA* network that has more reliable national coverage. An AT&T iPad can't jump on Verizon's network, and vice versa. If you don't know which to get, check the carrier's coverage map for your area. AT&T's is at *www.att.com/ wireless* and Verizon Wireless has info at *www.verizonwireless.com*.

As for whether you should use WiFi or 3G as your highway to the Web, in gen- eral, stick with WiFi when you can. It's likely to be faster. And remember, your carrier charges you to use their 3G cellular network and limits the amount of data you can gobble up each month (unless you're grandfathered into AT&T's old $30 unlimited-access deal offered with the original iPad). Depending on the plan you choose from either carrier, you can download from 250 mega- bytes (MB) to 10 gigabytes (GB) of data per month.

That said, if there's no WiFi hotspot in range, let 'er rip with the 3G. You'll always have 'Net, as long as there's an AT&T or Verizon signal nearby.

Get Your WiFi Connection

No matter which iPad you have, you can connect to the Internet over a *WiFi* network, known to geeks as an 802.11 or *Wireless Fidelity* network. It's the same technology that lets laptops, handheld game consoles, and portable media players get online at high speed. In fact, when you first turn on your iPad and try to use an Internet-focused app like Safari, the iPad may pop up a box listing a bunch of networks and suggesting you join one. Just find your own network, tap its name, and then enter your password.

If you're not prompted to join a network, here's how to set up the iPad on your home wireless network for the first time:

❶ On the iPad's Home screen, tap Settings→Wi-Fi. This brings you to the wireless settings area. Next to Wi-Fi, tap the On button.

❷ In the "Select a Wireless Network" box, pick one. The iPad samples the airwaves and displays the names of all the nearby WiFi networks (which could be a lot if you live in a big apartment building). Find the name of your home network on the list and tap it to join in.

❸ Type in the network's password if asked. The iPad tags secure networks—those that require passwords to keep freeloaders and intruders from glomming onto them and sucking up bandwidth—with a lock icon (🔒). You need to enter a password to get onto them.

Once you type in your network password, the WiFi icon (📶) in the iPad's top menu bar should bloom, indicating that yes, you are on the Internet. Fire up Safari, FaceTime, or Game Center and have fun.

If you don't get the happy blooming WiFi icon, repeat the steps above. Typos are a common error, so *carefully* retype your network password. You should also make sure that your home network is actually up and working.

The iPad is smart enough to know you're a busy person, so you should only have to run through this setup process the first time you successfully join a network. It remembers your network and password from then on.

Use Public WiFi Hotspots

Your iPad isn't confined to your home network. It can jump onto any other WiFi pipeline within range: the wireless network at your office or on campus, free public wireless networks in city parks, or any other place the iPad picks up the sweet scent of a hotspot. When it finds networks in the area and you're not currently connected to one, it lists the available networks you can tap and join. Most public-access networks don't require passwords.

Along with free networks, you can find *commercial* hotspots for the joining, but you need a little something extra with one of these: money, as in your credit-card number. You usually see these networks in large public places, like airports, megabookstore chains, hotel rooms, and other spots that dispense WiFi access for an hourly or daily fee.

To join a pay network, tap its name (it's probably something official-sounding) in the list your hotspot-sniffing iPad presents you. Next, tap open Safari. The network will be there, squatting on your browser's home page with a request for your plastic digits before you can engage in any Web activity.

If you do a lot of traveling and don't have the Wi-Fi + 3G iPad, you may want to consider signing up for a service plan with a commercial hot-spot provider like T-Mobile (*hotspot.t-mobile.com*), Gogo Inflight (*www.gogoinflight.com*), or Boingo (*www.boingo.com*). AT&T and Verizon have a hand in the hotspot business, too, and they may be a good choice, especially if you already use their services for residential Internet access. Check out AT&T's offerings at *www. wireless.att.com/sbusiness/wifi* or the deals from Verizon at *www22.verizon. com/residential/wifi/*.

Stay Secure: WiFi Network Safety Tips

The word "wireless" brings with it a sense of freedom: no wires, no cords, no strings attached. But with all that freedom comes the potential for danger, because your personal information isn't humming along inside a sheathed Ethernet cable from Point A to Point B—it's flying around in the air.

Most of the time, this isn't a problem. That is, unless someone evil is lurking nearby who knows how to snatch data out of the air. Then you could be at risk of identity theft or other ills if, say, you buy a pair of shoes with a credit card and the malcontent electronically nets your numbers out of the air.

To make things as safe as possible, keep these basic tips in mind when you ride the airwaves:

- **Make sure your home network is protected by a password.** Yes, it's an extra step when you set up your wireless network, and it may make the connection a tad slower overall. But it keeps intruders and squatters off your network where, at best, they hog your bandwidth and, at worst, they infiltrate all your connected computers and steal personal information.

- **Don't do any financial business on public wireless networks.** Since someone you don't know sets up public WiFi networks, you don't truly know how secure they are—or who else is lurking on them. So save the online banking or stock-trading chores for home. Use your iPad to check the score on the Saints game or catch up on the headlines while you sip your mocha latte.

- **Use a VPN for business on the road.** If you *do* have to take care of company business on your iPad while traveling, get the folks in your corporate systems department to let you access your company's *virtual private network* (VPN), a secure portal to the Web.

Remember, the Internet is a wonderful, glorious thing, but it's sometimes a dark place, too. Be careful out there.

Use a Mobile Broadband Hotspot

So you didn't buy the Wi-Fi + 3G iPad and now you're regretting it. What do you do—slap your WiFi iPad up on eBay and put the proceeds toward your Wi-Fi + 3G iPad Upgrade Fund? Lurch from hotspot to hotspot all over town? Sit on the couch and complain?

If trading up to a 3G iPad isn't in your future, you have another option: a *mobile broadband hotspot*. This portable hotspot-in-a-box pulls down a cellular network signal from a carrier—probably Verizon, AT&T, or Sprint—and divvies it up into a mini WiFi network so four to five wireless devices (laptops, Portable PlayStations, iPads, and so on) can get onto the Internet at once. Novatel's *MiFi* (above) and the *Overdrive* from Sierra Wireless are two models.

Newer mobile hotspots can use today's faster 4G data networks, which give connected WiFi devices an HOV lane to the Web. 4G nets are rolling out slowly, though, so hopping on a 3G wave is still more common. For now, anyway.

Sounds great, doesn't it? Yes, having a WiFi network wherever you go has its advantages, but there's a downside, too: cost. First, you have to pay for the box itself, which costs $100 to $250. Then you have to sign up for a service plan, which typically adds at least $40 a month to your bill and involves a contract.

If you do math, this is obviously more than the bare minimum $15 you'd shell out for AT&T's 3G service or the $20 that Verizon Wireless charges for its low-end iPad data plan. Plus, the Wi-Fi + 3G iPad models from either carrier don't require any additional hardware to drag around or possibly leave behind in a hotel room. (You pay for the convenience up-front when you buy the 3G iPad; adding that cellular chip tacks $130 onto the iPad's cost.)

But here's where the pocket network *does* make sense: when you need to get multiple devices online wherever you go. This could be a family with three WiFi iPads, an iPad and two laptops, and so on. The monthly service fee covers everyone—and it's way cheaper than buying individual 3G 'Pads and 3G plans.

Verizon Wireless offers a special deal that includes a WiFi-only iPad 1, a MiFi, and lower data rates, starting at $20 a month for a gig of wireless data.

If mobile hotspots sound attractive, investigate your options further at Verizon Wireless (*www.verizonwireless.com/b2c/mobilebroadband*) or Sprint (*www.sprint.com*). The regional carrier Clear (*www.clear.com*) even has mobile hotspots you can *lease* instead of buy, which may make more sense for travelers.

Pick an AT&T 3G Service Plan

If you paid a little extra for the AT&T Wi-Fi + 3G iPad model, you don't have to worry about going from WiFi hotspot to WiFi hotspot to stay connected. You have a connection wherever your iPad and AT&T's 3G network intersect. The iPad's WiFi works right out of the box, but before you can start using AT&T's network, you need to sign up for a prepaid cellular data plan. (If you already have an AT&T account, you can add an iPad plan to your overall bill as a post-paid option at *www.wireless.att.com*.)

You have your choice of two monthly AT&T DataConnect plans:

- **250 MB.** This $15 plan gives you 250 megabytes of data coming to and going from your iPad every 30 days. The iPad warns you when you get close to 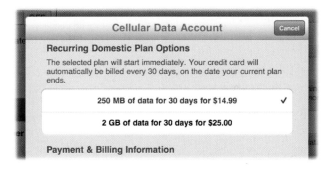 the limit and you can buy more, but how much data is 250 MB realistically? *PC Magazine* estimates that it equals about 500 medium-to-large web pages. So you may eat up 250 megs fast, especially if you send and receive a lot of big email attachments, like photos.

- **2 GB/Unlimited.** New iPad owners can download 2 gigabytes of data a month for $25 each month. But if you bought your iPad before June 7, 2010, you had the option of a $30-a-month unlimited data plan, but that plan is the relic of a lost era for new iPad owners.

There are three other things to know about AT&T's plans:

❶ You can cancel your service at any time because there's no contract lashing you to the mast of the AT&T ship for one or two years.

❷ If you don't plan to use your 3G service regularly (maybe you just signed up for one month for that cross-country trip), you need to remember to *cancel* your account. It automatically renews itself every month and bills your credit card until you manually put an end to it. See page 47.

❸ With any AT&T plan, you also get unlimited free access to any of its WiFi hotspots, which you often find in places like major airports, Starbucks coffee shops, and Barnes & Noble bookstores. This could be helpful for people watching the meter on a 250-MB plan, because you can switch off the 3G chip (page 44) and cozy up to some free WiFi.

Pick a Verizon Wireless 3G Service Plan

Verizon Wireless is the new kid on the block when it comes to working with Apple hardware, but the company got its start by bundling MiFi hotspots with WiFi iPads a few months before a Verizon-ready iPhone hit the scene in early 2011. So when the iPad 2 rolled out in March 2011, Verizon was there with a 3G model that worked with its own cellular network. The choices are good, especially for people who aren't exactly fans of AT&T.

Unlike AT&T, which has just two iPad data plans, Verizon doubles the fun with four, aimed to meet your simple—or extravagant—monthly mobile data needs:

- **1 GB.** At $20, it's the cheapest option on Verizon's menu, but filling enough for the person who mainly sends email or does a bit of web surfing on the go.

- **3 GB.** Add another $15 to move up a notch, and you triple your data allowance with this plan: 3 gigs for $35.

- **5 GB.** Moving up to the third-most expensive plan can save you money per gigabyte, as Verizon charges $50 for a monthly 5 GB of data. That breaks down to $10 a gigabyte.

- **10 GB.** For people who need to stream a lot of video, transfer hefty files, and do other data-intensive tasks when there's no WiFi network around, this top-shelf plan should cover you—for $80 a month.

As with AT&T, you can cancel your monthly Verizon plan any time. The tricky part is *remembering* to cancel it when you don't need it for a few months. Otherwise, it just keeps showing up on your credit-card bill each month, like that gym membership fee you keep forgetting to cancel, too.

Sign Up for 3G Service

Once you decide on a plan—or one to start out with, anyway—it's time to unleash your credit card. Keep in mind that this is a brand-new account that has nothing to do with any of the other wireless or iTunes Store accounts you may have (unless you contact AT&T and have it added to your overall services bill as a postpaid plan). The monthly charges on prepaid plans are billed directly to your Visa, MasterCard, Discover, or American Express card.

You can sign up for 3G service right from the iPad:

❶ From the Home screen, tap Settings→Cellular Data→View Account.

❷ Once you tap that View Account button, a window pops up. Here, you fill in your name, phone number, email address, and 3G account password. (You use your email address and 3G password later to log in and make account changes.) You also choose which plan you want and type in your credit card information. Tap Next when you're done.

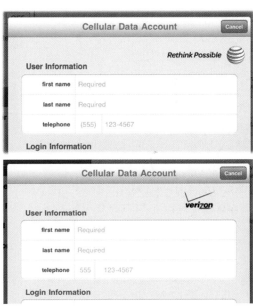

❸ The Terms of Service agreement, always delightful beach reading, appears on-screen. Read the fine print (so you know what you're in for) or skip it, but tap Agree to move on.

❹ On the next screen, verify your billing information and plan choice. Then tap the Submit button.

Once you send off all your information, your carrier goes to work, first processing the info and then giving you a glorious "Data Plan Activated" message.

Tip Still stumped on how much monthly data to sign up for? Check out the Data Calculator pages on the sites of Verizon (*www.verizonwireless.com/splash_includes/ datacalculator.html* or AT&T (*www.att.com/standalone/data-calculator*) to get an estimate based on your typical activities.

Use the 3G Data Network

When there's a WiFi network within range, the iPad automatically joins it (or asks you if you want to join it) so you can enjoy a speedier connection than you'd get with the 3G cellular network. But when you're out of WiFi range, the iPad maintains its link to the Internet via its 3G chip.

When the iPad is using your cellular network, you see the familiar signal bars (**·ıll**) in the upper-left corner of the screen. This is the same signal-strength graphic that cellphones use to indicate connection quality. The more bars, the stronger the signal.

The opposite of "full/five bars" is the dreaded No Service notice squatting in the top-left corner. No Service may not always mean you're out of net-work range, though. It may also mean that you forgot to turn on the 3G chip (page 46) or you haven't yet signed up for a 3G account yet.

The icons in the top-left corner tell you which network you're on, although the last two are exclusive to AT&T:

- **WiFi** (奈). You're connected to a WiFi hotspot, most likely the fastest of all the connections, but this can vary by individual network—some over-loaded coffee-shop or hotel networks can feel like dial-up.

- **3G** (ᴱᴳ). The second-fastest network option, 3G (which stands for the *third generation* of data networks), is available in most urban areas. *This* is what you pay for with your monthly bill.

- **EDGE** (ᴱ). The EDGE network is slower than 3G, but can handle most data transfers if you wait around long enough. The name, in case you were wondering, stands for Enhanced Data rates for GSM (or Global) Evolution.

- **GPRS** (°). The slowest of all network options, the General Packet Radio Service network has been letting mobile phones send and receive data for years.

Even though your iPad may drop to turtle speed when you're out in the thin-ner one- and two-bar coverage areas of a 3G network, just remember: a trickle of data is still *some* data, and better than no data at all.

Use an iOS Personal Hotspot

You know how you can buy a router and share your one broadband Internet connection among several household members? Wouldn't it be great if you could share a 3G cellular connection with other people, too? That's just what mobile broadband hotspots (page 40) do, but what if you don't want to buy an extra piece of hardware?

That's where iOS 4.3's Personal Hotspot feature comes in really handy—you can turn your iPhone into a mobile hotspot to share your AT&T or Verizon 3G iPhone connection with your iPad, laptop, or other Internet-enabled device. Other users can connect to the hotspot via WiFi, Bluetooth, or (in the case of laptops), USB. This is the practice formerly known as *tethering*, but since that term often brings to mind tying a horse to a hitching post or a certain playground game with a ball on a rope, *Personal Hotspot* makes much more sense.

To use it, you need a compatible iOS device—like the iPhone 4. You may soon be able to use your iPad as a Personal Hotspot, too, if Apple decides to add the feature to the tablet. Older iPhones can tether with Bluetooth or USB, but can't offer WiFi connections to other users. And your hotspot device needs to run iOS 4.2.5 or later.

Alas, you must also agree to give your wireless carrier more money. For AT&T customers, you need to have the $25 plan for 2 GB of data—and then add $20 for the Personal Hotspot, which, in turn, nets you 2 more gigabytes of data. Verizon users will pay $20 more for 2 GB of data, on top of your regular iPhone bill.

To use a Personal Hotspot on an iPhone 4, for example, tap Home→Settings→General→ Network→Set Up Personal Hotspot (circled). When you do, you can upgrade your plan through your carrier's website or with a phone call. Once you get your account adjusted, tap Home→Settings→Personal Hotspot→On. You can decide how other users connect to your hotspot—WiFi, Bluetooth, or USB—and set up a password.

The network name is the name of your phone. When other users (up to five of them) share your connection, a blue bar appears on the hotspot screen listing the number of connected users. To boot them off because your battery is draining fast (and it will), tap Settings→Wi-Fi Networks→Disconnect Wi-Fi Clients, turn off Bluetooth, or unplug the USB cable.

Turn 3G Service Off or On

Always having an Internet connection is convenient in today's data-munching world. You never have to worry about missing an important email message or sudden news development.

But there are times when you want to turn off your 3G service, such as when you're getting perilously close to your monthly data allowance and don't want to give AT&T or Verizon any more money. Another good time is when you travel to other countries and want to avoid monster charges for inadvertently roaming onto a third-party network (page 280).

In times like these, tap Settings→Cellular Data→Cellular Data→Off. You can also turn off Data Roaming by tapping Settings→Cellular Data→Data Roaming→Off. And if you need to turn off *all* your iPad's wireless powers, choose Settings→Airplane Mode→On. When it's safe to start surfing again, come back to these screens to turn everything back on.

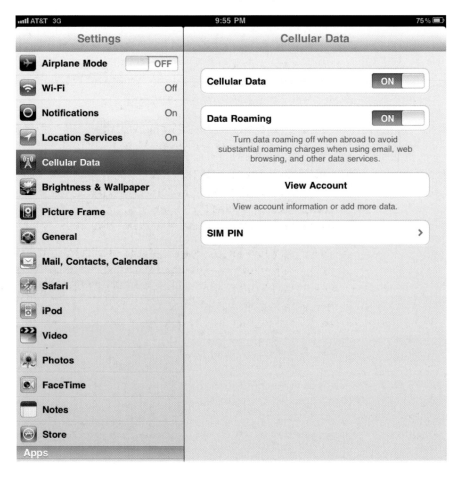

Change or Cancel Data Plans

If you need to upgrade your data plan, add another chunk of data because you're almost maxed out, see how much data your iPad has gobbled this month, cancel your monthly plan, or change the credit-card number your carrier has on file, there's one place to go: the Cellular Data account settings on the iPad.

To get there, tap Settings→Cellular Data→View Account. Since your account settings contain billing and personal information, you need to type in the same email address and account password you used when you originally set up the account on the iPad. (If you forgot your password, click the *Forgot Password?* link in the box.)

Once you get to the Cellular Data Account settings, your options are laid out before you. Tap Add Data or Change Plan if you want to tack on another batch of mega- or gigabytes, upgrade or downgrade to another plan, or outright cancel your plan. If you plan to travel overseas with an AT&T iPad, you can sign up for an International plan, explained on the next page.

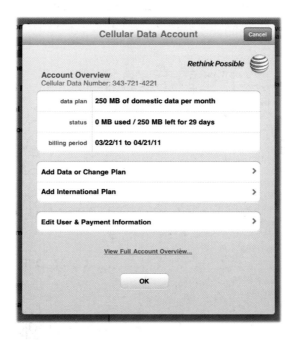

Tip You can also see your iPad's data meter by tapping Settings→General→Usage.

Travel Internationally with the iPad

Of the two 3G iPad carriers, only AT&T offers dedicated international data plans for the iPad. Much of Europe, along with other parts of the globe, use the same GSM network technology that AT&T does, but that's not so much the case with Verizon's CDMA network. WiFi iPads work wherever there's WiFi, though.

If you and your iPad plan to pop across the pond to London or attend a business meeting in Berlin, you may want to get a plan and micro-SIM card from a wireless carrier in the country you plan to visit.

If that's too much to bother with, AT&T does offer its own international plans to keep you connected. Be warned, however, that its prices are astronomical compared to the company's relatively low, low U.S. network prices. For example, a mere 20 MB of international data within a 30-day billing period is $25. There's no unlimited plan, so if you're a heavy Internet user, the maximum plan is 200 MB of data for the month—at a whopping 200 bucks. (And you thought the currency exchange rates were crazy.)

Still, if you must, you must. Tap Settings→Cellular Data→View Account and tap Add International Plan to see a list of countries and plans available.

Use Skype to Make Internet Calls

The iPad is not an iPhone, but that doesn't mean you can't make telephone calls with it. Well, certain kinds of calls, specifically *VoIP* calls. VoIP stands for *Voice over Internet Protocol*. It's a technology that basically turns Internet wires into telephone wires—and your iPad into a giant ad-hoc iPhone.

With special software and a microphone, VoIP lets you place calls from computer-to-computer or even from computer-to-regular-phone. And with programs like Skype, you can place calls from iPad-to-iPad, iPad-to-computer, or iPad-to-phone. Best of all, you can get Skype for free in the App Store.

To use Skype, you need to set up an account with the service. It's sort of like setting up an instant-messaging program. During the process, you pick a user name and password that appears in the Contacts list of people you make Skype calls with.

To make a call from Skype, just tap the name of a person (who also needs to be online) in your Contacts list. To call a regular phone line, tap the little blue phone icon (circled), enter the number on the keypad, and hit the green Call button.

Skype calls themselves can be free if they're going from computer or iPad to computer or iPad, but Skype charges a bit of coin to jump off the Internet and call a real phone number. The rates are low compared to standard phone services, and it's a popular way to make cheap overseas calls. For instance, with a $1.25 monthly subscription, you can make unlimited calls to landlines in the country of your choice (you can choose from more than 30 countries). Check out the prices for Skype's various calling plans at *www.skype.com*.

Skype can be a great way to keep up with the folks back in the Old Country on the cheap, but call quality can vary. The Internet can be a very busy network, which can affect the fidelity of the voice signals traveling across it.

> **Tip** With an iPad 2 and the latest version of Skype, you can also make video calls with your pals running the app on a camera-equipped iPhone, computer, or tablet.

4

 slide to unlock

Surf the Web

Sure, you can surf the Web on a smartphone. But odds are you strain your neck and squint your eyes to read the tiny screen, even when you zoom in for a closer look. For most people, microbrowsing is fine on a train or waiting in line at the cineplex, but who wants to do that in a coffee shop, campus library, or on the couch?

Browsing the Web on an iPad eliminates the old strain 'n' squint. Its 10-inch screen shows you pretty much a whole web page at once. And forget mouse-clicking—the iPad uses a touch-sensitive version of Apple's Safari browser, so your fingers do the walking around the Web. You jump from link to link with a tap, and zoom in on pages with a two-finger spread. And the latest version of mobile Safari, the one that arrived in March 2011, is the fastest one yet, displaying web pages more quickly than ever before.

From the basics of tablet-style browsing to tips on Web security, this chapter gives you the grand tour of Safari on the iPad, your wide-open window to the World Wide Web.

Take a Safari Tour

The iPad makes it easy to get to the Web. Just tap the Safari icon there on your Home screen (circled); the first time you open the browser, you see an empty window, ready to host web pages. Tap the address bar so the iPad keyboard pops up and type in a web address.

Except for the ability to play certain video files (those created with Adobe Flash), Safari has most of the features of a desktop browser: bookmarks, a history file, cookies, a pop-up blocker, and more.

When you go to a web page, 'Pad-Safari *behaves* just like a desktop browser, too. It highlights the address bar as it loads all the elements on the page and gives you Apple's "Yo! I'm still loading the page!" animated icon at the top of the screen, which looks like this: ❋.

Here's a quick tour of Safari's main screen elements, starting from the upper left:

- ◀, ▶ **(Back, Forward).** To flip back to the page you were just on before the current one, tap the ◀ button. You need to go back before you can go forward, so after you tap ◀, you can tap the ▶ button. This takes you to the page you were looking at before you tapped the ◀ button. Got it?

- ⬚ **(Pages).** Tap here to switch among open pages, sort of like tabs on a desktop browser. You can have up to nine pages open at one time.

- ⬚ **(Bookmarks).** Tap here to see your list of favorite sites. (Flip ahead a few pages for more info on working with bookmarks.)

- ⬚ **(Action menu).** Tap this multi-option icon to add a new bookmark, add a bookmark that lives on your Home screen, mail a link to the page, or print it (if you have an iPad-friendly printer, as page 32 explains).

- **Address bar.** This narrow white strip of typeable turf is where you enter a page's web address (also known as its *URL* or Uniform Resource Locator) when you're off to see the sites.

- ✖, ↻ **(Stop, Reload).** If you request the wrong page or get tired of waiting for a slow-loading site, tap the ✖ button on the address bar to stop the page from downloading any further.

If you don't tap the ✖ button and the page loads normally, the ✖ button turns into a ↻ button. Tap it to reload a page that doesn't look right (say a bunch of icons or graphics are missing) or if you want to see the latest version of a site that updates frequently—like a news or auction site.

- **Search box.** Safari has a separate little box for typing in search terms. Tap here and the keyboard pops up. Type in your keywords and tap the Search button that automatically replaces the Return key on your keyboard.

Zoom and Scroll Through Web Pages

As soon as many new iPad owners unbox their tablets, they spend hours zooming and scrolling through web pages because it's cool, fun, and novel to flick a finger across a piece of glass and see a web page respond to touch.

Even though the iPad has a fairly large screen, it's not quite the same experience as surfing the Web on your 17-inch laptop display or even bigger desktop monitor. Many companies offer mobile versions of their websites that bump up the size of text and graphics so you can see them better on iPads and smartphones. Better yet, many have free iPad apps that capitalize on the touchscreen for things like site navigation.

But not every site out there caters to iPad or smartphone users. You'll encounter plenty of regular old web pages that look perfectly fine, except that they're just a wee bit too small to read comfortably without some maneuvering:

Fortunately, the iPad gives you three ways to read pages more comfortably:

- **Rotate the iPad to Landscape Mode.** Turn the tablet 90 degrees in either direction and the screen rotates and enlarges the web page to fill the wider side of the iPad.

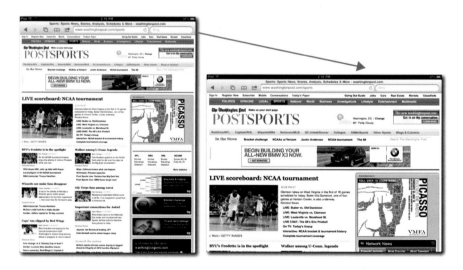

- **Zoom and pinch.** Place your thumb and forefinger (or whichever fingers you prefer) on the screen and slowly spread them apart to *zoom in* (enlarge) the part of the page between your fingers. To go in the opposite direction and *reduce* the size of the selected area, move your fingers closer together in a pinch formation.

- **Double-tap.** Web pages are made up of different sections, and Safari can isolate each one and magnify just that part. Find the section of a page you want to read and double-tap it with your finger to expand it. Double-tap again to reduce the section to its original size.

Double-tap

When you zoom in on a page and want to read a part that's out of view, simply drag your finger on the glass to pull that section to the center of the iPad screen.

You can also scroll around a page quickly by flicking your finger across the glass. As your finger flies around, you may inadvertently hit a link, but Safari knows that you're in transit and doesn't open the linked page or site. To actually click a link, stop scrolling and tap the link with your finger.

> **Tip** Every so often, you'll find, on certain web pages, a *frame* (a column of text) with its own scroll bar—an area of content that scrolls independently of the main page. (If you have a MobileMe account, the Messages list is such a frame.) The iPad offers its own way to navigate one of these frames without scrolling the whole page: It's the *two-finger drag*. To scroll within a frame, use two fingers instead of the usual one.

Create and Use Bookmarks

Did you set up your syncing preferences 'twixt iPad and computer when you first connected your tablet? If so, you'll find Safari already stuffed with a whole batch of bookmarks (Favorites)—that is, a list of sites you can re-visit with just a tap on the screen, so you don't have to remember and type in their URLs.

If you ripped your iPad out of its box as soon as you got it and haven't yet introduced it to your PC or Mac, you can easily copy your existing desktop computer's browser bookmarks from Internet Explorer (Windows) or Safari (Macintosh and Windows; page 192 has instructions).

To see all your bookmarks, tap the 🕮 button at the top of the screen. The Bookmarks box appears. Some bookmarks may be floating loose in the list, while others are neatly filed into folders, or even folders *within* folders. Tap a folder to see what's inside. Tap a bookmark to open the website it points to.

Tip The handy search box at the top right of the Safari window can do more than sniff around the Web for your search terms. When you tap in a keyword, it also shows you how many times the word appears on the current web page—which is really helpful if you're wading through a screen full of text looking for that one relevant term.

Add New Bookmarks on the iPad

As you surf, you can add new bookmarks right on your iPad. And any sites you bookmark there get copied *back* to your computer the next time you sync up.

To add a cool new site to your Bookmarks list, tap the icon at the top of the screen and then tap the Add Bookmark button. On the Add Bookmark screen, you have these choices:

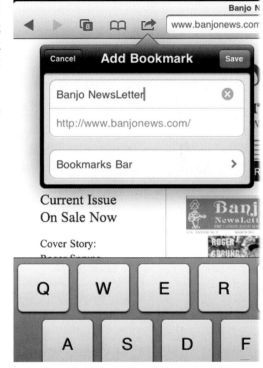

- **Rename it.** Some websites have hideously long names, like "Uncle Earl's Good-Time Five-String Finger-Pickin' Jam Session," but you can change that. Tap the top box on the Add Bookmark screen and rename the site something shorter, like "Banjos."

  The box right below that—which you can't mess with—displays the site's official web address.

- **File it.** The third line down in the Add Bookmark box lets you file the bookmark in a folder (see page 60) or add it to the Bookmarks bar on the browser window for quick 'n' easy access. Tap the Bookmarks link to open Safari's list of bookmark folders. When you find the one you want, tap the folder's name to deposit your bookmark there, where it awaits your return the next time you want to visit that site.

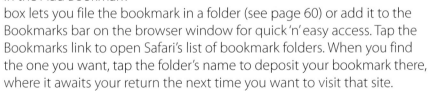

Tip If you make a mistake as you tap in a URL and don't notice it right away, you don't have to backspace all the way to the typo. Press your finger down on the text until a magnifying glass and a flashing insertion cursor appear, then drag your finger to the error, lift your finger, and correct the mistake. Then go back to where you were.

Make Home Screen Bookmarks

Are you one of those people who has shortcuts to your absolute favorite websites right on your computer's desktop? If so, would you like to continue the tradition on your iPad's Home screen? Not a problem.

When you're on a site you want to save, tap the button at the top of Safari and choose "Add to Home Screen" from the menu box. The site's icon now sits on your iPad's main screen. And don't worry about filling up your Home screen pages—you can have up to 11 of 'em and flick among them—or, if you run out of Home screen real estate, you can consolidate icons by storing them in a folder. See page 8 to create folders.

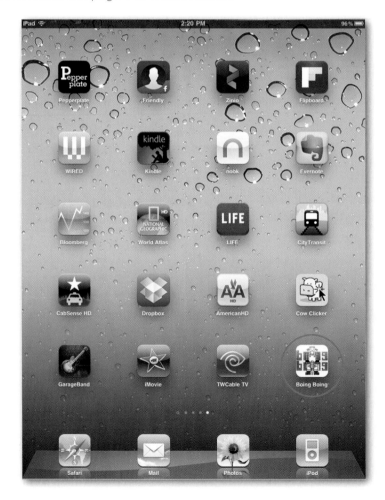

Jump to Other Web Pages

You may find yourself so mesmerized by navigating the iPad with a series of finger moves that you completely forget about the concept of clicking links, especially since you've probably been using a computer mouse to do that for the past 15 years or so.

Here's how you handle links on the iPad: Tap them with your finger, much the way you'd click them if you *did* have a mouse. As you know from desktop-computer browsing, not all links are blue and underlined. Sometimes, in fact, they're graphics, like pictures or icons.

Tip If you hold your finger on a link for a moment—press it rather than tap it—a box pops up identifying the link's full web address and offering three buttons: You can open the linked page, open it in a new browser page, or copy it to the iPad's clipboard to paste it elsewhere. Page 28 shows you how to copy and paste text.

Edit and Organize Bookmarks and Folders

Safari lists bookmarks in the order in which you save them, and that may not be the easiest way to remember where they are—especially if you wander around the Web saving site addresses every day. But iPad Safari is ready for this inevitability, as well as the probability that you'd like to delete old bookmarks every once in a while.

Editing your bookmarks—and folders of bookmarks—is quick and efficient on the iPad's version of Safari. To edit a bookmark or folder, tap the 🛱 button and then tap the Edit button. To edit bookmarks *inside* a folder, tap the 🛱 button, tap open the target folder, and then tap the Edit button.

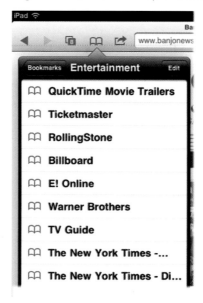

Tip If you're a newshound, there's one thing worth bookmarking: the *RSS feed* of your favorite news site—or all the RSS feeds from all your top sites. RSS feeds are subscriptions to a site's story summaries (the abbreviation stands for Really Simple Syndication). Subscribe, and you spare yourself the tediousness of checking sites for updated news and information manually, plus you get to read short summaries of new articles without ads and blinking animations. If you want to read a full article, just tap its headline.

Safari, as it turns out, doubles as a handy RSS *reader*. Whenever you tap an "RSS Feed" link on a web page, or whenever you type the address of an RSS feed into the Address bar (it often begins with *feed://*), Safari automatically displays a handy table-of-contents view that lists all the news blurbs on that page.

Here's what you can do to bookmarks and folders after you tap Edit:

- **Delete them.** When it's time for that bookmark or folder to go, tap the ⊖ button and then tap the Delete button.

- **Edit them.** Need to rename a folder or bookmark? Tap a folder to get to the Edit Folder screen so you can change the folder's name. To edit a bookmark, tap it to get to the Edit Bookmark screen, where you can change its name and address. Tap the Back button in the upper-left corner when you're done.

- **Refile them.** To make, name, or file a new folder, tap the New Folder button in the upper-left corner of the Edit screen. You can move an existing folder by tapping it, choosing a new location on the Edit Folders screen, and relocating the folder elsewhere in the Bookmarks list.

- **Rearrange them.** Need a new order for your bookmarks? As shown below, drag the three-bar grip strip (≡) up or down the list to move folders or bookmarks to a new place. (You can't delete or move the History folder, however.)

Tap the Done button when you're finished.

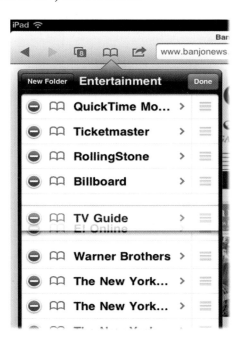

Sync Your Bookmarks

Saving bookmarks on the iPad as you go is fine, but over the years, you've probably built up a considerable collection of bookmarks on your desktop computer as well. In fact, you're probably very attached to some of those links. The good news is, you *can* take them with you—at least on the iPad.

To copy your entire Internet Explorer or Safari bookmark library from your computer to your iPad, all you need to do is turn on a checkbox in iTunes. Connect your iPad, click its icon in the iTunes window, and click the Info button at the top of the screen. Scroll down past things you can sync, like contacts, calendars, and mail accounts, until you get to the section called Other. Now, do the following, depending on the type of computer you have:

- **Windows PCs:** Turn on "Sync bookmarks with:" and then choose either Safari or Internet Explorer from the menu. Click Apply, and then Sync.

- **Macs:** Turn on "Sync Safari bookmarks," click Apply, and then click Sync.

As mentioned on the previous page, bookmarks you make on the iPad get synced back to your computer. But if things start to get too discombobulated and you decide you want to wipe out *all* the bookmarks on your iPad and start over with a fresh set from your computer, scroll down to the Advanced area of the Info screen (where it says "Replace information on this iPad"). Then put a check in the box next to Bookmarks before you sync again.

This is the wired way to sync. If you subscribe to Apple's MobileMe service, you can sync bookmarks on all your devices over the air, as page 271 explains.

Special Instructions for Firefox Fans

If Mozilla's Firefox browser is your preferred window to the Web, you can still move those foxy favorites over to your iPad. Apps like Firefox Home and Sync Browser can help, but you can also do it the long way—by first importing your bookmarks from Firefox into the desktop version of Safari. The next time you sync, your Firefox bookmarks land on your tablet (but bookmarks you add to Firefox on your iPad don't get synced back to your desktop browser).

- **Windows.** Grab your free PC copy of Safari (*www.apple.com/safari*) and, during the setup process, import your Firefox bookmarks. Press Ctrl+Shift+B to see them and trash the bookmarks you no longer need. Now set the iPad to sync with your PC's new copy of Safari bookmarks.

- **Macintosh.** Your Mac came with Safari. But if you spurned it to go browse with Firefox, hold your nose and open Safari anyway. Choose File→Import Bookmarks. Navigate to your Firefox book-marks file in your Home folder, and go to Library→Application Support→Firefox→Profiles→*weird scrambled-named folder like e9v01wmx.default* folder. Inside, double-click *bookmarks.html*.

  You have reeled in your Firefox bookmarks to Safari. Now, in Safari, press ⌘-Shift-B to show all your bookmarks onscreen. Delete the ones you don't want on the tablet, and then set the iPad to sync with Safari.

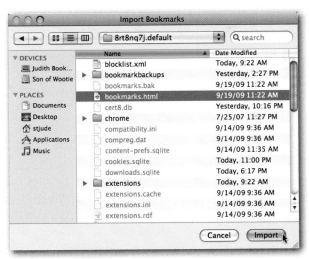

- **Both Systems.** Since most browsers (including Firefox here) usually have an Export Bookmarks feature under the File menu, you can use it to export your bookmarks file to your desktop. Then open Safari and choose File→Import Bookmarks to pull in your list of saved sites.

Call Up Your History List

The History button on desktop browsers has saved many a soul who can't remember the name of that really informative site from the other day. Safari on the iPad doesn't let you forget your history, either (well, not without some extra work), and it, too, quietly keeps a list of the sites you recently surfed.

To see your web trail, tap the ⊞ button and then tap the History folder, where Safari stores your past sites in tidy subfolders with names like "Earlier Today." Tap a bookmark within one of the History subfolders to go back in time—or at least back to that site. The link won't be in the History folder forever (time does march on, and so does the History list), so you may want to bookmark it for real within the week before it slips away.

Erase the History List

Don't want to leave a record of your browsing history in case someone picks up your iPad and snoops around? One way to prevent that is to set up a Passcode Lock on your iPad, as described on page 281. Then, anyone who wants to get into your iPad needs a four-digit code to unlock the screen.

Another way to clean up after yourself is to erase your whole History list. To do that, open the History folder and tap the Clear History button in the top-right corner (circled above). You've just wiped away your personal History. Many politicians probably envy you.

Save and Mail Images From the Web

Every once in a while, you come across an image on a web page that you just have to have on your computer. It could be a cool sports photo of your favorite ball player, an image of a house on a real-estate site, or a wacky picture of a disgruntled Pekinese. Now, on a desktop system, you just have to right-click (Control-click) the image with your mouse and choose "Save Image to Desktop." But how do you do that on the iPad, where there's no mouse, trackpad, or obvious way to right-click on anything?

Easy. Press the desired photo or graphic with your finger. A box pops up with a whole bunch of options like Open, Open in New Page, Save Image, and Copy. Tap the Save Image button to download a copy of the picture to your iPad's Photo library (page 256). From there, you can look at it any time you want, or email it to someone (page 259).

Tip Speaking of email (which is covered in the next chapter), you can also use the ol' press-and-save move with photo attachments to messages. And if you have a message with multiple photo attachments, the iPad is smart enough to offer you a button to save all the images simultaneously.

Stream Web Audio and Video

When the iPad was announced in 2010, there was much grumbling about the fact that it wouldn't play files in the Adobe Flash format—which is a large portion of the videos and browser-based videogames on the Web. In fact, some people thought the lack of Flash support would deal a crippling blow to the iPad's chances of success.

But guess what? Those naysayers were wrong. Sure, the iPad doesn't recognize Flash, RealPlayer, or Windows Media file formats, but it can do a fair amount of streaming in other formats. After all, it has that whole YouTube app (page 104) that plays plenty of videos. It can also play some QuickTime movies, like movie trailers, as long as they've been prepared in iPad-friendly video formats (page 250). It can also play MP3 and WAV audio files right off the Web. Here are a few sites to sample:

- **BBC News.** The Beeb's podcasts stream nicely, and you can search shows by radio station, genre, or get an A to Zed list; the company also has a fine iPad app (described on page 147). *http://www.bbc.co.uk/podcasts/*

- **"Meet the Press" audio stream.** You can find an MP3 edition of the venerable Sunday-morning talk show here: *http://podcast.msnbc.com/audio/ podcast/MSNBC-MTP.xml*

- **National Public Radio.** NPR has many of its signature programs, like "All Things Considered" and "World Café," plus "Morning Edition" and its other newscasts, online and ready to stream through your iPad's speaker at *m.npr.org.* (NPR has a news-focused iPad app in the App Store, too.)

- **New York Times podcasts.** Check out a whole page of news shows that start streaming when you tap the MP3 link. (The author is an employee of the *New York Times*.) *www.nytimes.com/podcasts*

Just about any MP3 file plays perfectly fine in the Safari browser. If you've already exhausted your iPad's music library, search for *free mp3 music* or check your favorite radio station's website for an MP3 stream of its live broadcast.

As for video, you have more to watch on the Web than just 'Pad-friendly streaming videos at Home→YouTube. And Apple hosts a huge collection of movie trailers at *trailers.apple.com*. Tap a movie poster to get started.

Work with Online Apps

With the rise of mobile Internet-connected devices came the increased popularity of *cloud computing*—using programs that reside and store files online, up in the clouds, where you can get to them from any Web-enabled machine. This means you don't have to drag around a seven-pound laptop stuffed with business software just to update a spreadsheet, because you can edit it *online* with a two-pound netbook. Or an iPad.

Not every cloud-computing site works with the iPad—Adobe's Flash-based Photoshop.com site, which lets you edit pictures online, is one example. Other sites may have limited functionality, like the ability to read files, but not edit them. Still, if you need to quickly look up something in a document stored online or check the status of an ongoing project, point your iPad toward the cloud.

Google Docs is probably one of the most popular cloud-computing apps, partly because it's free, partly because it can handle Microsoft Office documents, and partly because it belongs to the ever-growing Google Empire of Free Programs. To use it, you need a Gmail or Google account (also free at *www.google.com*). Once you sign up, you can create, edit, and share files right in your computer's web browser—including word-processing documents, spreadsheets, and basic presentations.

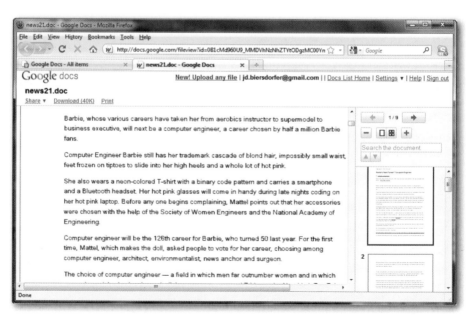

Since all those files are online, you can get to them through the Safari browser on your iPad. There are some limitations, though. For one, you currently can't edit documents or presentations on the iPad, so these files are pretty much read-only copies for reference when you're on the road. You can, however, do basic editing on your spreadsheet files.

And unlike Google Docs on a standard computer, you can't use the "offline" feature that lets you edit and save files even when you don't have an Internet connection. (That's because a piece of necessary software, called Google Gears, doesn't work with the iPad's operating system.)

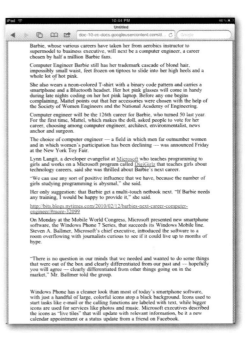

Another cloud-computing company, Zoho (*www.zoho.com*), has a whole slew of business and productivity apps that work through your computer's browser. Many of them are free for personal use; you just need to sign up for an account. Zoho Writer, Sheet, and Show roughly correspond to Microsoft Word, Excel, and PowerPoint, and can open and edit files in those formats. The company also has a front door for mobile devices at *mobile.zoho.com*; you can log in through the iPad if you need to refer to a file stored online in a less-cluttered interface than logging in to the standard web page.

If you're a big fan of cloud computing and already use services like the Basecamp project management site (*http://basecamphq.com*) or DropBox for file-sharing (*www.dropbox.com*), take a run through the Productivity section of the App Store for iPad-friendly programs that work specifically with those sites. For example, the free QuickOffice Connect app gives you a convenient portal to files you store on Dropbox, Box.net, Google Docs, and MobileMe (Chapter 16).

Dedicated Basecampers have several App Store choices as well. Programs like Satchel ($10) and Outpost 2 ($20) let you keep tabs on ongoing projects, tasks, and deadlines by checking in through your iPad.

Social Networking on the iPad

With your iPad, you can keep connected to all your favorite social networking sites whenever you hop onto a wireless network—because, after all, a large part of many people's day is spent keeping up with events on Facebook, Twitter, Flickr, and the like. Some sites even have their own iPad apps.

Chapter 7 has info about shopping the iTunes Store for iPad apps and instructions for installing them. Once you're ready, here's some of what's out there:

- **Facebook** and **MySpace.** Both sites have free apps in the App Store—but they're made for the iPhone. They do scale up to iPad size with a tap of the 2x button, but that means a blotchy display. Several third-party apps, like the Friendly and MyPad lines, give you alternative ways to tap social sites. The apps are streamlined for the touchscreen, but if you're not into them, there's *www.facebook.com* and *www.myspace.com* in Safari.

- **Twitter.** Using this widely popular micro-blogging service is much easier on the iPad than trying to text out pithy thoughts on a tiny mobile phone (unless, of course, it's an iPhone). Most Twitter apps are still iPhone-oriented, but *Twitter for iPad*, free and shown below, does an excellent job of turning your tablet into an easy-to-tweet dashboard for all your thoughts of 140 characters or less.

- **Flickr.** Several apps are available for browsing pictures on this massive photo-sharing site, but many exist just to ease photo-uploading. Perhaps the best way to experience Flickr is to point Safari at *www.flickr.com*.

- **AIM.** You can't get more social or networked than with instant messaging, which keeps you in touch with all your online pals through real-time, typed conversations. *AIM for iPad* works just like its computer and smartphone counterparts: Pick a friend off your Buddy List and shoot over a message to start a conversation. But the iPad edition doesn't end with AIM—you can also pull in updates from Facebook, MySpace, Foursquare, Twitter, YouTube, and other social sites.

- **Photobucket.** If you choose to share your pictures on Photobucket, check out the free *Photobucket for iPad* app. You can download any image to the tablet, easily search the entire site, and create albums right on your iPad.

- **G-Whizz! Social.** Designed for folks using Google Talk and Google Buzz to chat and share their lives, the *G-Whizz! Social* app hooks into one's Facebook, MySpace, and Twitter accounts as well.

Use Autofill to Save Time

Some people will love the iPad's simple virtual keyboard, and some will hate it because it feels like typing on a glass coffee table. And some will use it only when buying things online while relaxing in the hammock out back. No matter how you feel about the keyboard, there's one feature built into Safari that's bound to please everybody: *Autofill*.

Autofill, as its name suggests, automatically fills in your name, address, and phone number on web forms—saving you the drudgery of typing in the same information all the time. It's convenient, reduces your keyboard time, and speeds up purchases for power shoppers.

Along with your contact info, Autofill can remember passwords for websites that require them, but be careful with this. If you accidentally lose your iPad or someone steals it, the thief can retrieve your password, waltz right into your password-protected accounts, and steal even more from you.

To turn on Autofill, start on the iPad's Home screen and tap Settings→ Safari→Autofill. On the Autofill screen, tap the On button next to Use Contact Info. Tap the My Info line below it and choose your own name and address from your Contacts list. (See page 96 if you don't have a contact file for yourself.) Now when you come to a web form that wants your info, you'll see an Autofill button on the iPad keyboard; tap it instead of doing all that typing.

If you want to go ahead and use the password-supplying part of Autofill, tap the button on the Settings screen to On. Now, whenever you hit a site that requires your password, Safari gives you three choices: *Yes*, *Never for this Website*, and *Not Now* (the latter means you'll get pestered again on your next visit). Say Yes and the browser logs you into the site automatically from then on.

To play it safe, say Yes only to non-money-related sites, like online newspapers. Tap "Never for this Website" for any bank, stock-trading, e-commerce, or other site that involves money and credit-card numbers.

Use Multiple Web Pages

Tabbed browsers, like Internet Explorer and Firefox, have changed the way people surf. If you need to compare two pages or flip back and forth between them, you no longer have to open them in two separate windows. Tabs let you easily click back and forth between pages in the *same* window, making your personal space-time continuum much more efficient.

Safari on the iPad gives you a variation on the concept of tabbed browsing. You can push older pages off to the side when you need to open a new one, but still have both within a finger's reach. Here's what you can do:

- **Open a new page.** Need to check something on another site? Tap the ◫ button in the Safari toolbar. Your current page shrinks into the background. Tap inside the dotted outline of the New Page silhouette on the black screen (shown in the bottom-right corner) to get a fresh blank page to address and visit. You can open up to eight other pages this way. To see how many pages you have open at once, check the ◫ icon, which now has a tiny number inside it. If you see ▣, for example, you currently have three pages open.

- **Switch to another open page.** Go back and tap ▣ again. You return to the black screen and a grid of up to nine open pages, looking sort of like baseball-card versions of their larger selves. Find the page you want to revisit and tap it to open it full-screen again.

- **Close a page.** Tap that useful ▣ icon again and locate the mini-page you're ready to close. Tap the ⊗ button in the top-left corner to do so.

 Fans of tabbed browsing, rejoice! The new version of Safari, to be included with iOS 5 (due Fall 2011), comes with real tabs atop the browser window.

Use Safari Security

The Web is full of wonders—it's like the collective consciousness and accumulated knowledge of everyone who's ever used it, right there for you to explore. The Web is also full of jerks, criminals, and general-purpose evildoers, so you have to take care to keep your *personal* information safe in this Playground of Information. To see how Safari can help protect you, go to the iPad's Home screen and tap Settings→Safari. Your defenses include these:

- **Fraud Warning.** Some websites aren't what they appear to be; their main purpose is *phishing*—masquerading as legit sites to get you to enter personal info, like bank account and Social Security numbers. Turn this setting on so Safari can warn you when a site stinks like bad phish.

- **JavaScript.** This coding tool lets developers run little programs within web pages. Many are innocent, and most people leave JavaScript turned on. But some are not. Poorly written or malicious scripts have the potential to cause security problems, and JavaScript can also slow down page loads. Turn it off or on here.

- **Block Pop-ups.** Once a web surfer's lament, these unwanted extra windows (often hawking cheesy products and services) have been largely shattered by pop-up blocking controls in most browsers. Still, you

may need a pop-up window here and there to order concert tickets or to fill in web forms. You can block or unblock pop-ups here, but it's a universal setting for all sites.

- **Accept Cookies.** A cookie is a little file that helps a website recognize you. This can be good—you get a personal greeting from sites you revisit, for example—or bad, because some cookies track and report (to paying third parties) the ads you respond to. Here, you can choose to have Safari take a cookie *Never*, *Always*, or only from sites you actually visit.

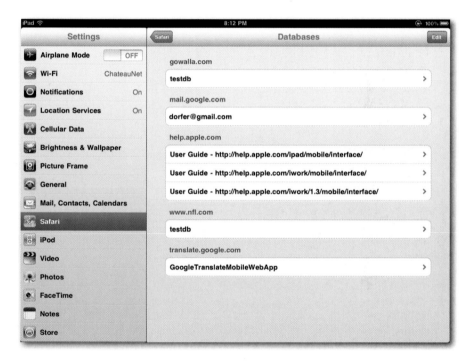

- **Databases.** Tap here to see which sites store info locally on your iPad. As shown above, many of Apple's help guides stash a bit of data here.

- **Clear History.** Tap this button to erase your Safari history (page 64).

- **Clear Cookies.** Tap the Clear Cookies button to delete them all.

- **Clear Cache.** The cache is where your iPad stores downloaded graphics and other web page parts to speed up your surfing. You can jettison these files by tapping Clear Cache here.

- **Developer.** If you create websites and want to see if they have errors in iPad Safari, tap Debug Console and get ready to stomp bugs.

slide to unlock

Keep in Touch with Email

Email is part of daily life. You wake up and check your inbox, you go to work and check it all day, and you come home and check it once more to make sure you haven't missed anything. Today, the ability to compose, send, and receive mail on mobile phones means you spend less time in front of a computer, but still, there you are—hunched over a smartphone, squinting and pecking on a tiny screen.

The iPad changes all that. Now you can lean back on your couch, flip on the tablet, and read and write mail on a spacious 10-inch screen. No more terse, abbreviated messages inspired by a cramped little keypad. With the iPad's full-size onscreen keyboard, you can compose your thoughts completely, without having to drag the laptop out of your home office and wait for it to boot up.

This chapter gives you a tour of the iPad's email program, from setting up your mail accounts to hitting the Send button on that first message. And remember, when you're done checking email, you'll find movies, music, and that new best seller are just a tap away—and you don't have to leave the couch, either.

Set Up an Email Account (or Two)

Thanks to its WiFi or WiFi + 3G connectivity, the iPad can grab your email out of thin air. Using it, you can read, write, and send messages so you stay in the digital loop of your life.

But to get your messages flowing *into* the iPad's Mail program, you need to supply it with your email account settings so it knows where on the Internet to look for your mailbox. You do this in a couple of ways:

Sync mail settings with iTunes

You get email on your desktop computer, right? If you're using a dedicated program like Microsoft Outlook or Apple Mail, you can copy your account settings over to your iPad without having to fiddle with server addresses and other arcane tech matters.

To do so, connect your iPad to your computer, click its icon in iTunes, and then click the Info tab. Scroll down to Sync Mail Accounts and put a check in the box next to "Sync selected mail accounts." Pick the accounts you want to tote around on your iPad. Click Sync or Apply to copy the settings—but not your computer-based messages—over to the iPad, where you can now check for mail from your tablet.

Set up mail accounts on the iPad

Tap the Mail icon. If you use Microsoft Exchange, MobileMe, Gmail, Yahoo, or AOL, tap the appropriate icon. If you don't use any of those, tap Other.

On the next screen, type in your name, email address, password, and a brief description ("Personal Gmail," say). If you tapped Other, be prepared to type in the settings you got from your Internet provider when you signed up for your account. This includes your email account user name, password, and the addresses of your ISP's incoming and outgoing mail  servers (which usually look something like *mail.myserver.com* and *smtp. myserver.com*, respectively).

If you don't happen to know this information off the top of your head and can't find the paperwork from your ISP, check the technical support area of its website for "email configuration settings" or "email server addresses." Or just peek at the account settings in your desktop computer's mail program.

Click Save, and the Mail program goes out and gets your new messages. Repeat the process if you have more than one account. (And you can always add more accounts later at Settings→Mail, Contacts, Calendars→Add Account.)

If you *do* have more than one email account, the iPad now (with iOS 4.2 and later) offers a *unified inbox* view at the top of the Mailboxes screen, as shown on the right. This means you can see all your new messages in *every* account at once just by tapping All Inboxes.

Of course, you can still check each inbox individually by tapping the account's name. And if you want to see other mailboxes, like Sent, Trash, and Drafts, flick down to Accounts, tap one, and then tap the name of the mailbox you want to see.

Tour the iPad's Mail Program

Once you get it set up, the iPad's email program works pretty much like any other: You read messages, you write messages, you send messages. But instead of popping open overlapping windows for Inbox messages, messages you're reading, and messages you're composing, the iPad keeps things in tight formation.

You don't have to click a thing to see your inbox along the left side of the screen and an open message displayed alongside it: Just hold your iPad *horizontally*. Your inbox appears as a vertical list, showing the sender's name, the message subject, and a two-line preview of each message.

A search box lets you scan mail for specific keywords. A blue dot (●) next to a message means you haven't read it yet. A numerical gray icon on the right side of a message preview (❸ ›) refers to the number of messages in that *thread*, or set of messages grouped together because they share the same subject line. Tap a message preview in the Inbox to see the missive open up and fill the rest of the screen, complete with message header, text, and attachments.

To reply to a message (or forward it on to somebody else), tap the ← icon. This brings up a fresh mail message with a copy of the original below it, ready for you to write back—or fill out a new address to forward along. It also brings up the iPad's virtual keyboard for the heavy fingerwork.

If you find the screen a little too busy with all these window panes, hold the iPad *vertically*. This 90-degree move re-architects the screen—all the background boxes disappear, and the one message you need to deal with sits front and center, filling the screen, with a toolbar on top.

This streamlined toolbar doesn't have a lot of room for button labels, so here's a guide to those cryptic Dan Brown-ish symbols, generally moving from left to right along the screen:

- **▲,▼ (Previous Message, Next Message).** When you have a message open on-screen, you don't have to switch back to the Inbox view to go on to the next one (or back to the previous one). Just tap the ▲ button to revisit the message you were reading earlier—or tap the ▼ icon to move on to the next message.

- **Č (Check Mail).** Tap the Č button to have the iPad check for new messages and load your inbox with fresh arrivals.

- **📁 (Move to Folder).** Want to save an open message to a different folder (Drafts, say) within an account? Tap this icon and pick the new folder.

- **🗑 (Delete).** Tap here when you're done with this message for good—or if it was an annoying piece of spam to begin with.

- **↩ (Forward, Reply, Print).** When you want to respond to a message or send it along to another recipient, tap the ↩ button and select its destination from the menu that pops up. (See page 32 for information on setting up the whole print-right-from-my-iPad thing.)

- **✎ Compose New Message.** Need to fire off a fresh note to somebody? Tap here to get started with a brand-new, blank message.

Read Mail

So how do you get started reading your messages once you get your mail accounts all set up? Like this:

❶ Tap the Mail icon on the iPad's Home screen. Unless you moved it, it's in the bottom row of icons, between Safari and Photos.

❷ If you're connected to the Internet, the iPad checks all the email accounts you set up and downloads any new messages it finds.

❸ If you're holding the iPad horizontally (landscape mode), your Inbox sits along the left side of the screen. Tap a message preview to see it displayed in full in the middle of the screen. If you're holding the iPad in its vertical position (portrait mode), the first or currently selected message fills the window; tap the Inbox button in the upper-left corner to see what else awaits you. If you're in another mailbox, like All Mail, tap the mail account name in the left corner to retrace your steps to your individual mailboxes.

❹ Work your way up and down the mailbox, either by tapping the message previews in the inbox or by using the ▲ and ▼ buttons (page 81) to scoot up or down the list from the main screen. Tap the "Mark as Unread" button on a message if you want it to appear as new mail so you can deal with it later.

File Attachments

Email messages often come with attached files. The iPad can open and display Microsoft Office and iWork files. It can also handle PDF, RTF (rich text format, a cross-platform text standard), .vcf (a Contacts file standard), and text files, as well as several photo and graphics file types, along with some types of video and audio files (as long as they aren't copy-protected).

File attachments like photos usually appear open and visible in messages, so if someone sends you a few snaps from their vacation on Italy's Amalfi Coast, you don't have to hunt around for icons at the bottom of the message to tap a photo open—you get instant envy without any extra effort.

Some attachments—like word-processing documents, spreadsheets, and presentations—typically appear as icons at the bottom of a message. Tap that Excel chart icon, for example, and the whole spreadsheet pops open to fill the iPad's screen.

Use Information in Messages

Ever notice how a lot of email messages involve setting up dinner dates, appointments, meetings, and other gatherings that use addresses and peo-ple's contact info? The iPad's Mail program knows this—and is ready to do something about it.

For example, say you get a message suggesting din-ner at a new restaurant— with the address helpfully pasted in the message. If it's an unfamiliar location, press down on it. The iPad recognizes this as a street address and turns it into a link. Tap it, and a box pops up offering four options—including the ability to see the address in the iPad's Maps program. Now *that's* service!

The other options include:

- **Create New Contact.** If your sender includes personal information, like a name, address, and phone number, in a message, you can add him or her to your Contacts list with a tap

- **Add to Existing Contact.** If you have the name but not the number of a friend or colleague in your Contacts file, you can add in the new info.

- **Copy.** Need to move this information into another message or program? Select Copy and, when you get to the destination file, hold your finger down and select Paste from the pop-up menu.

If the message has an underlined date, time, or phrase ("dinner tomorrow"), press and hold that bit of text to get a menu option for adding it as an event to the iPad's Calendar program. And now that you've mastered reading email, turn the page to find out how to write and send messages on the iPad.

Write and Send Email

When you're ready to write—or write back—the iPad is there for you. If you're starting from scratch with a new message, tap the ✏️ icon at the top of the screen. If you're replying to (or forwarding) a message you received, tap the ← icon and select *Reply*, *Reply All*, or *Forward*. Either way, you get a new message.

❶ If this is a brand-new message, tap the "To:" field at the top. The iPad keyboard appears for your text-entry pleasure. If the recipient is in your Contacts list (page 96) or you've written to the person before, the iPad cheerfully suggests addresses and fills in the "To:" line on your tap. Filling in the "Cc:" (carbon copy) field works the same way. If you're replying to a message, the address or addresses of your correspondents are already there for you.

❷ Tap the Subject line and type in whatever this message is about. If you're replying to a message, you can tap and edit the Subject line using the handy delete key on the iPad keyboard.

❸ Tap the message body area and type your missive.

❹ If you have multiple mail accounts, tap the "From:" field and choose the account you want to use here.

❺ When you finish, tap the Send button in the top-right corner to fire off your note. Hit Cancel if you change your mind.

> **Tip** Want to email a photo? Bop into the Photos app from the Home screen and tap open the album containing the image or images you want to send. Tap the 📧 icon at the bottom of the screen and then tap the photos you want to mail. Then tap the Share button to create a new message with the images attached. If you already have the message started, you can also paste in a pic.

Take Control of Your Email

Messages can pile up quickly, especially if you have several accounts funneling mail into your tablet. If you find yourself splashing around in a rising tide of mailbox flotsam, here are a few quick things you can do to get things back under control:

- **File messages in different folders.** Some mail providers, like Yahoo and AOL, let you create your own folders to sort messages the way you prefer, like by topic or sender. If you had your own folders set up with the service before you got your iPad, the folders should be there after you add the account to your tablet. To file a message into one of these personal folders, tap the 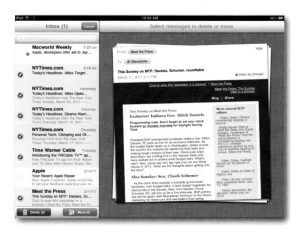 icon and choose the folder you want to use as the message's new home.

- **Delete all the junk at once.** Zapping unwanted messages out of your Inbox one by one with a finger swipe is tedious, but there's a faster way. Just tap the Edit button at the top of the Inbox pane. Buttons for Delete (🗑) and Move (📁) appear at the bottom of the screen. In the message list, tap the ones you want to either nuke or refile. Each message you select slides out into a "pile" next to the Inbox list— these are readable versions, so you can make sure you aren't dumping messages you still need. Once you make your selections, tap the appropriate button below to send all those messages to the same place at once: either the trash or a different folder.

- **Scan for spam.** Want to see the messages that are personally addressed to you, either in the "To:" or "Cc:" fields—and not mail addressed to you and 500 other people from bulk mailing lists or junk-mail dealers? The iPad can identify your personal messages by sticking a distinct little **To** or **Cc** tag on them. To turn on the tags, choose Settings→Mail, Contacts, Calendars and flip the On switch next to "Show To/Cc Label." Messages without these tags stand out and make more obvious targets for the mass-deletion method described above. The next page has more adjustments you can make to the Mail program's settings.

Adjust Mail Settings

Like most programs, the iPad's mail app comes with standard settings for things like the size of the text that appears onscreen. If you don't like the way the type looks or you want to tweak the program in other ways (like how many lines of a message appear in the Inbox preview), take a trip to Home→Settings→Mail, Contacts, Calendars.

From here, you can:

- **Change the minimum font size.** Unlike paper mail, you can easily make message print bigger or smaller for more comfortable reading. Size choices range from Small to Giant.

- **Add a custom signature.** As with a regular email program, you can add a personalized tag at the bottom of each outgoing message. Popular signatures include your contact information or quotes from *The Matrix*.

- **Show more (or less) preview in your message list.** Out of the box, the iPad's mail program shows you a two-line preview of each message so you have some idea of what it contains. You can change this from one to five lines, or select None to turn off the preview entirely.

- **Set a default mail account.** If you have multiple email accounts on your iPad, use this setting to designate one of them as your default account for all outgoing messages (and for messages you create by tapping mail links in other programs). Remember, you can always tap the "From:" field in a message to switch to a different account.

- **Load remote images (or not).** Some people don't like embedded graphics in a message, as they can transmit a signal to the sender that you opened the message. Turn off the images here.

- **Organize by thread.** Hate threaded messages clumped together under one subject line? Turn off the threading (and those ❸ ❯ icons) here.

- **Delete unwanted mail accounts.** Need to ditch an account because it's become too spam-laden or you need to streamline things? Flick up to the Accounts section, tap the name of the doomed account to get to its settings, and tap the Delete Account button.

Webmail on the iPad

Despite the fact that you can get your messages on the iPad through its dedicated Mail app, that's not the only way to monitor your inbox. As you may remember from the last chapter, the iPad has a nice, sturdy web browser. With it, you can check your Web-based email accounts (Yahoo, Gmail, Hotmail, AOL, and so on) by logging in through Safari. Doing it this way can be helpful if you just want to deal with your mail on the website it belongs to, no matter what device you're using.

Depending on the service you use, you may find that it offers a mobile version of your mailbox when you log in through the iPad's browser, like the Yahoo mailbox shown here. Some big services (like Google) even have their own free apps in the App Store, designed to make it easier to check mail, news, and other features on your iPad. Check the App Store and search for your service.

 Note To help you keep a copy of each message in your account no matter where you read it, Google turns the Delete button into an Archive button when you try to zap a message from the iPad's Mail app. Instead of getting deleted from your inbox, the message moves into the All Mail area of your account, where you can still read it on the Gmail website or on other devices you use for Gmail. If you prefer to delete those unwanted messages, tap Settings→Mail, Contacts, Calendars, and then tap the name of your Gmail account. In the account's settings area, tap the button next to Archive Messages from On to Off.

POP3 and IMAP Accounts on the iPad

Web-based mail—especially if it's *free*—works for many people. But millions of others don't use webmail for one reason or another, perhaps because they have accounts from their Internet providers, use employer-provided accounts, or worry about privacy and security. At any rate, these mail accounts are typically one of two types:

- **POP accounts.** Short for "Post Office Protocol," these accounts use an older messaging technology, but are still quite common around the Internet. The main drawback to POP is that it wasn't really designed for checking mail on *more than one* computer (yes, it pre-dates the mobile boom).

  Unless you're allowed by your ISP to save mail on its server, a POP server transfers incoming mail to your computer (including your iPad) before you read it, which works fine as long as you're using only *that machine* for your email. You won't get a copy of that message when you log in from another computer because you already downloaded it.

- **IMAP accounts.** IMAP (Internet Message Access Protocol) is a newer mail system that folks on the go tend to like much better than one-stop POP. Instead of downloading a message to just one machine and leaving it there, IMAP servers keep all your mail online. That means you can get the same mail from any computer (or trusty iPad). These thoughtful IMAP servers remember which messages you've already read and sent off. They also keep tabs on your other mail folders. (Yahoo, MobileMe, AOL, and Gmail all use IMAP, as do corporate Microsoft Exchange servers.)

  Now for the bad news: Since all this mail roosts on the IMAP server, you need to deliberately delete old messages or your mailbox will eventually runneth over. On IMAP accounts that don't come with a lot of storage, the server could start bouncing new messages when it gets full, annoying your friends. And you don't want that.

No matter which kind of account you have, the iPad will work with it. You just need to have all the user account information for it.

 Tip Since you're on the go, the iPad generally copies your IMAP messages to itself, so you can deal with mail even when you're not online. If you want to direct these messages to a specific mail folder, you can. Open Settings→Mail, Contacts, Calendars→[IMAP account name]→Account→Mail→Advanced. On this screen, tell the iPad where to put draft, sent, and deleted messages.

Syncing your mail accounts with iTunes (described at the beginning of this chapter) is one way to get each type of account set up correctly on the iPad. If you skipped that step, you can do it the old-fashioned, manual way.

Start on the iPad's Home screen and tap Settings→Mail, Contacts, Calendars→ Add Account. On the next screen, tap Add Mail Account and then enter your name, email address, password, and an optional description. Tap Next to start working through the account-creation screens.

The Mail app attempts to pin down which kind of account you have (POP or IMAP) by your email address. If it can't figure it out, it takes you to a second screen, and grills you for information like the host name for incoming and outgoing mail servers. At the top of the box, you can tap either IMAP or POP, to inform the iPad of your account type.

If you don't have this information written down (or stored in your own memory bank), ask your Internet service provider or the office tech guru for help.

When you're finished, tap Save.

6

 slide to unlock

Use the iPad's Built-In Apps

Apps, also known as "programs that run on the iPad" (and iPhone and iPod Touch), make Apple's tablet a versatile device, beyond its role as a Web window and portable email reader. As mentioned back in Chapter 1, the iPad gives you a few of its own apps right on the Home screen, alongside the previously discussed Safari and Mail apps.

Three of these apps handle personal organization tasks: Calendar (for keeping your appointments), Contacts (your address book), and Notes (for jotting down bits of text to yourself). One app, Maps, helps you find yourself and chart your course, and two other apps (iTunes and the App Store) point the way to shopping Apple's online stores.

Aside from the Settings app (described in Appendix A), the rest of the iPad's Home screen icons are there to entertain you: YouTube, Photos, Videos, and iPod. And if you have a second-generation iPad, you have three other fun apps to play with: Camera, FaceTime, and Photo Booth, all devoted to creating pictures and video clips right there on your tablet, wherever you may be.

And remember, these are just the apps that come *with* the iPad. Once you get to know these built-in apps, you'll be ready to tackle any of the gajillion other goodies in the App Store. But that's for another chapter (7, to be exact).

Set Up Your Calendar

Just as iTunes can sync bookmarks and mail settings from your computer to your slab, so it can snag and display a copy of your daily or monthly schedule on your iPad—*if* you happen to use Outlook on your PC or iCal on your Mac. You can also use Entourage 2004 or later by choosing, in Entourage, Preferences→Sync Services and checking the option to have Entourage share its info with iCal. (Alas, Outlook 2011 for the Mac doesn't sync calenders yet.)

To get your life in sync between computer and iPad, fire up iTunes and then:

❶ Connect your iPad to your computer and click the iPad's icon when it shows up in iTunes' Source list.

❷ In the main part of the iTunes window, click the Info tab. Scroll down past Contacts to Calendars.

❸ Turn on the checkbox next to "Sync Calendars with Outlook" (Windows) or "Sync iCal Calendars" (Mac). If you have multiple calendars—like for work, home, and school—select the ones you want to copy to your 'Pad.

❹ In the lower-right corner of the iTunes window, click the Apply button.

❺ If your iPad doesn't automatically start updating itself with your date book, choose File→Sync iPad. If you haven't changed any calendar settings (like turning off the iCal sync) but want to update your appointments, you won't see an Apply button; rather, you'll see just the Sync button, and you can click that instead of going up to Menuville.

> **Tip** If you prefer to sync wirelessly, and you have a MobileMe or Microsoft Exchange account, you can update your MobileMe/Exchange calendar over the airwaves. Choose Settings→Mail, Contacts, Calendars and then tap MobileMe or Exchange. Tap the Calendars button to On to keep your calendar current across devices you configured to work with MobileMe or Exchange.

On the iPad, tap the Calendar icon on the Home screen to see your schedule unfold in glorious color. If you have multiple calendars, tap the Calendars button to select one and see its events—or you can consolidate your appointments into one uber-calendar. Use the search box to find specific events.

Along the top of the screen, tap List, Day, Week, or Month to see your schedule for the short or long term, color-coded by calendar type (home, work, school, and so on). Tap the Today button to see what's in your immediate future. List view displays your scheduled events one after the other. No matter which view you choose, the iPad shows the year's months in a bar below the calendar. Tap the triangles on either side of the bar to go forward or backward in time.

Use the iPad Calendar

The iPad isn't a static version of your calendar. You can add events to and delete them from it and sync them back to your computer (or to your MobileMe or Exchange accounts). The iPad's calendar also lets you subscribe to online calendars to keep you apprised of events on Web-based Google and Yahoo calendars—or even your favorite sports team's schedule.

Add a Calendar Event

To punch in a new appointment or event, tap the **+** button in the lower-right corner of the calendar screen. In the box that pops up, fill in all the necessary information, like the name of the event, location, and starting and ending times. (There's also an All-Day option for those outdoor rock festivals and softball tourna-ments.) Tap Alert to be reminded about an appointment in advance—from five minutes to two days beforehand.

If you need a standing appointment, like a weekly banjo lesson or staff meeting, you have the option to repeat the event every day, every week, every other week, every month, or every year (like for your wedding anniversary or spouse's birthday). There's also a little Notes field in the Add Event box in case you need to remember some additional information about the appointment, like "Bring Q3 report" or "Take cat-allergy meds before leaving."

Edit or Delete an Event

Schedules change, especially if you work in the high-powered corporate world or have teenage children—or both. To change the time of an event, find it on the calendar, tap the event, and then tap the Edit button. If you need to cancel an appointment completely, flick down to the bottom of the box and tap the red Delete Event button.

Set Up an iPad Alert

To make the iPad pipe up with a text and audio alert for a looming event, tap Settings→General→Sounds and flip Calendar Alerts to On. At the prede-termined nag time, a reminder box flashes on-screen, accompanied by an R2-D2-like booping noise. If the iPad is off, the message appears when you turn it on, but the audio alert doesn't play.

Subscribe to an Online Calendar

To see a shared calendar or one you subscribe to, add it to the iPad. If it's a specific calendar on the Web, choose Settings→Mail, Contacts, Calendars→Add Account→Other. Select the Add CalDAV Account option (when you want to add a datebook like a Google calendar; see *http://bit.ly/iYvA5* for instructions) or Add Subscribed Calendar. Enter the calendar's URL and any other account information you need to subscribe, like your user name and password.

Want to instantly add customized online calendars for all sorts of topics, including religious holidays, schedules of your favorite sports teams, movie release dates, and more— right on your iPad? Crank up the Safari browser and visit iCalShare.com (*http://icalshare.com*). When you find a calendar you want to add to your iPad's collection, tap the Subscribe to Calendar button on the page, and

then confirm your decision in the box that pops up. The new calendar gets added to your subscription list, and you see its events on your schedule. Tap the Calendars button and select it to show (or hide) those dates.

Calendars you add by subscription over the Internet are read-only, so you can't add your own events to them. If you want to delete a calendar subscription, tap Settings→Mail, Contacts, Calendars. In the Accounts list, tap the name of the calendar and tap the red Delete Account button.

 Tip If you have an iPad calendar set up to sync with an Exchange account, you can respond to Outlook or Entourage meeting invitations that your colleagues send you. When you get a new invite, it lands on the scheduled date and time in your calendar with a dotted line around the event. You respond to it by tapping it on the calendar or by tapping 🔲 to see pending invites. Select the one you wish to reply to. Tap Invitation From to get all the details, like who called the meeting and who else got invited. When you get an invitation, you can tap Accept, Maybe, or Decline to send off your RSVP. And if you get your meeting invitations by email instead, tap the Invite icon attachment on the message to open it up and respond to the sender. If you accept, the iPad adds the event to your calendar.

If you get a lot of meeting invitations and want to know as soon as they arrive, tap Settings→Mail, Contacts, Calendars. In the Calendars area of the screen, tap the On button next to New Invitation Alert.

Maintain Contacts

Putting a copy of your contacts file—also known as your electronic address book—on your iPad is quite easy, as long as you use up-to-date software. Windows users need to have their contacts stored in Outlook Express, Outlook 2003 or later, Windows Contacts, or the Windows Address Book (used by Outlook Express and some other email programs).

Mac folks need to use at least Mac OS X 10.5 and the Mac OS X Address Book, which Apple's Mail program uses to stash addresses. You can also use Outlook 2011 or Entourage 2004 and later, but you first have to *link* before you *sync*: In Entourage, choose Preferences and click Sync Services. Then turn on the checkboxes for sharing contacts with Address Book. Outlook or Entourage share the info, and Address Book syncs it up.

To turn your iPad into a big glass address book, follow these steps:

❶ Connect your iPad to your computer and click its icon when it shows up in iTunes' Source list. (If you use Outlook or Outlook Express, launch that now, too.)

❷ In the main part of the iTunes window, click the Info tab.

❸ Windows owners: Turn on the checkbox next to "Sync Contacts with" and then use the drop-down menu to choose the program whose contacts you want to copy. Mac owners: Turn on the "Sync Address Book con-tacts" checkbox. If you want to sync contact groups, select them from the "Selected groups" box. You can also choose to import the photos in your contacts files.

❹ Click the Apply button in the lower-right corner of the iTunes window.

The iPad updates itself with the contact information stored in your address book. If you add new contacts while you have your iPad plugged in, choose File→Update iPad or click the Sync button in iTunes to manually move the new data over to your tablet.

> **Tip** You can add contacts right on the iPad as well—tap the **+** button at the bottom of the screen and type the person's information into the form. If you're on a synced Exchange server, tap Settings→Mail, Contacts, Calendars, tap your account name, and tap the Contacts button to On to pull new addresses into the iPad over the air.

To look up a pal on the iPad, tap the Home screen's Contacts icon. Use the search box or, on the Contacts list, flick to the person's name on the left side of the screen (take a shortcut by tapping the letter tab on the outer edge). Tap the name to see the person's details. Here are some of things you can do now:

- **Change the information.** Need to update an address or change a phone number? Tap the Edit button at the bottom of the contact screen.

- **Add a photo.** Pictures in your desktop contacts program should be here on the iPad. You can also add a picture to a contact from your iPad's Photos app. Open the contact file, tap Edit, then tap Add Photo. Find the picture you want, then pinch and zoom to crop it to the right size.

- **Map an address.** Tap an address to open the Maps app and see the location highlighted.

- **Send a message.** Tap the person's email address to open up a pre-addressed Mail message.

- **Pass along the information.** Tap the Share Contact button on the contact's page to attach the information as a *.vcf* file (the format most computer address books use) and attach it to a new message.

- **Start a FaceTime video call.** Tap the FaceTime tab and then tap the phone number or email address your pal uses for FaceTime (page 102).

To delete a contact, whack it from your computer's address book and the person will disappear from your iPad the next time you sync up. To delete a contact directly on the iPad, tap it open, tap Edit, and then tap Delete Contact.

Take Notes

Need a piece of virtual scratch paper to jot down a few thoughts? Have to type up a memo to email to colleagues, but don't own the Pages app described in Chapter 10? Want to copy a recipe off a web page and save it for future reference, when you may not have online access? The iPad's Notes program is here to serve. To get started, return to your Home screen and tap Notes. The program opens, and here's where Apple's designers got really creative.

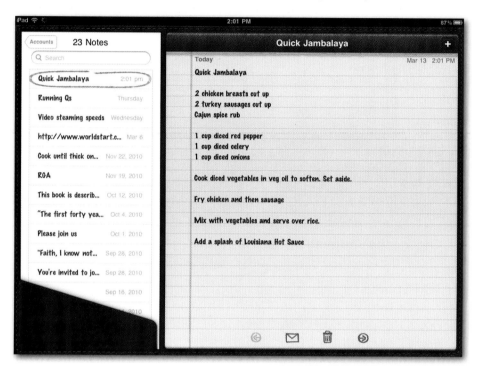

When you hold the iPad in portrait mode, it looks like one of those yellow lined pads of paper you used to scribble lecture notes in school. But hold the iPad in landscape mode, as shown above, and the yellow pad shrinks down to size and shares the screen with a virtual slip of index paper, all tucked inside a faux leather folio, the kind made to sit on top of your desk and look fancy. You can even see stitches in the digital leather.

 Tip Although it's hard to change your own handwriting in a real pen-and-paper situation, the iPad's Notes program gives you a choice of three fonts to hold your thoughts. To see your options or to change the current font, go to the Home screen and tap Settings →Notes. Here, you can choose from Chalkboard, Helvetica, and a font called Market Felt, which was the jaunty original (and, at that time, only) typeface Notes used.

When you hold the iPad in portrait mode, you can see the same index of all your stored notes by tapping the Notes button in the upper-right corner of the screen. Tap any entry in the list to jump to that particular note and open it so you can read it—or add more text to it. All of the Cut | Copy | Paste | Replace functions described back in Chapter 2 work in Notes, so you can paste in gobs of text you copy from web pages and elsewhere. You can't, however, paste picture files—you just get a string of text with the image file's name and location.

To start a new note, tap the **+** icon in the upper-right corner to generate a blank sheet of "paper." Tap the yellow Note itself to summon the iPad's keyboard for a little good-old-fashioned text entry. You can sync notes to and from a MobileMe or Windows Outlook account, too (see page 192).

If you're looking for a certain word or words, type them into the search box to call up a list of all the notes where the words appear. To flip forward or backward through your collected notes, tap the arrow keys at the bottom of the screen. You can even email the contents of a note by tapping the ⊠ icon down below. (Hey, it costs the price of a stamp to do that with a paper note nowadays, so you just saved a little cash.)

Use the Camera for Photos and Videos

The second-generation iPad arrived in March 2011 sporting a feature many had hoped for and wanted: cameras on the front and back. This one-two camera punch gives new iPad owners the same hardware iPhone and iPod Touch folks have for FaceTime video calls, shooting movies, and snapping photos.

With its huge slab screen, the iPad is probably one of the more unwieldy point-and-shoot cameras out there, but it's not exactly bursting with megapixels. While the rear camera can shoot 720p high-definition video at 30 frames per second, still photos from the rear camera have a resolution of just 1280 × 720 pixels (an average digicam has a resolution of about 1600 × 1200 pixels). And while the front camera's VGA quality—640 × 480 pixels—is fine for online video chats, your regular digital camera shouldn't feel threatened.

Taking Still Photos

To shoot a digital photo, make sure you set the little slider in the bottom-right corner to ◙ (still camera). Line up your shot and press the shutter button (◙). Your newly snapped picture ends up in Photos→Camera Roll. A preview of the last shot you snapped also appears in the bottom-left corner of the screen; tap it to jump right to the photo in the Camera Roll album.

The iPad cameras offer a few controls for better photos:

- **Exposure adjustment.** Lighting is an important part of photography, and while the iPad doesn't have a flash, it does let you adjust the *exposure* (the overall lightness or darkness) of an image. If you have a shot lined up, but one part of the frame is cast in shadows, tap a lighter area of the image. A blue-white square (right) appears briefly and the iPad's camera adjusts its exposure settings based on that area. Now you can snap the pic.

- **Zoom.** Tapping the screen to readjust the photo's exposure also brings up the zoom slider (right). If you want to narrow in on your subject and lose distracting background elements, tap the screen and drag the slider to the right until you have the framing you want. Drag the slider the other way to zoom back out.

To change cameras and take a self-portrait with the front camera, tap the Switch Cameras icon (⟳) in the upper-right corner of the photo screen.

Shooting Videos

To shoot a video, tap the Camera icon on the iPad's Home screen and nudge the slider over to ◼◀. When you're ready to start filming, tap the ⊙ button. It flashes red to indicate that you're recording. The time stamp in the upper-right corner of the screen shows the current length of your video-in-progress. The tiny microphone on the back of the iPad records the audio. When you're ready to virtually yell "Cut!", tap the ⊙ button again to stop recording.

Like the still camera, you can tap an area of the screen to adjust the exposure, but there's no zoom feature for video. You can hold the iPad vertically or horizontally to shoot video, but portrait-shot clips may get letterboxed if you upload them to a site that displays video in the horizontal orientation.

Share and Upload Photos and Videos

Now that you've taken all these great photos and videos, don't you want to share them? You can do that in several ways:

- **Email.** Tap Photos→Camera Roll to see your photos and videos; if you have the Camera app open onscreen, tap the thumbnail preview icon in the toolbar to jump to your collection. Next, hit the ➦ button, tap the thumbnails of the photos and videos you want to send, and then tap Email. A Mail message appears with your files attached, ready for you to address and send. The Copy option lets you copy and paste the file into a message you've already started. (You can also use the ➦ button to select files for deletion out of the Camera Roll.)

- **Upload to YouTube or MobileMe.** With a video clip open onscreen, tap the ➦ button and select Send to YouTube or Send to MobileMe.

- **Transfer to the computer.** Connect your iPad to your PC or Mac and use the Import command in your photo-organizer program (like Adobe Photoshop Elements or iPhoto) to copy over photos and videos. Once you have the files on your computer, you can post them online.

Want to polish your work before sharing? Consider an iPad video-editing app (page 248) or photo-editing app (page 260).

Make Video Calls with FaceTime

Since the early days of science-fiction movies and TV shows, the videophone has been a staple of fantasy communication. Cheap webcams and teleconferencing systems made the fantasy real, but they're *so* last year. For modern convenience, the iPad makes and takes video calls thanks to FaceTime, its built-in mobile video-chat app. It's like a real-time talking picture frame.

To use FaceTime, you need an Apple ID (Chapter 7) and a WiFi connection (sorry, no 3G). You also need folks to talk to, namely people running around with fourth-generation iPhones or iPod Touches, fellow second-generation iPad owners, or folks with Apple's FaceTime program for Mac OS X.

Once you have all that, getting started with FaceTime is easy:

❶ Tap the FaceTime icon on the Home screen and sign in with your Apple ID. If you don't have an Apple ID, see page 118 for how to get one. You can also use a different email address for your FaceTime login.

❷ Once you have your account set up, tap Home→FaceTime and tap the Contacts icon at the bottom of the screen. In the Contacts list, tap the name of the person you want to call, and then tap the iPhone number or email address they use for their own FaceTime accounts. (No contacts? See page 96 to get some and for another way to start a FaceTime call.)

❸ When your buddy picks up the call, prop up your iPad so they can see you and start chatting. You see them, too. If the little picture-in-picture window of your face is in the way, use your finger to drag it around.

❹ After you wave goodbye, tap the End button (📞 **End**) to hang up.

If you need to temporarily turn off the sound during a call (like when the baby starts screaming), tap the Mute icon (🎤) in the screen's bottom-left corner.

Want to show your friend what you're seeing without physically flipping the iPad around? Tap the 📷 icon ion the right side of the toolbar to switch to the iPad's rear camera. Tap the icon again to return the view to you.

Take Portraits with Photo Booth

Remember those old-fashioned instant-portrait kiosks that can still be found in arcades or along the boardwalk? You know, the kind where you get a strip of four black-and-white shots for a buck, and you and your pals all cram together to make goofy faces for the camera? The second-generation iPad can do the same thing, but better—the pictures are free and in color. Meet Photo Booth.

Like its predecessor (part of Mac OS X for years), Photo Booth is a simple app for taking your own picture, say, if you need a quick headshot for your Facebook page. You can use Photo Booth with the rear camera as well; just tap the ⟳ icon to switch back and forth between cameras. But for loads more fun, you can also add one of eight special effects to your photo, including several funhouse-mirror style distortions, a thermal camera simulation, or even a creepy faux x-ray filter.

Here's how to get going with Photo Booth:

❶ Tap the Photo Booth icon on the iPad's Home screen.

❷ You can take a regular photo, or you can pick a special effect. Tap the ⊠ icon to see a preview of all the effects. Tap the one you want to use. (If you pick one of the funky funhouse-mirror distortions, you can distort it further by dragging your finger around on the screen.)

❸ Snap the photo by tapping the ◉ button.

A small thumbnail version of your photo slides into the photo tray underneath the mail screen. Tap the photo to see it full-size. Tap the ➦ button to email or copy the image. To delete a photo from Photo Booth, tap its thumbnail in the photo tray. Then tap the ⊗ button in the corner of the thumbnail image and tap Delete Photo.

Copies of your Photo Booth pictures are also saved to Photos→Camera Roll, so you can share the pictures from there, too (page 259).

Watch YouTube Clips

YouTube, which started in 2005, has become *the* spot to share and see video from around the world. While YouTube videos on the Web usually come in the Flash format, a technology foreign to the iPad, Apple convinced the site to re-encode its millions of videos into H.264 format, a *much* higher-quality rendering than Flash—*and* one you can play via the iPad's YouTube app. Here's how.

Find Videos on YouTube

The iPad is full of entertainment options, and its YouTube app is no exception. Tap the YouTube icon on the Home screen to see:

- **Featured.** This list highlights videos that folks on the YouTube team think are interesting or worth your while to watch. Tap a thumbnail to see 'em.

- **Top Rated.** When someone watches a video on YouTube, they can give it a thumbs-up ("Like") or a thumbs-down ("Dislike") rating to reflect their opinion of the clip (this binary system replaced the old one- to five-star ratings). Tap here to see videos with the most upward thumbs.

- **Most Viewed.** If you constantly get emailed the same videos, odds are they're on this list. Tap the *Today*, *This Week*, or *All* (as in "of all time") tabs to see. When you get to the end of the list, tap "Load 25 More" to load up the next set of vids.

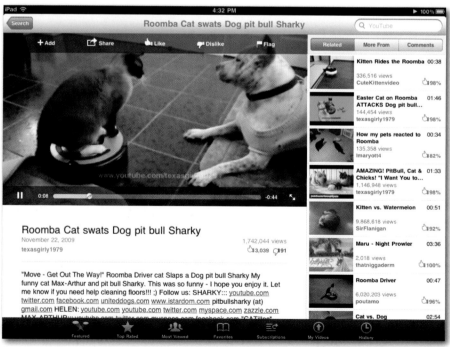

- **Favorites.** If you have a YouTube account (it's free, and it also means you can upload your own clips), you can mark videos as your faves so you can find them easily in your Favorites list.

- **Subscriptions.** Many organizations and celebrities have their own YouTube "channels" that you can subscribe to. Once you sign up, tap here to see the latest video dispatches from Oprah or the Queen of England.

- **My Videos.** Tap here to see a list of the clips you've uploaded to YouTube (you need to be logged into your YouTube account to do so).

- **History.** Like a web browser, the YouTube app keeps track of what you've looked at. Also like a browser: Tap the Clear button to wipe out the evidence that you checked out those skateboarding dogs videos again.

There's also a search box in the upper right corner to seek out videos by keywords. Tap any video thumbnail to open a Details screen for that video, featuring a description, date, category name, keywords, the contributor's name, length, number of views, links to related videos, and so on.

That same Details screen offers an Add button (**+**) so you can add the video to your list of favorites. Tap the Share button (**⮕**) to send a link to the clip by email. You can also Like, Dislike, and "Flag as Inappropriate" selected videos.

Control the Playback of YouTube Videos

To play a video, tap its thumbnail. You can watch it in portrait or landscape mode. Tap the **⬛** button to expand the clip to the screen's width.

The standard playback controls (**⏭**, **⏮**, **⏸**, the volume slider, and the progress bar that lets you jump around in the timeline) appear when the clip starts playing. After a few seconds, the controls disappear and get out of the way, so they don't block the picture. Tap the screen once to make them reappear (or disappear again).

YouTube videos can have black bars on the sides of the playback screen. To see a video full-screen, tap the **⬛** button in the top-right corner or double-tap the screen itself. To beam the clip to your Apple TV with AirPlay, tap the **⬛** icon. You can also watch YouTube on your TV with a cable connection (page 246). Tap the **Done** button in the top-left corner when you finish watching.

YouTube in the iPad's full-screen mode offers two other icons on the control bar: On the left side, the **⌘** button, quickly adds the clip on screen to your YouTube Favorites list. Tap the icon on the right, the **⬛** button, to shrink the video down from the full-screen mode so you can see its Details page.

Find Your Way with Maps

The iPad's Maps app makes you forget all about those folded paper roadmaps that always end up stained and crumpled in the back seat of the car. Tap open the Maps app on the Home screen. Type any address into the Maps app—and you instantly see it on the screen, its location marked with a virtual red pin. All your usual iPad finger moves work on the maps, so you can zoom, scroll, pinch, and flick your way around the world.

Like Safari, though, Maps needs an Internet connection to pull its data down from the Web, so it's not the best thing in the world for emergency directions when you're lost in a bad part of town with only a Wi-Fi iPad. (If you ponied up the big bucks for a Wi-Fi + 3G model, you don't have to worry about lack of an Internet connection, but you may still have to worry about getting mugged.)

To plot your course, tap the Maps icon on the Home screen. Here are some of the things you can do with Maps and a network connection:

- **Find an address.** Tap the Search button. In the Address box at the top of the screen, type in an address—or tap the ⊞ icon to call up your bookmarks list. Here, you can tap places you've previously marked, see your recent locations, or map an address from your contacts list. When the red pushpin drop onto the map, tap your ❶ in the bar above it to get an info box for that address, like the one shown on the next page.

- **Mark the spot.** Press and hold any spot on the map to drop a marker pin on it. If you miss slightly, press and drag the pin to the right address. Tap ❶ to see the full address, get directions (to or from there), or remove the pin. You can also add the location to your contacts or bookmarked places, or share the address by email—very handy when you set up a group dinner at a new restaurant. If the pin's infobar has an ❶ icon, tap it to see a photo of the location from Google Street View that you can zoom, pan, and rotate 360 degrees; tap the map inset in the bottom-right corner to go back to the regular view. You can plant a pin the long way by tapping the bottom-right corner of the screen (where it looks like the map is peeling away), tapping the Drop Pin button, and then dragging the pin around the map to the right location. And you can mark your current location by tapping the ➔ icon in the menu bar.

- **Pick a view.** The Maps app doesn't skimp on the scenery. Tap the bottom-right corner to see your available map styles: Classic (traditional cartography), Satellite (a high-quality photo from a camera high in the sky), Hybrid (street names overlaid on the streets' photo), and Terrain (shaded elevations of the area). Tap Show Traffic if you want to see current road congestion and maybe take that antacid *before* you leave the house.

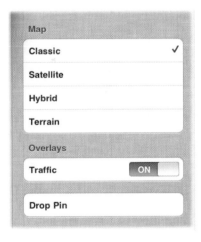

 Ever wonder what those green, yellow, and red lines actually mean when you look at a map of traffic conditions? The color-coding is all about the need for speed—or the lack of it. Green means traffic is moving at a rate of 50 miles an hour or more, and yellow means slower going, at 25 to 50 m.p.h. Red means traffic is creeping along at less than 25 m.p.h., so you may find some very crabby cabbies out there.

Locate Your Position Using GPS

Ever look at a map and wonder exactly where you are in relation to the place you're trying to get to? Unless that map has one of those You Are Here arrows, you usually have to guess—but not if you have an iPad.

Just make sure you have an Internet connection and your Location Services turned on (page 279), too. Then tap the Current Location icon (➹) at the top of the Maps screen. The iPad drops a blue dot on the map to mark your position to within a few hundred yards. While the Wi-Fi iPad doesn't have a GPS chip inside it like the 3G 'Pad does, it does have software that calculates your position based on a big database of Wi-Fi hot spots and cell towers.

You can even combine the ability to instantly find your current location with getting directions to someplace else. Just tap the Directions button at the top of the screen. Unless you're offline, the iPad usually starts with your current location in the first box. In the second box, type in a destination address or tap the ⊞ button to get to your contact addresses. Once it has the starting and ending points of your journey, the iPad pops up a blue bar offering driving, mass transit, or walking directions (see the next page for more on getting directions).

If you want to use your current position and navigate your way Boy Scout-style, the iPad includes a built-in digital compass. To use it, tap the Current Location icon once to get your position, and then tap it again to activate the digital compass, which appears on the iPad screen. To rotate the compass-point north, hold the iPad parallel to the ground. To get back to regular map view, tap the Compass icon (◨) in the toolbar.

If a message with a ∞ symbol appears on the screen as shown here, you need to calibrate the compass, which is normal the first time you use it. Firmly grip the iPad and wave it in an "air Figure 8" pattern to fine-tune its sense of direction.

Get Directions on the Map

Need to find your way from Point A to Point B, or at least from Albany to Boston? To map your route, tap the Directions button at the top of the screen. A two-field box appears. If you don't want to use your current location, tap the ❌ in the Start box and type in a point of origin. In the End box, type in the destination address or tap the 📖 icon and choose one from your list of book-marked sites, recent visits, or contacts.

Once the iPad gets the starting and ending points, it calculates how to get there by car, mass transit (like train or bus), or foot. Tap the car, bus, or walking-person icon to get a set of step-by-step directions. If you're in the middle of nowhere, driving directions may be all you see here. (If you need to reverse the starting and ending points of the trip, tap the ⇆ icon.)

The iPad delivers your directions in the blue bar. Tap the Start button to get going. You can see each step of your journey in one of two ways:

❶ To see all the turns in a list, tap the ☰ icon and flick down the Route Overview directions; tap the square icon to close the box.

❷ To see one turn at a time in the blue bar, tap the ← and → buttons to get each new direction displayed on the map as you go.

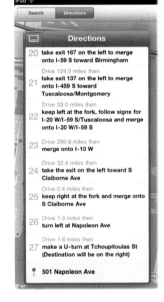

Unless you chose the mass-transit directions, you also get an approximate travel time for the trip. (If you did ask for mass-transit directions, tap the clock icon to get a list of transit schedules.) If you have an Internet connection as you go, the route can also update current traffic conditions.

View Photos

All the photos you sync to the iPad from your computer, take with the iPad's camera, save from email messages, web pages, and iPad screenshots (see the Tip on page 257), all live in the Photos app. Tap the Photos app icon (represented by a happy sunflower) to open it up and see what's there.

After you get some photos on the iPad, this app takes care of the sorting for you. You'll find photos that were in albums on your computer in same-named albums on your iPad. You can also see all your pictures in a loose collection by tapping the Photos button at the top of the screen.

Tap any photo thumbnail to open an album or the photo itself to full-screen size. Chapter 15 has all the information about getting pictures on your iPad, showing them off, making slideshows, and more. So if you're a photography enthusiast and want flip ahead right now, this chapter *understands*.

Watch Videos

Tap the Videos icon to find all the movies, TV shows, video podcasts, and music videos you have on your iPad. If you use the iPad's Home Sharing feature (page 198), you can also check out the iTunes libraries of the computers in your Home Sharing network, too; look under the Shared tab.

If you don't have any stuff yet, you can get video content in a couple of ways—download it directly to the iPad from the iTunes Store (Chapter 11) or sync compatible clips from your computer to your iPad (Chapter 14). And for the record, the Videos app is where your downloaded content lives; the YouTube app (mentioned earlier in this chapter) is for streaming cool clips from YouTube's perch on the Internet. Videos you shoot on the iPad land in Photos→Camera Roll, though, as page 101 explains.

Once you have videos, tap Home→Videos. The iPad sorts your collection by type: movies, TV shows, podcasts, and music videos. Tap an icon to play the video. In the case of TV shows, where you may have multiple episodes, tap the show's icon and, on the following screen, tap the episode you want to see.

The iPad's high-resolution screen shows off high-quality video files quite nicely. With a folding case or an extra pillow propped up on your stomach, you have a whole new way to watch TV in bed now—without having to dig around under the blankets for the remote control.

Use the iPad as an iPod

The original boxy white-and-chrome iPod from 2001 is one of Apple's greatest success stories, and its legacy lives on with the iPad. To listen to music or see what tunes you have on your tablet, tap the orange-and-white iPod icon on the iPad's Home screen.

The iPad's iPod is an elegantly designed and organized app, made to help you find your music quickly, sorted by songs, artists, albums, genres, or composers. The items in your library (music, spoken-word podcasts, audiobooks, and custom-made playlists) appear in a neat vertical list along the left side of the screen, all awaiting your tap. If you're tapping into your computer's iTunes library with the iPad's Home Sharing feature (page 198), you see a gray Library bar at the top of the left column; tap it to get the goods.

If this all sounds perfectly fine but you don't actually have any music loaded or shared on your iPad, take a stroll to Chapter 13 for further instructions. You can also download music directly to your iPad, right from the iTunes Store, as the next page explains.

Shop iTunes and the App Store

The purple iTunes icon and the blue App Store icon on the Home Screen are all about *shopping*. Some people will find this very exciting, the chance to buy fresh new things directly on the iPad, with no cables, cars, or crankiness involved. All you need is a live Internet connection and a working credit-card number.

For much more on the iTunes Store—where you can buy music, audiobooks, movies, TV shows, and download free audio and video podcasts—take a stroll to Chapter 11.

If apps are your thing and you want to find new programs to run on your iPad, you don't have as far to go. Just turn the page to leave this chapter and move on to Chapter 7, which is all about the App Store.

 Note "Hey," you say, "there's another icon on the Home screen that wasn't mentioned! What about Settings?" Settings is a collection of iPad set-up screens, and it gets an entire index all to itself. See Appendix A if you just can't wait.

slide to unlock

Shop the App Store

In the beginning—2003 to be exact—there was the iTunes Music Store. Apple's perfectly legal online emporium sold songs for 99 cents a pop and quickly became a hit itself. The premise and the promise were simple: inexpensive entertainment you could instantly download and use. Just a few years later, the renamed iTunes Store added (and still sells) TV shows, movies, and simple arcade-style video games for iPods. And then in 2008, Apple added the App Store for iPhone and iPod Touch programs.

The App Store is where you download *apps*, or programs, that run on your iPhone, iPod Touch, and now, iPad. You can find thousands of apps, including foreign-language tutors, e-newspapers, restaurant guides, hurricane trackers, tiny word processors, and sophisticated handheld videogames, in the App Store, with developers writing new programs every week. It's a hugely popular part of the Apple empire, with more than 10 billion apps downloaded as of January 2011.

With the iPad out for more than a year now, you can choose from more apps than ever—of the 350,000 apps that work on iOS devices, more than 60,000 were written just for the tablet. This chapter shows you how to get shopping by setting up an account in the store, buying and installing your first apps, and keeping them organized once you start loading up your 'Pad.

Go to the App Store

Remember when computer stores displayed shelves and shelves worth of software in colorful shrinkwrapped cardboard boxes? The App Store ditches the physical racks and crowds of people but still offers thousands of programs, neatly organized into 20 categories right on the other side of your Internet connection. Once you're online, you can either:

❶ Click the iTunes Store icon in the Source list and then click the App Store link at the top of the screen. Or, if you're looking for a specific category of program, like, say, an expense tracker, click the small triangle that pops up in the App Store tab to open a submenu of app categories and go right to the Financial section. (Chapter 11 has more about the music and video sides of the iTunes Store.)

❷ Tap the App Store icon on the iPad's home screen.

Either action gets you to the App Store. If you choose the iTunes path from the comfort of your laptop or desktop computer, you may end up with a bigger screen to browse the store's selections—but you also have to take the extra step of syncing your purchases from iTunes to your iPad (page 195).

Tour the App Store

No matter how you get there, the App Store has plenty to offer your iPad. In most cases, you land right on the store's home page, where Apple employees regularly spotlight new, timely, or interesting apps and games. You also see the list of top apps, both in the budget-friendly Free Apps section and in the more feature-friendly Paid Apps department.

If you tap any app's name or icon, you go to the program's App Store page, where you can read more about what the app does. You can also view sample screenshots, read reviews from people who bought the app, and check out the app's system requirements to make sure it's compatible with your iPad model's hardware and software. For apps intended for both the iPhone and the iPad, some developers give you a choice of screenshots to inspect. Next to Screenshots, click the iPad button (circled) to see just the iPad images.

Many games include an age rating to help parents decide if a game is appropriate (or not) for children. There's also a Free App button to download the apps that are gratis, or a Buy App link if you have to shell out some simoleons. (If you buy an app, it gets billed to your credit card. Turn the page for instructions on setting up an account with Apple.)

Across the top of each app's page, you'll see a category listed, like Weather, Sports, Games, Photography, Music, and so on. You can click the category name to see similar apps if the one you're looking at doesn't quite fit the bill.

Set Up an iTunes/App Store Account

Before you can buy any of the cool stuff you see in the Store, you need to set up an account with Apple. If you already have one from previous purchases, you can use that name and password here—all your bills will go to the credit card you have on file with Apple.

If you've never bought any of Apple's online products, like iTunes movies or prints from iPhoto, you need to set up an account before you can buy any-thing. To do so, click the Sign In button in the upper-right corner of the iTunes window, and then click Create New Account. (If you're on the iPad, scroll down to the bottom of the screen, then tap Sign In→Create New Account.)

Then follow these three steps:

❶ Agree to the terms for using the Store and buying music.

❷ Create an Apple Account.

❸ Supply a credit card or PayPal account number and billing address.

As your first step in creating an Apple Account, you must read and agree to the terms of the legal document on the first screen. This long, 27-page state-ment informs you of your rights and responsibilities as an iTunes Store and App Store customer. It boils down to two core points: *Thou shalt not down-load an album, burn it to CD, and then sell bootleg copies of it at your local convenience store*, and *Third-party crashware apps are not our fault.*

Click the Agree button to move on to step 2. Here, you create an Apple ID, password, and secret question and answer. If you later have to click the "Forgot Password?" button in the Store sign-in box, this is the question you have to answer to prove that you're you. Apple requests that you type in your birthday to help verify your identity. (You must be over 13 to get an account here.)

On the third and final screen, provide a valid credit card number with a billing address. You can also use a PayPal account.

Click Done. You've got yourself an Apple Account. From now on, you can log into the App Store by clicking the Sign In button in the upper-right corner of the iTunes window.

Sign Up Without a Credit Card

But what if you just want to download free apps from the App Store? You don't have to cough up a credit-card number, but you do need to make sure you're in the App Store and not the main iTunes Store (where only podcasts are regularly free). In iTunes, click the App Store link on the main iTunes Store page. Once you're in the App Store:

❶ Find a free program you want and click the Free App button.

❷ When the sign-in box pops up, click the Create a New Account button.

❸ Agree to the "Terms and Conditions" document and then fill out your account name, password, and birthday information.

❹ On the screen for payment options, click None.

❺ Fill in your name and email address, and then click the link used to verify your new account.

❻ When you get the Store's confirmation email, click the embedded link to verify your account.

Once you finish up step 6, you get prompted to log into your account with your new user name and password. When you do, you land back in the App Store, ready to gobble up free apps for your 'Pad.

 Need to change billing or other information in your iTunes/App Store account? Sign into the store, and then click on your account name. In the box that pops up, retype your password and click the View Account button. On the account settings screen, click either the Edit Account Info or Edit Payment Information button.

Buy, Download, and Install Apps

Okay, you've found the App Store, maybe even created an Apple account ahead of time: Now you're ready to start loading up your iPad with all the cool programs, games, and utilities you can fit on it.

- **Get apps from the iTunes Store.** Click the App Store link on the main Store page and browse away. When you find an app you want, click the Free App or Buy App button to download a copy of the program to iTunes. You can see all the apps you've purchased by clicking the Applications icon in the iTunes Source list. When you finish shopping, connect the iPad to your computer, and sync 'em up, as Chapter 11 explains.

- **Get apps on the iPad.** When you've got a WiFi or 3G connection, tap the blue App Store icon on the Home screen and browse away. At the top of the Featured screen, you can see what's new and hot. At the bottom of the screen, you can tap to see what the iTunes Genius thinks you might like, see a list of the most downloaded apps (Top Charts), and check out apps listed by category. When you find an app you want, tap the Free App or price button; the latter turns into a Buy Now button, so hit that. Type in your Store name and password (even if it's a free application), and the download begins. After the program finishes loading and installing, tap its icon to launch it. Download times vary by app size. For example, the beautiful interactive textbook pictured here, *The Elements: A Visual Exploration*, is a honking 1.71 gigabytes—so give it time.

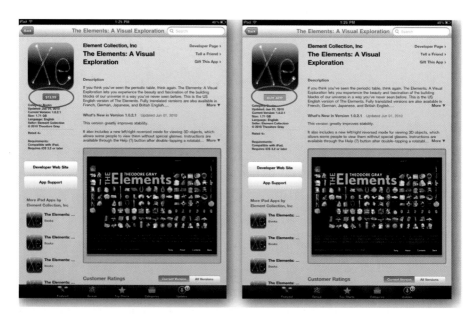

Uninstall Apps

Not every app is a five-star winner. One may turn out to be different from what you envisioned when you bought it or not live up to your expectations in other ways. Or maybe some of those bigger games and programs are just taking up too much of your limited iPad real estate. Some apps may even be buggy and crashy, and perhaps you want to just remove them instead of waiting for the developer to post an update (page 127).

Here are two ways to uninstall an app:

- **Remove apps in iTunes.** Connect the iPad to your computer, and then click its icon in the iTunes Source list. In the main iTunes window, click the Applications tab. In the list, turn off the check-boxes next to the apps you want to remove and then click Sync to unin-stall them. The removed apps stay in your iTunes library, but you won't be carting them around on your iPad until you select them here and resync. Page 195 has pictures.

- **Remove apps on the iPad.** As shown here on the Home screen, press and hold the unwanted application's icon until it starts wiggling around and an ⊗ appears in the corner. Tap the ⊗, confirm your intention to delete, and wave goodbye to that app. Press the Home button to return to business as usual.

> **Tip** While all App Store sales are final, you may be able to get a refund if an app is mislabeled or seriously doesn't perform as advertised. It's certainly not a sure thing, and you need to make your case to the iTunes Support folks calmly and clearly about why the app fails for technical reasons ("I just don't like it" is not a valid excuse). Contact customer service at *www.apple.com/support/itunes*.

Search for Apps

Just as you can buy apps on either your computer or tablet, so you can search for them or specific types of programs through iTunes or the iPad. This comes in handy if you don't know the exact name of the app you seek, or you want to throw a few keywords into the search box and see what comes up.

Here's how to search:

- **On the computer.** The upper-right corner of the iTunes window has a nice little search box. When you're in an iTunes library, typing keywords into the box brings up results from your own collection. But when you search with the iTunes Store selected in the Source list, your results come from the apps, games, music, and other items for sale in the online store. If you don't immediately see what you want, click the Power Search button in the top-left corner to get a set of boxes (circled) that let you narrow your results even further—by developer name, category, or device.

- **On the iPad.** Tap the search box (🔍) at the top of the App Store screen to summon the keyboard. Type in the keywords for the app you seek, and tap the keyboard's Search button. The iPad matches what you type as you go and presents a list. At the top of the results screen, you can filter the apps by category, price, and other criteria.

Once iTunes completes a search, click or tap an app name to get more information about it from its page in the App Store.

Scale Up iPhone Apps

The bulk of the App Store's more than 350,000 programs are for iPhone and iPod Touch owners (for now, anyway). But don't let that stop you from shopping, because most iPhone apps can run just fine on the iPad, so there's no software shortage for the slab here.

And while iPhone/iPod Touch apps can run on the iPad, most of them weren't *designed* for it. As a result, they may seem a little sparse on the bigger screen. Still, you can run iPhone and iPod Touch apps on the iPad in two ways:

- **Run the apps at actual size.** While this maintains the original look of the app, it looks kind of silly floating there in the middle of your iPad, like a tiny island surrounding by an ocean of dark screen. And you have to reach in much farther across the iPad to tap the screen buttons.

- **Run the apps at twice the size.** If you don't want to squint, you can super-size that old iPhone app—just tap the 2X button in the bottom-right corner of the iPad screen (circled). The iPad doubles each pixel in the iPhone app to scale it up to tablet size. Depending on the program, though, Hulk-ing up your apps with the 2X button can make them look a little blotchy and weird compared to running them at the size they were intended. But you do make use of your iPad's expansive vista.

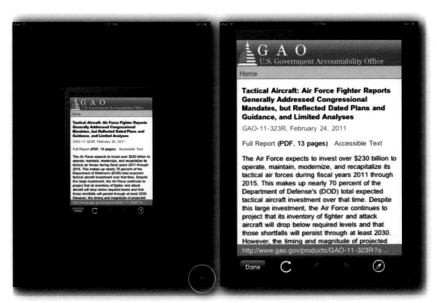

The longer the iPad is available, though, the more apps will appear written (or rewritten) expressly to fill its big glorious screen. In a year or so, the 2X feature may seem a quaint little kludge.

Organize Apps

Back in Chapter 1, you learned how to rearrange the icons on the Home screen of your iPad. And after reading the first few pages of this chapter, you may now have a *ton* of groovy new app icons all over your iPad—but not in the order you'd like them. Sure, you can drag wiggling icons all over your 11 pages of Home screen, but that can get a little confusing and frustrating when you accidentally drop an icon on the wrong page. Plus, that iPad screen is awfully large and you could throw your shoulder out dragging those apps such a long distance.

iTunes offers an easier way to fine-tune your iPad's Home screens: You can arrange all your app icons on your big-screen computer:

❶ Connect the iPad to your computer. Click its icon in the Source list.

❷ Click the Applications tab. You now see all your applications—a complete list on the left, a giant version of your iPad screen in the middle, and individual pages to the right-hand side of or below the Big Screen.

❸ Select the icons you want to move. Click an icon you want to move on the JumboTron and drag it to the desired page thumbnail below—iTunes recreates both iPad screen orientations so you can fine-tune the look of your screens: Landscape mode pages appear along the bottom, portrait mode screens stacked vertically on the far right. Hold down the

Ctrl or ⌘ keys and click to select multiple apps. It's much easier to group similar apps on a page this way—you can have, say, a page of games and a page of online newspapers. If you prefer grouping like apps in themed folders (page 8), drag them into the folder with the mouse. You can even swap out the four permanent application icons in the gray bar on the bottom of the iPad screen (either here or on the tablet itself) with other apps—and squeeze in two more for a total of six apps in the bottom row.

❹ Click Apply or Sync. Wait just a moment as iTunes rearranges the icons on your iPad so they mirror the setup in iTunes.

But what if you have too many apps for the iPad's limit of 11 Home screens? Even if an app's not visible, you can find it on the tablet by flicking your finger from left to right on the first Home screen and typing in the app name in the search box that appears.

Tip Just as you can on the iPad itself, you can whack an app in iTunes by clicking it to select it and then clicking the ⊗ that appears in the app icon's upper-left corner (circled above). This just deletes the app from the iPad—not from your overall iTunes library.

Adjust App Preferences

Many apps have all their functions and controls within each program; you can get to them by tapping Setup or Options (or something similarly named) while you run the app. Some apps, however, have a separate set of preferences in the iPad's Settings area.

For example, your nifty little weather program may include the option to display temperatures in either Fahrenheit or Celsius and wind speeds in either miles per hour or kilometers per hour, depending on the measuring standards of your country. You set these app preferences by choosing Home→Settings and flicking all the way down the screen to the collection of individual apps. Tap the name of the app whose settings you want to adjust.

Tip Want to keep your iPad in sync with all your App Store purchases? While you're tromping around in the iPad's Settings area, tap the Store icon on the left side of the screen. Here, you can turn on automatic downloads, which deposit a copy of any music, apps, or books you bought through your iTunes account onto your iPad, no matter whether you originally bought the item on your computer, iPhone, or iPod Touch.

Update Apps

When you see a red circled number on the App Store icon, you know you have some updatin' to do. The number in the red circle represents the number of apps that have updates waiting for you to download. Updates usually fix bugs and improve program performance, and that may help wobbly apps stop crashing. Some updates include new features. All updates for a particular version of an app are free.

To see a list of which apps have an update pending, tap the App Store icon. Tap the name of the program you want to update, tap the Price button, and then tap Install. If you have multiple programs with updates ready, you can install them all in one fell swoop by tapping the Update All button. The update downloads after you type in your Store password. (Already in the App Store? The Updates icon at the bottom of the screen shows the number of updates; tap it to see them and get all the new stuff at once.)

You can also check for app updates in iTunes. Click the Applications icon in the iTunes Source list to display all your downloaded apps, and then click the "Check for Updates" link at the bottom of the window. If you have updates, iTunes alerts you with a box and gives you a button to click to see a list of the apps. (The number in the gray circle next to Apps in the Source list also gives you the total number of updates available.)

When you view a list of the updates, iTunes gives you a button in the top-right corner to install all the updates at once, but you can also update programs individually by clicking the Get Update button next to each app's name. Once you download the updates, sync the iPad to install them on your tablet.

Troubleshoot Apps

Most App Store programs work perfectly well at what they were designed to do, but things can occasionally go wrong. Maybe a little bug made it through the testing process. Or maybe an iPad software update changed the way the operating system interacts with the app.

In any case, you can take a few basic troubleshooting steps for apps that aren't playing nice with the iPad:

- **Restart the iPad.** If you just installed an elaborate videogame like *Star Wars: Trench Run* or some other complex application, it's a good idea to restart the iPad (page 288 has the steps) to get all this new software off to a fresh start with the operating system—sort of like how it's a fine notion to restart your computer after you install new programs.

- **Check for updates.** Some apps may have been sold just a tad too soon. The developer, facing cranky customers and bad reviews in the App Store, quickly posts an updated version of the app that fixes the problem. Flip back a page for information on updating apps. (It's also a good idea to plug the tablet into the computer and check for iPad software updates every once in a while; see page 292 to learn how.)

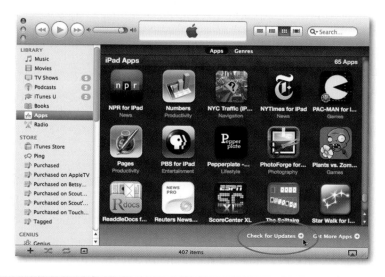

 Note Some apps are designed to work only with certain iPad features, like its global positioning system (GPS) or 3G network. Before you tear your hair out trying to figure out why your brand-new app won't do what it's supposed to, revisit its App Store page and re-check the system requirements to make sure it's actually *supposed* to run on the iPad, Wi-Fi + 3G model or otherwise.

- **Remove and reinstall the app.** Perhaps something tripped up the installation process when you first bought the app or a little piece of it somehow got damaged during a crash. If a certain app wigs out on you, try uninstalling it (page 121), restarting the iPad (page 288), and then downloading the program again from the App Store (page 120) to install a fresh copy. If it's a paid app you previously purchased, you can download a new copy of the same version for free. (Just to be sure you know that you already downloaded this app, the App Store displays an alert box that asks you to tap the OK button to confirm your desire to download it again.) But a clean install with a new copy of the software just may do the trick if, say, your Facebook app bombs out every time you try to upload a photo.

Other steps to try include deauthorizing (page 186) and re-authorizing (page 185) your computer for purchases from the iTunes and App Stores, or reinstalling the whole iTunes program on your computer (page 290). Sometimes, just logging out of your Store account and logging back in can resolve an issue.

If all that fails, it's probably the app's fault. You can, however, report your problem. If you're on the iPad, tap the App Store icon, find the app's page in the Store, and flick down to the part of the page where the Developer's Web Site and App Support and buttons live. Tap Developer's Web Site to see other apps from the company and get contact information, or tap App Support for technical help and information on this specific app.

If you're logged into your iTunes Store account on the computer, click your user name in the top right corner. In the sign-in box, click the View Account button, sign in again, and click the Purchase History button on the Account Settings page. Click the "Report a Problem" button at the bottom of the page, and then click the arrow next to the problem program in your list of recent purchases. Now you get an electronic form you can fill out and send to Apple.

> **Tip** If you need help from a human at Apple, you can either call (800) 275-2273 or email them. From the iTunes Store's main page, click the Support link. Your web browser presents you with the main iTunes service and support page; click any link in the Customer Service area and then, at the bottom of the page that appears, fill out the Email Support form. Live online chat is also available for some issues.

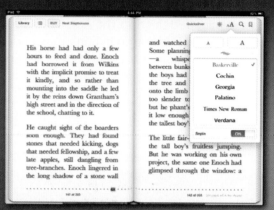

Read iBooks & ePeriodicals

Books in easy-to-use, page-turning form have been around since the second century or so. Now, after a few years of false starts and dashed hopes, *electronic* books are wooing many people away from the world of ink, paper, and tiny clip-on book lights for nighttime reading. And as the eBook goes, so go eBook readers. The Amazon Kindle, Barnes & Noble Nook, and Sony Reader are among the big names in the eBook reader playground.

Enter the iPad.

With its glorious, high-resolution color touchscreen, the iPad takes the eBook experience to a new level. True, the Nook has a color screen and the Kindle is dramatically cheaper, but the iPad's big bright display makes books, newspapers, and magazines look amazing. And turning the page of an eBook no longer involves one screen abruptly replacing another, either—it's a fully animated re-creation of the page-flip on a real book.

The books themselves have evolved into interactive creations, with built-in dictionaries, searchable text, hyperlinked footnotes, and embedded notes and bookmarks that make the whole process of reading more engaging and efficient. So flip *this* page to see how much fun you can have reading books on your iPad in the 21st century.

Download the iBooks App

Before you can buy and read eBooks on your iPad, you have to do two things: recalibrate your brain, because Apple calls eBooks *iBooks*, and then pop into the iTunes App Store to download Apple's free iBooks app. You have your choice of how to get there.

- **On the iPad.** Grab the iBooks app by tapping the App Store icon on the iPad's Home screen. If you don't get an invitation to download the app right off the bat, as shown here, you can always find it yourself. You might see an iBooks icon on the App Store's main page, or you can tap the Search box at the top of the screen, type in *iBooks*, and wait for the app to pop up. Then tap the Install App button.

- **On the computer.** If your iPad's out of network range or you prefer to get all your apps via the desktop, you can get iBooks through iTunes. Fire up the media manager, click the iTunes Store link, tap the App Store tab, and search for the iBooks app there. Once you download it, you need to sync your iPad with iTunes to install it on your tablet. You can buy iBooks through the app (see opposite page) or through the desktop iTunes Store—to do the latter, just click the Books tab and then browse and sync away.

 Note Did you jump right to this chapter because you really wanted to learn more about Apple's approach to the whole eBook thing? If you're feeling lost, flip back to Chapter 7. It gives you the lowdown on this App Store business and shows you how to open an iTunes account—which you need to buy books.

Go to the iBookstore

To get to all the electronic books Apple has to offer in its iBookstore, you first have to open the iBooks app. Find it on your home screen and tap it open. You see a virtual rendition of a handsome wooden bookshelf. This is where all your downloaded books eventually come to live.

For now, the shelves likely hold a single electronic volume, the one that came with the iBooks app: *Winnie-the-Pooh*, the illustrated children's classic by A.A. Milne. (Surely you remember the story? Honey-loving bear hangs out in the woods and learns life's lessons with his pals, who include a hyperactive tiger and a depressed donkey.)

Apple has thoughtfully included this free title so you can see an iBook for yourself before you go tapping off to buy books of your own choosing. If you want to stay and play with Pooh, there's no rush. Just tap the cover to open the book. Page 140 explains how to further navigate through the bright electronic pages of an iBook.

If you've moved beyond the Hundred-Acre Wood and want to get to the Malcolm Gladwell and Doris Kearns Goodwin tomes, tap the Store button in the upper-left corner of the bookshelf. As long as you've got an Internet connection, you land in the iBookstore. Turn the page to find out what happens next.

> **Tip** If you delete your free *Pooh* accidentally (or on purpose, to save drive space), you can usually get it back by downloading it again from the Children's & Teens section of the iBookstore. And don't sweat the file size. Compared to music and video files, most books are rather small—about 2 megabytes per title.

Browse and Search for Books

Once you tap iBooks' Store icon, you're transported into the iBookstore—which looks quite a bit like the iTunes Store and the App Store, but with book titles instead of music, videos, and TV programs. Browsing and searching works pretty much the same way.

The main storefront features best-sellers, popular titles, and books the iBookstore staff finds interesting. If you're browsing for books on a specific subject, tap the Categories button (circled at right) and select from the pop-up menu.

A row of four icons at the bottom of the screen sort the books into groups:

- **Featured.** The main storefront displays new and notable titles and spotlighted genres. Flick to the bottom of the screen for links to books on sale, books made into movies, books Apple's staff thinks you should read, books so enticing people are pre-ordering them, free books, and books Oprah likes. Buttons at the bottom of every Store screen let you log into or out of your Apple account, redeem iTunes gift cards, or get technical support with an iBookstore problem.

- **NYTimes.** This button reveals the weekly rankings of books on the venerable *New York Times* Best Sellers list, which has been charting books since 1942 (the author is an employee of the *New York Times*). The iBookstore's version gets updated each week, in tandem with the *Times* list.

- **Top Charts.** Tap Top Charts to see a list of the most popular books people buy though their iPads, as well as a list of the most popular *free* books (page 137) readers are snapping up.

- **Browse.** Tap Browse for a list of alphabetized authors and categories to peruse. You'll find both paid and free titles listed.

- **Purchased.** Can't remember what you bought? Tap here to see a list of your previous purchases. If you delete a purchased book from your iPad, find it in the list here and tap the Redownload button. You don't have to pay again.

To search for a title or author, tap the Search box at the top of the Store screen. When the keyboard pops up, start typing in a book title or author name. A suggestions box appears to help complete your search. If Apple has titles that match your criteria, you see them listed. Tap the Cancel button to quit the search.

Tap any book cover to get more information about the title—the cover spins around to reveal a book description, star ratings, reviews from other readers, examples of books other readers also bought, and even a button to download a free sample of the work. (Isn't this easier than leaning against hard wooden shelves and getting jostled by other customers or unleashed toddlers when you browse in a regular bookstore?) You can also tap the price button to buy the book right away.

After you read a book, you can go back to its info page and offer your own two cents about the story or writing. Tap the stars to give it a wordless ranking or tap the "Write a Review" link to give it a more thoughtful critique. You need to log into your store account to rank and review books, so it's not an anonymous undertaking.

Buy and Download a Book

When you find a book you simply must have in your digital library, tap the price button, which then turns into a Buy Book button. Tap it, type in your iTunes/App Store/iBookstore account name and password so Apple has a credit-card number to charge, and let the download begin.

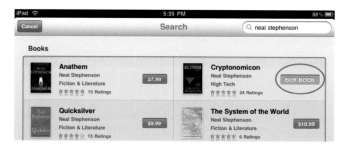

Back in your iPad's library—which you can always get to by tapping the Library button in the top-left corner of the Store screen—the book cover appears on your library shelf. A blue progress bar (circled below) creeps across the cover to indicate how much of the file you've downloaded.

Most books take just a couple minutes to arrive on the iPad, but this can vary with network congestion and other factors. When the download is complete, your book appears on the Library shelf with a sassy blue "New" ribbon on the cover. (Free-sample chapters get a red "Sample" ribbon.)

Find Free iBooks

Most iBooks cost between $6 and $15, significantly cheaper than the $25 to $30 you pay for the brand-new hardcover treeware versions. But the iBookstore isn't all about the money, all the time. It offers more than a hundred *absolutely free* eBooks on its virtual shelves.

To find this Treasure Chest of Free Literature, tap the Browse button at the bottom of the iBooks screen. An alphabetical list of author names appears on the Browse screen. Tap the Free button (circled below) and then tap an author to see if he or she has any works in the ultimate bargain bin. (Hint: Authors writing before 1923 often appear here.)

If you want to narrow down your field of interest beyond the fiscal, tap the Categories button at the top of the Browse screen, and choose a topic. Tap a cover to read a synopsis and find out what other people think of the book. Tap the Get Book button to download it; you can also get a sample, but the book itself is free, so just go for it.

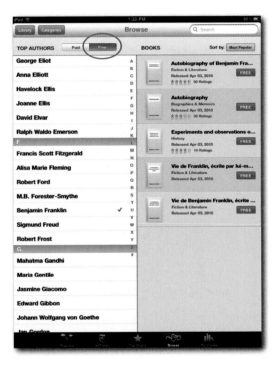

Most of these free titles tend to be classic works of literature that have fallen out of copyright and into the public domain. In fact, you may have read some of them in school (or at least the Cliffs Notes guides). The offerings include *Middlemarch* by George Eliot, *The Art of War* by Sun Tzu, *Washington Square* by Henry James, *The Adventures of Sherlock Holmes* by Arthur Conan Doyle, and many of Shakespeare's plays.

You can also download *Ulysses* by James Joyce. Even though the iPad weighs a pound and a half, it's still probably lighter than paperback copies of this epic Irish novel of more than 700 old-fashioned printed pages.

Free books aren't the fanciest ones on the shelf—on the outside, anyway. But while you don't get colorfully designed mini book covers (they all sort of look like they're covered in plain brown wrappers), you sure can't beat the price.

Sync Books with iTunes

As Chapter 11 explains, iTunes is your conduit to moving files between your computer and the iPad. True, you buy iBooks from the iBookstore on the iPad—but you back them up (to your computer) by syncing your 'Pad with iTunes. Once you sync—and therefore back up—your iPad's contents, it's much less of a stomach-churning event if you have to restore the tablet's software (page 294) or if you accidentally delete books you weren't quite done with.

To sync your iPad with iTunes, connect the tablet to the computer with its USB cable. If you previously purchased some iBooks, choose File→Transfer Purchases from iPad to copy them into iTunes for safe-keeping.

Since your computer probably has more hard drive space than your iPad does, you can also use iTunes to sync books on and off the tablet as you need them, conserving disk space. To do so, click the iPad's icon in the iTunes Source list, then click the Books tab in the middle of the screen. Turn on the checkbox next to Sync Books. If you want to selectively sync titles, click "Selected books" and turn on the checkboxes next to the relevant books. Click Apply and then click the Sync button to make it happen. (You can sync audiobooks this way, too.)

In addition to eBooks, the iBooks app also handles PDF files like those that arrive as email attachments (tap the attachment and choose "Open in iBooks" at the top of the screen) or those you sync to your 'Pad by dragging them into your iTunes library. To find them on your iPad, fire up the iBooks app, tap the Collections button in the top-left corner, and then select PDFs from the menu.

Add Other eBooks to the iPad

The iBookstore isn't the only place you can get electronic books. Bookstore behemoths Amazon and Barnes & Noble both have their own iPad apps that let you tap into the inventory from *their* online bookstores.

All you need is the official store app and an account with the company so they can bill you for your purchases—your existing Amazon or B&N account (with your payment info on file) will do fine. If you don't have a prior purchase history with the company, install the app (*Kindle* for Amazon and *Nook* for Barnes & Noble) and follow the on-screen instructions to create your account.

Once you set everything up, you can buy and download books from these stores—and read them by tapping open the app and selecting the new title from your collection.

You can also download eBooks from the many book-download sites out there—type *ebooks* into your favorite search engine to find them. iBooks uses the popular ePub format for its digital books, so you can read eBooks that have the extension *.epub*—just make sure the file doesn't have any fun-killing, copy-protecting DRM (digital-rights management) built in that requires a password before you can read it. Most eBook sites identify a book's format.

One place to get unprotected ePub files is the Project Gutenberg site. Founded in 1971, Project Gutenberg is a volunteer effort that collects and freely distributes great works of literature. To browse and download books from the collection, visit *gutenberg.org*.

You can search Project Gutenberg for specific books, which are often available in several file formats. Find a book in ePub format as highlighted here (it'll have the extension *.epub*) and download it to your computer. To get the book onto your iPad, choose File→"Add to Library" in iTunes. Once you get the file in iTunes, sync it to the iPad as described on the previous page. Once it's on the iPad, it looks just like a regular iBook.

Read an iBook

Of course, reading an iBook isn't the same as cracking open the spine of a leather-bound volume and relaxing in an English club chair. But really—who reads books that way anymore (except for the impossibly wealthy and characters on *Masterpiece Mystery*)?

Reading books in the 21st century can involve anything from squinting through Boswell's *Life of Johnson* on a mobile phone to gobbling down the latest Danielle Steel epic on the oversized Kindle DX e-reader.

Then there's the iPad way. Tap the screen to see these iBook controls:

❶ **Library.** Tap here to leave your current book and go back to the iBook-store bookshelf.

❷ **Contents.** Tap this button to see the book's chapter titles; tap a title to jump to that point in the book. You can also see your list of bookmarks (page 145).

❸ **Buy.** Reading a sample chapter? If you like what you read, tap the Buy button for a near-instant library acquisition.

❹ **Page Navigator.** Drag the little brown slider along the bottom of the page to quickly advance or retreat through a book's pages. Keywords and page numbers flash on-screen as you drag.

> iPad 📶   4:3
>
> Library   ☰   BUY   Neal Stephenson
> ❶   ❷   ❸
>
> it kindly, and so rather than mounting into the saddle he led it by the reins down Grantham's high street and in the direction of the school, chatting to it.
>
> He caught sight of the boarders soon enough. They had found stones that needed kicking, dogs that needed fellowship, and a few late apples, still dangling from tree-branches. Enoch lingered in the long shadow of a stone wall and watched the apple project. Some planning had gone into it—a whispered conference between bunks last night. One of the boys
>
> ❹
>
> 140 of 350

The iPad displays books in either portrait or landscape mode (the latter shown across these two pages). When you tap the screen in either view, the iBook controls appear. Reading iBooks is probably the reason most people use the iPad's Screen Orientation Lock (page 3). Turning on the lock prevents the screen from spinning all over the place (and giving you motion sickness) when you try to read in bed.

To turn the page in an iBook, tap the right margin to go forward and the left one to go backward. And you can always drag the page corner with your finger for that dramatic looks-like-a-real-page-turning animated effect.

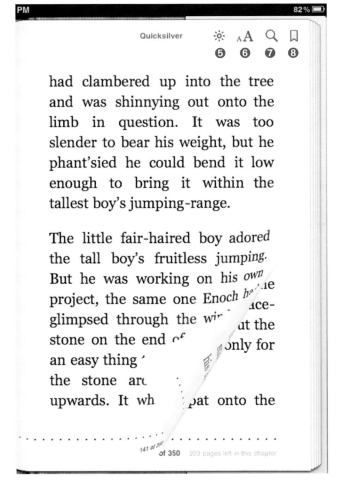

❺ **Screen Brightness.** The iPad's color display is bright—too bright, sometimes. To dim the screen, tap the Sun icon and drag the slider (this move affects iBooks only).

❻ **Type.** Is the font and size not to your liking? Tap here to fix it; page 142 has more.

❼ **Search.** Tap the magnifying-glass icon (Q) to get a box where you can type in keywords to find mentions of a word. Page 143 has details.

❽ **Bookmark.** Tap here to save your place in the book you're reading. Page 145 tells you more, along with info on making notes in the margins.

Change the Type in an iBook

One thing you can't really do with a printed book is make the type size bigger or smaller to suit the needs of your eyes, not the book designer's. And if you don't care for a book's typeface, you're stuck with that, too—in a printed book, that is.

But not on the iPad. Thanks to the iBooks software, you can make book type bigger or smaller, or change the look altogether. Just tap the Type icon (**AA**) at the top of the page. A box like the one shown below appears. Tap the little **A** to make the text on-screen smaller, or tap the big **A** to make it bigger. The size changes as you tap, so you can immediately see which works best for you. Hate reading on white pages? Tap the Sepia button to give the page a brownish tint.

To change the typeface (font) used for the text, tap the name of another typeface in the list. The font name itself appears in its namesake typeface so you can preview what it looks like on-screen. Tap the page when you're done.

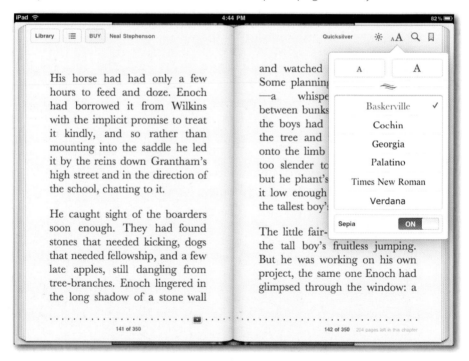

 Note Some of these typeface names may seem odd, but several are named after the typographers who designed or inspired the font. Baskerville, for example, was created by John Baskerville in 18th-century England. Cochin (designed by Georges Peignot in 1912) is named after the French engraver Charles Nicolas Cochin. Little did they know they'd show up in a book about the iPad.

Search an iBook

Need to pinpoint a certain word or phrase in a book to find a particular passage—or to see how many times the word appears? The iPad helps you out here, too. And if you want more information about that searched word, the tablet even offers buttons to bring up search results from Google or Wikipedia. Let's see that hardback copy of *Abraham Lincoln: Vampire Hunter* do *that*.

You have two ways to start up a search.

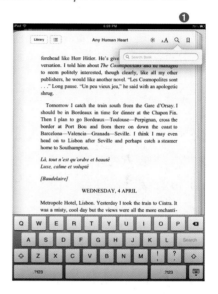

1. Tap the Q icon on the top of the book page. When the keyboard slides into view, type in your keywords and hit the Search key. Your results arrive quickly.

2. When you're in the middle of a book page, press and hold your finger down on the word you want to search on. A box appears on-screen over the selected word with four choices: Dictionary | Highlight | Note | Search. Tap Search and let the iPad bring you a list of results—in context.

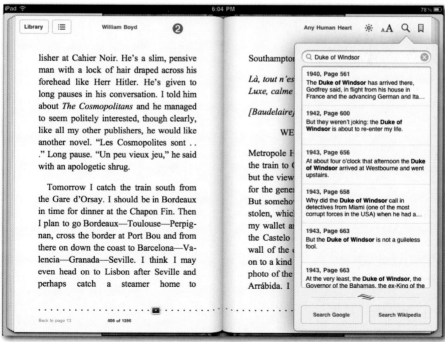

Use the Dictionary

Reading a book on the iPad means you don't need Webster's Dictionary riding shotgun to look up word definitions. This sort of thing can happen when you read scientific or historical texts, or if vocabulary was never your strong suit in high-school English class.

To see the meaning of a word you don't recognize, double-tap it (or press and hold it for a second) until the Dictionary | Highlight | Note | Search box appears. (If you want information about a full name or a phrase, drag the blue selection dots around all the words.) Tap Dictionary to see the definition.

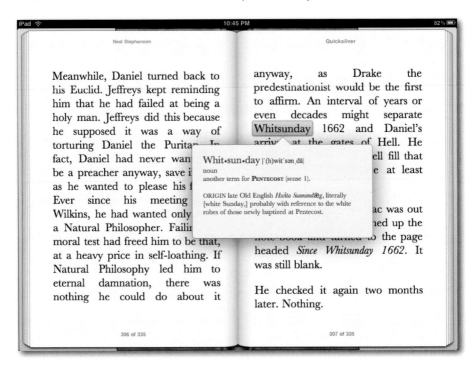

The dictionary recognizes some proper names, but as you can see here, the results can be a bit mixed—and sometimes unintentionally funny.

Create Bookmarks and Margin Notes

Even if you abruptly bail out of the iBooks app and jump to another program, the iPad remembers what book you were reading and what page you were on. If you happen to be reading a dense, brain-burning book and want to remember *exactly* where you left off (or you want to mark a passage for later reference), you can set digital bookmarks or highlight text right on the page.

Tap the bookmark icon (▤) in the upper-right corner to save your place. To mark a specific spot in the text, double-tap a word to select it (or drag the blue selection dots around more words). When the Dictionary | Highlight | Note | Search box pops up, tap

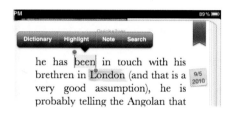

Highlight to swipe color across the selected text. Choose Note to make a digital Post-It note that you can leave in the margins. (You can also select, copy, and paste text in and out of margin notes [page 28] when you tap them open.)

To see the places you marked in an iBook, tap the Contents icon (▤) and then tap the Bookmarks button (circled). You see the list of bookmarks, highlights, and notes—and *when* you created them. Tap a bookmark to jump to it or tap Resume to go

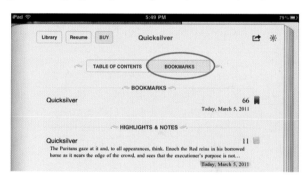

to the page you left, bookmarked or not. Swipe a bookmark or note and tap Delete to remove it. Tap the 🖅 icon to print or email your book notes.

Hate the text's hue or want to get rid of the highlight? Tap to select it and in the box that pops up, choose a different color of the rainbow by tapping Colors or tap Remove Highlight.

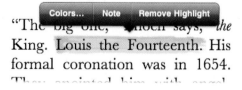

Use Newspaper and Magazine Apps

It's safe to say that the iPad got a huge share of media attention from the time Steve Jobs announced it in January 2010 until early April, when the tablet arrived in stores. This isn't unusual for an Apple product—remember that little cellphone Apple unleashed in 2007?

But to some observers, that Tidal Wave of Media Coverage had a few Surfers of Self-Interest riding along. That's because, in addition to changing how people consume books, videos, and other content, the interactive iPad was supposed to reinvigorate printed magazines and newspapers—a business that has seen its fortunes plummet since a little thing called the Internet came along.

Here's the good news: The iPad has inspired many news organizations to create beautiful apps to show off their content. Some are free (for now, anyway), some charge a fee just for the content, and some charge for the app *and* the content. You can find all the iPad-worthy news apps at App Store→Categories→News, but here are a few of the big ones:

- **The New York Times.** It's the full daily paper, but only free for the first 20 articles (it's $20 a month after that for Web and iPad access). The app offers up the day's top stories in several categories, like Technology and Opinion. Tap a story summary to see it expand to the full screen.

- **The Daily.** An electronic newspaper designed specifically for the iPad, The Daily presents the day's news in an interactive blend of text, graphics, and video. A subscription costs 99 cents a week, or you can pay $40 for a full year, and each day, a fresh issue downloads itself to your iPad when you start up the app.

- **USA Today.** Just as colorful as its print counterpart, the Nation's Newspaper is hoping to be the Nation's iPad App. Automatically updating headlines, sports scores, and the local weather forecast greet you when you open the app. Tap the section name in the top-left corner to jump to the separate Money, Sports, and Life pages.

- **The Wall Street Journal.** Since the early days of the Internet, the WSJ has been one of the few news sites on the Web to charge for full access, and its app continues the tradition. The app is free, and you can get a limited selection of stories when you register with the company. You can sign up for a full-content paid subscription ($4 a week) with the Subscribe Now link in the bottom-left corner.

- **Zinio Magazine Newsstand.** Want to browse a whole bunch of magazines and flip through a few before you buy? Try the Zinio app, which offers full-color sample pages from many printed mags (like *The Economist*, *National Geographic*, *The Sporting News*, and *Cosmopolitan*), all digitized and zoomable for your reading pleasure. The app is free, but the magazine content costs money. For example, one issue of *Us* magazine is $3.99, while a yearly subscription is $67.08.

In addition to newsstand publications, news services—which often supply stories to some of those publications—also have great apps. All of the ones mentioned below include video clips of news events as well as text stories.

- **AP News.** The Associated Press compiles the day's top stories into a free-form flow of little news bars on the screen in this no-cost app (shown on the right). Tap one to get the scoop. Photos and videos of the day are also here.

- **BBC News.** The British Broadcasting Corporation's beautifully designed app neatly organizes the day's stories in an easy-to-read, easy-to-navigate grid on the screen (shown here). Along with video clips, the Beeb—once and still a radio broadcaster—gives you a live radio stream with a tap on the Live Radio button at the top of the screen.

- **Reuters News Pro.** With its quick access to the world stock-market charts and a built-in currency converter, this free app from the Thomson Reuters service is great for the financially minded. The app also showcases the top stories and photographs of the news day.

Love news? The App Store also has apps from National Public Radio and international newspapers like *Le Monde*. You can also find apps that aggregate (collect) headlines from around the world.

Subscribe to ePublications

As mentioned on the previous page, some big news organizations don't give content away for free. To get all the publication's stories (and not just a Whitman's sampler of summaries or selected articles), some ask that you pay for them in the form of a subscription.

Some publications still handle the subscription process by having you pay for and download a new version of its app (with new content) each month. When you choose to subscribe to one of these titles, instructions guide you through the delivery and payment process.

But in early 2011, Apple made the whole subscription thing easier by absorbing the payment-and-renewal process into the App Store. Many periodicals, including *The Daily*, *Elle*, and *Popular Science*, hopped on board right away and others soon joined, despite grumblings that Apple was taking a 30-percent cut of the fee (as it does with all App Store wares).

Still, subscribing through the App Store makes it easier to keep track of your regular electronic material—the fee gets billed to your existing Apple account and you can renew or cancel your subscriptions right on the iPad. Here's how:

❶ Tap into the App Store from the home screen.

❷ Flick to the bottom of the screen and tap the Account button to log in.

❸ Tap the View Account button and retype your password if asked.

❹ In the box that appears, flick down to the Subscriptions area and tap Manage My Subscriptions.

Now you can see your subscription details and also turn off the Auto-Renewal setting (circled above). Remember, you'll keep getting billed for the subscription until you cancel it here, so it's good to keep tabs on your tab regularly.

 Tip Magazines and newspapers aren't the only periodicals you can read on your iPad—comic books also look amazing on the big, bright screen. Just search the App Store for *comics*, and DC Comics, Marvel Comics, and the ComiXolgy's Comics app (which has the big publishers and tons of indie titles, too) all pop up.

Delete or Rearrange iBooks

Bibliophiles know how easy it is to amass piles and piles of books and magazines. Magazines are usually emotionally easier to toss out since they don't have the feeling of permanence that a book does. (On the iPad, you typically delete old issues from within the magazine or newsstand apps.) But with books—some books you want to keep forever, while others, well, not so much. So let's get some iPad drive space back now.

If a book has to go, here are some ways to do it:

❶ On the Bookshelf screen, tap the Edit button in the top-right corner. Tap the books you want to remove, tap the red Delete button, and then confirm your choice.

❷ Connect the iPad to your computer, click the Books tab, turn off the checkbox next to the unwanted titles, and click Apply or Sync. iTunes removes the book from the iPad, but keeps a copy for future reference.

❸ You can not only delete books from the iBooks List View screen, but rearrange the order of the ones left on the shelf more easily. Tap the List View icon (▤), tap Bookshelf, and then tap the Edit button. Tap the button next to each book you want to toss and tap the Delete button at the top of the screen.

❹ You can do further tidying in List View. For example, use the grip strip (≡) to drag existing titles into a new order in the list.

❺ Select a book (or books) and tap the Move button at the top of the screen. A box pops up that lets you create a new grouping from the selected titles—say, all your British murder mysteries—that you can jump to later by tapping the Collections button at the top of the Library screen.

Tip If you have a huge multiscreen list of books, the Search box at the top of the List View screen lets you find titles and author names across your iLibrary.

Play Games

With digital music, videos, and books tucked inside your iPad's slim glass-and-metal form, you have plenty choices for entertainment. But if you want to *play* instead of just sitting back and *pushing* Play, your tablet makes a nice high-def game console as well. You can zap zombies, thwart governments, and channel your inner Dale Earnhardt Jr. You can also relive your glory days at the arcade. But instead of facing a machine the size of a phone booth, your fate lies in your hands—literally.

iPad games aren't simply iPhone games blown up to tablet proportions, either. Savvy game-makers have taken popular titles back into the shop to super-size them for the iPad's big 9.7-inch screen. As a result, you get richer graphics and more precise gameplay, with plenty of room to move around. That bigger screen makes it easy for two people to play against each other, too. And thanks to Apple's online Game Center network, you don't even need to be in the same room as your fellow joystick jockeys.

The iPad can handle everything from basic low-speed card games like euchre, all the way up to high-speed shooters with detailed 3D avatars and pulsating soundtracks. This chapter shows you how to find the games you want and get them onto your iPad. It doesn't tell you how to win, though—you have to figure *that* out for yourself.

Find iPad Games

To start your big-game hunt, you have to hit the App Store. You can buy and download games in iTunes and then sync them to your iPad, or you can buy them on the 'Pad itself.

To browse the iTunes Store on your Windows PC or Mac, choose App Store→Games. To find games on your iPad:

- Tap Categories→Games and flick through the screenshots flowing across the Spotlight section until you see a game you like.

- Tap through the New & Noteworthy titles to see what's recently arrived.

- Tap the Top Charts button at the bottom of the screen, tap the Categories button in the menu bar, and then choose Games to see the best-selling titles—and the most popular free games. (Games, being a popular pastime, are often the top-sellers of *all* the App Store's wares.)

- Tap the Search box in the upper-right corner and type in keywords to find a specific type of game ("cards") or game title ("Table Poker").

Tap any game listed to see its Store page, which includes system requirements, age ratings, sample screens, and reviews. When you check out a game, make sure it's made for the iPad and not for the iPhone and iPod Touch—unless you like pixellated graphics. Many iPad games have an HD tag (as in Plants vs. Zombies HD) or title themselves appropriately (Pac-Man for iPad).

When you find a game you like, tap the price button, and then tap Install.

Play Games

Once you download your game, it appears on your iPad's Home screen, just like any other app. Tap it open when you're ready to play. Don't know how? Look for a "How to Play" or "Info" or "Rules" button on the opening screen. Some games even have a link to YouTube demos or trailers explaining the game's rules and backstory.

Your iPad didn't come with an Xbox or PlayStation-style game controller, and it certainly doesn't have one of those motion-sensitive magic wands, like the Nintendo Wii. But with its accelerometer, sensitive touchscreen, and crisp high-resolution display, the iPad offers game makers a variety of ways to build in gameplay controls.

For example, in some driving games, like *Real Racing HD* (shown here), you zoom around a course holding your iPad like a steering wheel—just be careful not to drop it mid-race. Other games are just as creative. As its name suggests, *Flick Fishing HD* lets you cast a virtual line into the water with just a flick of your wrist.

Old-school joystick games like *Pac-Man* put a virtual version of the familiar red-handled knob in the corner of the screen, but you can lead the munching yellow disc with your finger as well. And in *Flight Control HD*, you guide an increasing number of incoming planes into their landing zones with a finger-drag along the runway.

> **Tip** Stuck on a certain level of a game or having trouble figuring it out? A quick Web search for the name of the game and "cheat codes" can return links to tips, tricks, and hints for moving forward. Cheaters may never win, but they can level up.

Sign Up for Game Center

Unless you're playing solitaire, games are usually more fun when you play with someone. Apple's Game Center network lets you compete against thousands of other players on iOS devices around the world. You can add pals to a Friends list for quick competitions, do battle with strangers in multiplayer games, and compete for the top spot on leaderboards.

Here's how you get started with Game Center:

❶ Tap the Game Center icon on the iPad's Home screen and sign up for an account (or use your Apple ID, as described on page 118). Apple bills the games you buy to this account. Then, pick an online nickname—it may take a few tries to find an available one.

❷ Configure your settings so you get invitations to games and update notifications, and so Game Center members can find you based on your email address. (If you're already a Game Center member and didn't turn on push notifications when you signed up, you can do that now by going to the Game Center's home screen, tapping your account name, and then tapping View Account.)

❸ Start a Friends list by tapping the ✚ icon; you can send an invitation to an email address or a Game Center nickname. Once your buds accept, Game Center adds their names to your list of friends. (Tap the Requests button to see pending friend requests from other players.)

❹ When you have your account set up, it's time to get a game. Tap the Game Center icon and then tap Find Game Center Games. Not every App Store game is hooked into Game Center, so it's best to pick from within the app.

❺ Play. Tap the Friends button to pick a buddy, tap the name of a game, and then tap the Play button. Your pal gets a game invite, and once she accepts your challenge, throw down and start whooping.

If your invitation goes ignored, send a request to another friend or tap the Auto-Match button to have Game Center pair you with an available player. Game Center tracks players' individual high scores, even when you compete in multiplayer games. To check these leaderboard scores, go to the Game Center's home screen and tap Games→[name of game]→Leaderboards.

Many games in the App Store can also connect to OpenFeint, an older gaming social network used by both iPadders and people playing on devices running Google's Android operating system. If an App Store game is compatible with OpenFeint, the iPad prompts you to sign up for or log into that network the first time out. Thereafter, when you launch a game that's compatible with both networks, the iPad presents you with a box so you can tap your preferred playground.

Play Multiplayer Games

Game Center is great if you're in a different room from your opponent, but what about those good old-fashioned face-to-face multiplayer games? You know, the ones people played around a card table, back when gaming was inherently social because your challenger sat right across from you.

Many iPad games are still like that, but with a twist: The tablet's size and powerful processor has encouraged developers to make titles that two people can play on two different iPads over a WiFi or Bluetooth connection, as well as games that two can play on the very same iPad—face-to-face, just like playing Scrabble around the kitchen table.

Speaking of Scrabble, it's one game that takes multiplayer contests into the modern age, with a whole new level of creativity. The $10 iPad version has several modes of play, including one where friends can compete against each other by passing the tablet back and forth. And if everyone at your Scrabble party is an Apple hardware fan, there's a free app that turns your iPhone or iPod Touch into a very expensive tile rack— while the iPad serves as the game board. (You keep your letters to yourself on the handheld until it's time to magically flip them onto the iPad over the wireless connection.)

Many of the App Store's multiplayer games are electronic versions of popular tabletop games like air hockey, poker, Uno, and mahjong, which basically turn the iPad into an exquisitely designed game board. Dig deep enough, though, and you'll find all sorts of games meant for group play, including *Monster Ball HD* and the over-punctuated *Call of Duty: World at War: Zombies for iPad*. So, how to find all these games? Search for *multiplayer* in the App Store.

 Some multiplayer games feature a Wi-Fi logo or Bluetooth symbol on the game's icon to let you know that you can play with another person over a wireless connection.

Troubleshoot Games

Some games work flawlessly, while others may be a little more unstable, acting erratically, bombing out on you, and frustrating you (especially if you paid good money for them). If that happens, first shut down and then restart your iPad. If that doesn't help, return to the App Store to see if there are any updates for the game—many developers quickly issue fixes if enough people complain. (Complaining to Apple probably won't help much since they just sell the games.)

In general, if a game begins to crash on you, uninstall it (press down on its Home screen icon until a ⊗ appears, tap the ⊗, and then press the Home button again). Then return to the App Store and re-download the game to see if that clears things up. Don't worry, you won't have to pay for the game again.

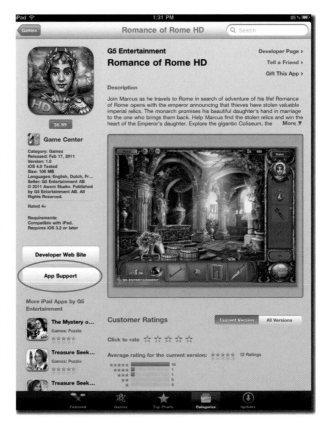

If you're still having trouble, go to the game creator's website. Most major developers have support and troubleshooting information there, and the game's Store page often includes links to the developer's site or an App Support button (circled above).

And if you really like a certain game and want to see more titles from the same company, check the game's App Store page again —it sometimes includes a list of other games the company created for the iPad.

An iPad Games Gallery

The App Store has just about every type of game you can think of: casual games, action games, shooter games, goofy games, mind-numbingly-repetitious-but-still-better-than-working games, and old favorites. Apple adds new games every week, so if you're serious about gaming, it's worth a regular visit to keep an eye out for new releases. If you want a few games to get started with, here are the ones that proved popular with iPad owners right off the bat:

- **Angry Birds.** On the surface, this game starts out as a straightforward tale of a band of kamikaze birds trying to take revenge on a herd of chartreuse swine who raided their nest. But this $5 green-ham-and-eggs story teaches a few lessons about physics—you have to figure out the right  angle and trajectory at which to catapult the avenging avians and knock down a series of increasingly complex structures the pigs try to hide in.

- **Mirror's Edge.** This action game has been around for years and was previously released for the Xbox 360 and PlayStation 3. The $13 iPad version re-creates the tale of Faith, who lives under a totalitarian regime and works as a covert courier. As a "runner," she gallops across rooftops and clambers  up walls on a mission to deliver messages and avoid government surveillance. The game's Hollywood action-picture soundtrack and bright visuals bring to mind the rooftop scene in *The Matrix*—another story about communication and rebellion in an oppressive society.

- **Fruit Ninja HD.** Your fingertip becomes a razor-sharp samurai sword, and your mission, young apprentice, is to slice fruit tossed in the air. While this can be relaxing (or even therapeutic after one of *those* days), your reflexes need to be as honed as your blade when the produce comes flying. If you miss three times, it's Game Over. To complicate things, sometimes a bomb floats up instead of fruit. The two-player mode lets you go head-to-head with fellow salad warriors.

- **Plants vs. Zombies HD.** One of the first iPad titles available from PopCap Games (maker of Bejeweled, Peggle, and several other multiplat-form casual games), this $10 app relies on you to protect your home against an invading zombie army by sowing flowers and other plants that attack the badly dressed undead as they advance across your lush green lawn.

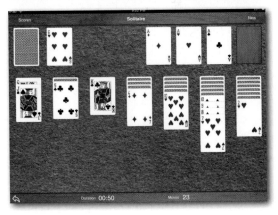

- **The Solitaire.** Need something free and familiar? Look no further. This particular version of the solo card game finally added an automatic three-card draw, and, well, the price is right. As you can imagine, though, there's more than one version of solitaire in the App Store to search out.

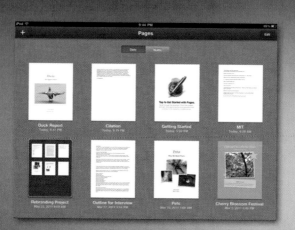

 10

 slide to unlock

Get Productive with iWork

Word processing, spreadsheets, and presentations probably aren't the first things that come to mind when you think of the iPad—unless they're the first things that come to your mind on any topic. After you've used the iPad for longer than two hours, you realize that it's a great little device for consuming stuff (videos, eBooks, web pages), but not so much for *creating* stuff, like, well, word-processing documents, spreadsheets, and presentations.

Apple's iWork suite for the iPad attempts to change that impression. For many years, iWork—consisting of Pages (word-processing), Numbers (spreadsheet), and Keynote (presentations) programs—lived on some Macs in the giant, looming shadow of Microsoft Office. After all, from corporate offices to college campuses, Microsoft Word, Excel, and PowerPoint are the de facto industry standards for documents, spreadsheets, and presentations.

If you're considering buying iWork (or you have it already and don't know where to start with it), this chapter is for you. iWork isn't a do-all, be-all desktop suite, but neither does it take up gigabytes of hard drive space for files and features you'll never use. It can, however, keep you productive— even if you'd rather use your iPad to watch *The Office* instead of working on a spreadsheet *for* the office.

Meet iWork

If you've never heard of iWork, you're not alone. It's oldest component, the Keynote presentation program, has only been around since 2003, with Pages and Numbers debuting a few years later. All iWork programs are Mac-only, which means that more than 90 percent of the computing population has never used iWork or doesn't care because darn it, there's new antivirus software to install!

Apple created iWork to cover much of the same ground as Microsoft Office, Corel WordPerfect Office, OpenOffice.org, StarOffice, Google Docs, and any other software suite that contains the holy trinity of business productivity applications: a word-processing program, a spreadsheet program, and a pre-sentation/slideshow program.

With the tablet version of iWork, Apple transformed the point-and-click desk-top version of the suite into tap-and-drag iPad software. It isn't just a half-baked copy of an overstuffed office suite, either. Who wants a screen clogged full of toolbars, menus, and floating palettes when your screen *is* your workspace? Apple's iWork re-engineering takes this into account, tucking your formatting, function, and design controls neatly into tappable buttons that deliver tool-bars only when you need them—leaving most of the screen free and clear. And those iPad finger moves—where you zoom in on and pinch onscreen elements—work in iWork, too.

You can buy the iWork pro-grams in the App Store—just tap the Categories button and look in the Productivity area (circled). Apple sells each program separately for $10 apiece. This is convenient if, say, you just need to compose memos and wouldn't know a GPA calculator if it bit you—you don't have to buy the whole suite. And if you *do* buy the whole suite, it'll set you back just 30 bucks—a bargain compared to desktop suites that cost $80 or more.

 Note The App Store doesn't sell the whole iWork suite as one big app—you have to buy each $9.99 program separately. But all three apps show up if you search for "iWork" in the App Store.

Here's the iWork lineup:

- **Pages.** Pre-stocked with 16 templates for all kinds of documents (résumés, letters, flyers—even a *blank* page!), the iPad version of Pages aims to make word-processing as efficient as possible. Granted, it's no Microsoft Word in the features department, but it's versatile enough to let you do more than just type words. You can add photos, charts, and tables to documents, and format text with features like bullets and numbered lists. And here's one way Pages trumps Word: As with all iWork apps, Pages automatically saves your file at least twice a minute.

- **Numbers.** A spreadsheet-making alternative to Microsoft Excel, Numbers also has its own collection of templates so you can create things like budgets and travel planners. It lets you convert a table into a form for speedy data input and create formulas with more than 250 functions (for those who really like to rock a spreadsheet). Numbers isn't all about numbers, though; it can tap into the iPad's Photos app so you can jazz up your spreadsheets with pictures, too.

- **Keynote.** With 20 slideshow transitions and 12 themes to choose from, Keynote was made for crafting slick presentations for audiences of any size. Although it's not as powerful as Microsoft PowerPoint, Keynote is a nimble app, designed for creating shows on the go. And once you design your presentation on the iPad, you can *run* it there, too—by hooking it up to a projector with one of Apple's Dock Connector video adapters (see page 246).

At this point, you may be thinking, "It's all well and good that iWork can do all this stuff, but does it really matter if nobody besides iPad and Mac owners can *open* these files?" Here's the answer: iWork can export files in PDF format, the *lingua franca* of the computer world, whose files everyone with the free Adobe Reader can open. Makes iWork all that more appealing, eh?

Get Started with iWork

As with any word-processing, spreadsheet, or presentation program, the first step in using one of iWork's apps is to create or open a document so you have a place to process your words, numbers, or slides. Start by tapping open an app, say Pages, on the iPad's Home screen. If this is your first time with the program, you land on the app's main screen, where all the documents, spreadsheets, or presentations you create will live. (Apple organizes all the iWork apps the same way; Pages is used here as an example.)

The Pages main screen starts out fairly sparse, except for the introductory Getting Started guide (circled below). But as you create new documents, the screen fills up with pint-sized versions of your files, as shown below. Here's how you create and manage documents to fill up your own app screen:

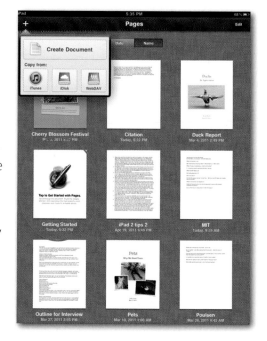

- **Create a document.** Tap the ✛ icon (right) to create a file from a blank page or iWork template.

- **Import a document.** Tap the ✛ icon and then, under "Copy from," tap the relevant source button (right). To copy a file to your iPad via iTunes, follow the import/export instructions on page 173. You can also copy files from an iDisk (soon to be renamed iCloud) or a WebDAV (collaboration) server.

- **Duplicate a document.** On the main Pages/Numbers/ Keynote screen, tap the Edit button or press and hold the document you want to duplicate until the thumbnail wiggles and a yellow border appears around your selection. Then tap the ⊞ icon in the upper-left corner.

- **Delete a document.** Don't need the selected file anymore? Press and hold its icon (or tap Edit) on the main Pages screen until it wiggles and the yellow border appears. Tap the 🗑 icon in the menu bar to delete it.

- **Send a document.** Ready to pass a file along by email, iTunes sync, or to an online server? Open the file, tap the wrench icon to reveal the Share and Print menu (shown on page 172), and choose an option.

When you're ready to create a fresh file in any of the apps, tap the **+** icon in the top-left corner and choose Create Document. To start from scratch, choose the blank-page option. To create a specific type of document, like a résumé or that flyer for the school bake sale, flick through the template catalog and tap the page style you like.

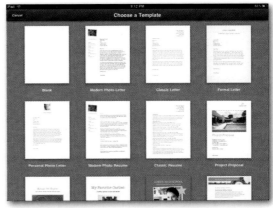

Want to rename a file? Tap Documents to go to the main Pages screen, tap the document's thumbnail, and then press the generic name underneath the preview until the Rename Document screen pops up (right). Now you can change the document name to a more personalized or appropriate one ("Duck Report"). Tap the document to go back to the main Pages screen.

Want to switch to another file or start a brand-new one while you're working on a document? Tap the Documents button in the upper-left corner of the open file. iWork saves the file and returns you to the main Pages, Numbers, or Keynote screen, which has your previously created files. To open one, locate its thumbnail and then tap it.

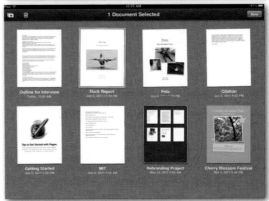

You can also store files in "folders," just as you can with apps on the iPad Home screen (page 8). Press and hold a thumbnail on the main screen and drag it onto another to create the folder (circled above), then drag in more files.

Create Documents in Pages

Unless you started with the Zen of a blank page, you'll notice that the Pages templates all use dummy type and stock photos as placeholders for your own text and pictures. In its simplest form, Pages lets you craft your documents by just tapping the fake text and typing in your own words; the program adds new pages as you need them. Tap the corner of the template's placeholder picture and replace it with one of your own from the Photos box that pops up.

When you tap into a text field (as opposed to a picture box), Pages displays a formatting toolbar at the top of the screen. It includes a ruler for tab stops and margins, plus buttons for things like formatting headlines, making characters boldface, and changing text alignment. (Tap the ❸ on the end if you want to slide the toolbar out of the way.)

A simple set of four icons in the top-right corner of the screen contains all the program's other formatting tools. With these, you can:

❶ **Style text.** Select some text on-screen and tap here to open a three-tabbed box with the labels Style, List, and Layout. The Style menu has pre-configured type styles for titles, subtitles, and so on, along with bold, italic, underline, and strikethrough buttons. Tap the List tab to turn the selected text into a bulleted or numbered list. Tap the Layout tab to change the text alignment (centered, flush right, and so on), the number of columns on the page, or the space between lines.

❷ **Add images and graphics.** Use this four-tabbed box to add visual elements to your documents. The Media tab lets you insert photos from the iPad's Photos app. Tap the Tables tab to stick in an adjustable table, and tap the Charts tab to insert bar charts, pie charts, and other infographics. Tap the Shapes tab to add pre-packaged geometric forms and arrows to your document. Hate the colors in a chart? Replace it; swipe the box with your finger—there are six mini-pages of each type of chart to choose from, as indicated by the dots at the bottom.

❸ Tools. Tap the Wrench icon to get to the Find option, which helps you search documents; the Print command (page 32); and the blueprint-y Document Setup screen, where you change a file's headers, footers, and margins. The "Go to Help" shortcut takes you to the full Pages manual online. The Settings menu lets you turn on guides for aligning text and photos, and launch the spell-checker and word-counter.

❹ Go to full-screen view. Tap these arrows to lose the toolbar and expand your document full-screen.

You can use Pages in either portrait or landscape view, but you'll only see the toolbar and other controls in portrait mode. Want to jump to a different page in a document? Press your finger down on the right side of the screen to see the Page Navigator preview tool, then move it up or down until you find the page you want.

Tips for Working with Text and Photos

Pages may have a ton of templates, but you're not locked into cookie-cutter documents. If you want, you can use text-formatting tools to change a document's type size, style, and even color (tap ❶→Style→Text Options→Color) to make it look the way *you* want it to look.

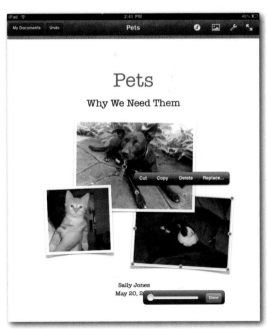

And you're not locked into rigid photo sizes or placement, either. After you import your own pictures or choose stock graphics, tap the element to get a slider bar so you can resize the image in the frame, or use the blue handles to resize the image itself. Drag a selected photo around the page to reposition it. You can even delete photo boxes you don't want.

Miss those Ctrl-Z (Undo) and Ctrl-S (Save) lifesavers? If you mess something up, don't worry. Pages, like all the iWork programs, has a handy Undo button on the top-left corner of every screen. And it automatically saves your document every 30 seconds as you work along.

Create Spreadsheets in Numbers

When you think of the iPad, you tend to think of shredding a game or cruising the Web, not wading deep into a spreadsheet. But if you need to get a little work done on your trusty tablet, the Numbers app can graph your data, crunch your digits, and handle other nerdy tasks.

As with Pages, Numbers offers a collection of 16 pre-fabricated templates for the most popular types of spreadsheets: a mortgage calculator, personal budget tracker, travel planner, weight-loss log, expense report, and more. There's also a blank template with an empty grid of cells awaiting you. Tap a template to select it. Tap the fake text and numbers in the cells to overwrite them with your own facts and figures. To add new sheets or forms to a spreadsheet, tap the **+** button on the tab at the top of the screen.

As with Pages, the four icons hanging out in the top-right corner of the screen hold the formatting tools for table text and graphics. With a tap, you can:

❶ **Style text, rows, and cells.** You get different options here depending on whether you highlight text or tables. For text, you get a box with Style, Text, and Arrange tabs. Here, you can choose typefaces, type colors, and effects (like opacity and shadows), as well as flip objects. When you have a table selected, the ❶ menu becomes a four-tabbed box for changing the color and style of the table. Tabs for Headers and Cells hold the controls for tweaking those elements, and the Format tab lets you dictate how Numbers represents numbers, like currency and percentages. With a chart selected, the ❶ menu gives you color and style options for the chart's text and type (pie chart, area chart, and so on). In short, if you need to format anything on this sheet, the ❶ has it.

❷ **Add images and graphics.** Just as in Pages, this menu holds the tabs (Media, Tables, Charts, and Shapes) to all the photos, tables, charts, and geometric shapes you may want to add to your spreadsheet. For example, you can press and hold a pie chart on the page until the Delete button appears, zap the pie chart off the screen, and drag a bar chart out of the menu and onto the sheet to replace it. Then tap or drag a table to add its data to the chart.

❸ Change settings. Tap here to open the Tools menu. The Find option at the top of the menu lets you search for keywords within a file, but it's the last menu item that should answer your Numbers questions. That's the link to the online Help guide, where Apple's detailed manual for Numbers (and all its formulas and functions) hangs out. The other two items on the Tools menu are the Print command and Settings—off/on switches for guides that help you align elements as you finger-drag them around the screen, as well as the program's spell-checker to help catch typos in your charts.

❹ Go to fullscreen view. Tap here to dismiss the toolbar for an uncluttered full-screen look at your sheet. Tap the top of the screen to get it back.

You can pull and push pretty much every element in a Numbers template to accommodate your data set. Need to expand the standard chart by a few rows or columns? Tap the chart and, when the gray bar appears, tap the circular handle on either the horizontal or vertical bar and drag it in the direction you

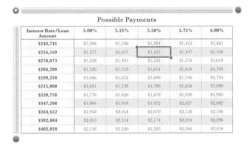

need to add (or delete) rows and columns. If you don't like the position of a table or chart in a template, tap it so the same gray adjustment bars appear. Then press the dotted circle in the top-left corner and drag the table to a new location on the page.

Need to edit the data the chart references? Give it the old double-tap and when the ✿ icon appears at the top of the screen, tap it and choose "Plot Rows as Series or Plot Columns as Series."

Numbers wouldn't be a spreadsheet program if it didn't do sums and calculations. Double-tap any cell where you want to execute an automatic calculation, and the Numbers keypad for punching in math and logic arguments appears. It offers more than 250 formulas and functions in several mathematical specialties, including engineering and statistics, for a value-calculating good time.

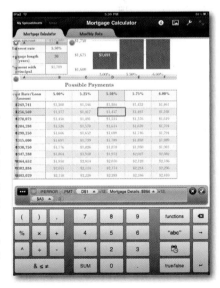

Create Presentations in Keynote

If there's an app in the iWork trio that shows off the iPad's looks best, it's Keynote—it shines when your slides and snazzy animated transitions play on its high-resolution screen. Made to let you show off photos, graphics, and short bits of bullet-pointed text, Keynote is the most intuitive of iWork's three apps.

It comes with 12 templates, some of them extremely plain for your more serious talks about how the company missed its financial goals for Q4, and some fancier for middle-school book reports and vacation essays. Once you pick a template, fill it up with your own pictures and text. (You have to 'Pad horizontally—Keynote doesn't do portrait mode.)

During your presentation, you don't have to progress statically from slide to slide. Keynote comes with several animated transitions. You can spin, twirl, pop, flip, dissolve, or zoom to get you from one slide to the next—and you can apply a different transition for any slide in the presentation.

Keynote gives you control over the text on your slides, building in animated effects where your titles disappear in a hail of flash bulbs, for instance. Here's a tour of the Keynote toolbar:

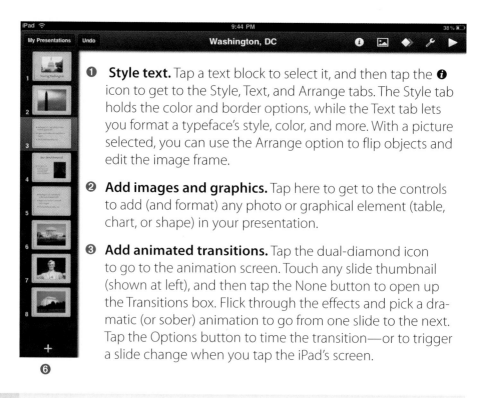

❶ **Style text.** Tap a text block to select it, and then tap the ❶ icon to get to the Style, Text, and Arrange tabs. The Style tab holds the color and border options, while the Text tab lets you format a typeface's style, color, and more. With a picture selected, you can use the Arrange option to flip objects and edit the image frame.

❷ **Add images and graphics.** Tap here to get to the controls to add (and format) any photo or graphical element (table, chart, or shape) in your presentation.

❸ **Add animated transitions.** Tap the dual-diamond icon to go to the animation screen. Touch any slide thumbnail (shown at left), and then tap the None button to open up the Transitions box. Flick through the effects and pick a dramatic (or sober) animation to go from one slide to the next. Tap the Options button to time the transition—or to trigger a slide change when you tap the iPad's screen.

❹ **Change settings.** Tap here to see the Tools menu. As in Pages and Numbers, visit this menu to use the Find feature to search for certain words in your presentation or to print out the presentation. Tap the "Go to Help" option for Apple's online Keynote manual. The rest of the tools consist of Presenter Notes (little iPad crib sheets you can refer to while projecting your presentation on the big screen), and settings for the built-in edge guides (used to align the elements on a slide), the display of each slide's number, and the embarrassment-saving spell-checker to catch giant typos in slide titles and text.

❺ **Play.** Tap the familiar ▶ icon to start your presentation. If you set your slides to advance automatically, sit back and enjoy the show. If you opted to manually advance each slide (if your presentation is part of a live talk and you need to time the slides with your narration), tap or swipe the iPad's screen to march through the show.

❻ **Add Slide.** Tap the ✚ button at the bottom of the vertical column of slides to call up a box full of slide styles (shown at right) so you can add new ones to the show. Some slide templates are just text blocks, some are photo-only, and some have both text and photos. If you don't see quite what you want, pick the one closest to your vision and use the text and object formatting controls to rework the slide.

To animate text or images so they move on or off a slide, tap the relevant element and then tap the toolbar's dual-diamond icon. Tap Build In (to move the item in) or Build Out (to move it off the slide), and then select an effect from the menu (shown at right). It's good fun.

For an even cooler way to grab your audience's attention, press and hold your finger on a slide for a second or two. A red laser pointer dot appears on-screen and follows your fingertip around as you drag it to point out something...important.

Import, Export, and Share iWork Files

So what good is all this work (and iWork) if you can't share your files with the people who need them? And what can you, as an industrious iPad owner, do with your fancy iWork suite if you can't view, open, and edit files that people send *you*—especially if your correspondents cling to Microsoft Office and don't even *have* iWork? No problem. Here's why:

- All the programs in the iWork suite let you import, open, and edit files created in Microsoft Word, Excel, and PowerPoint.

- All the programs in the iWork suite let you export files in just about any format you need. You can, for example, export files in their native iWork formats so you can edit them in the desktop version of the program on your MacBook or iMac. You can also export iWork files in the format of the corresponding Microsoft Office program: Pages exports files in Word's .doc format, Numbers spits out Excel .xls files, and Keynote exports presentations as PowerPoint .ppt files. And finally, you can export files as Adobe Acrobat-ready PDF documents.

You can move files on and off your iPad multiple ways—by email, using iTunes, or via Apple's document-sharing site, iWork.com. You can also copy your iWork files to your iCloud/MobileMe account or to a WebDAV server (the latter so you can work collaboratively).

iWork by Email

How do you normally get most of the files people send you? If the answer is email, you're in luck. If you get an attached Word, Excel, 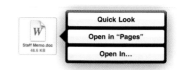 PowerPoint, or .csv (comma-separated values) file, or a Numbers, Pages, or Keynote file, you can save it in the corresponding iWork for iPad program. Just press and hold the file attachment icon until the "Open in Pages" (or whatever) option pops up; if you have another app that can open the file, choose "Open In..." and select the app. Just tapping the file once opens the attachment as a Quick Look preview for reading, but not editing (though Quick Look does give you a button, in the top-right corner, to open the file in the appropriate app).

Likewise, you can export iWork files by email. Select the file and tap the toolbar's wrench icon, tap Share and Print, and then tap Email Document (right). For Pages, Numbers, and Keynote, you can export iWork files in their native formats for the desktop editions of the program. You can also send documents as Office-ready .doc, .xls, or .ppt files. And finally, you can export any iWork file as a PDF document. (See the export options

for Pages at right.) Tap your choice to convert (if necessary) and attach the iWork file to an outgoing message.

iWork by iTunes Sync

File too big to email? You can use iTunes' file-sharing option to sync files back and forth between your computer and iPad.

To *import* a file to the tablet, connect your iPad, click its icon in the iTunes window, and then click the Apps tab. Scroll to the file transfer settings area at the bottom of the screen.

In the Apps column, click the icon for the program whose file you want to copy to your iPad (Pages and so on), click Add, and then navigate to and highlight the file. Sync your iPad to

copy the file over to it. Then, on your iPad, tap the ✛ icon on the Pages/Numbers/Keynote main screen, and then tap Copy from iTunes. In the box that appears (above), tap open the transferred file to import it into your chosen iWork app.

To *export* an open file from your iPad to iTunes (and then to your computer), tap the wrench icon in the toolbar, choose Share and Print, tap Send to iTunes, and then tap your preferred format for the exported file

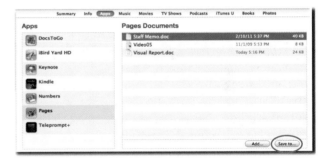

(like .doc or .pdf). Connect the iPad to your computer, select it in iTunes, and then click the Apps tab. Once you sync up the iPad and iTunes, the file appears in the shared files list. Select it and click the "Save to" button (circled above) to copy it to a folder on your computer, where you can open it in Word or whatnot.

iWork by Online Server

To share a file with others on the iWork.com site, iCloud/MobileMe iDisk, or a WebDAV server, open the file, tap the wrench icon in the toolbar, and choose Share and Print. From the menu (shown on the opposite page), tap your preferred online destination, choose an export format, and then type any user name and password needed to transfer the file.

Troubleshooting iWork Files

The dynamic trio of Pages, Numbers, and Keynote lets you create fairly sophisticated documents, spreadsheets, and presentations right there on your iPad. But let's face it—until iPads rule the galaxy, most of the world is still crouched in a Microsoft Office cubicle.

While many files can go back and forth between iWork and Office perfectly fine, intricately formatted files or those that use some of Microsoft's more complex features may have some trouble in iWork. If the apps have problems with an imported file, you see a warning box like the one below, detailing the iComplaints. Here are some of the issues to look out for:

- **Fonts.** The iWork for iPad trio has a selection of at least 40 fonts (and the family members within those fonts, like Plain and its cousins Bold and Italic), but it comes nowhere near the bulging font library found on most computers. When a file uses fonts the iPad doesn't itself possess, the tablet substitutes a font it thinks looks close to the original. Your results may vary. To be on the safe side when moving an Office file to iWork, you may want to stick with those standard desktop typeface classics like Arial, Baskerville, Cochin, Copperplate, Courier, Georgia, Gill Sans, Helvetica, Palatino, Times New Roman, and good old Verdana.

- **Tracking changes.** Two of Office's most-used tools are its Track Changes and Comments modes. These let several people collaborating on one file see each other's changes and embed notes to each other within the text. Unfortunately, these features don't work in iWork: It automatically accepts all the proposed changes when you pull the file into iWork—and it strips out comments entirely.

- **Linked files.** Unless it's a regular old Web URL, other elements that were linked in the original Office file will probably get zapped, especially clip art and other graphics in file formats iWork doesn't work with.

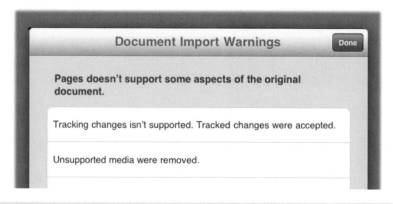

Getting Help with iWork

Even if you're not flinging files back and forth to and from Microsoft Office (or even the Mac desktop version of iWork), you may still have questions about how to do things, like, say, setting tab stops or rotating objects. Thankfully, iWork's creators anticipated your needs and wrote a tappable online user manual for each program in the suite.

When you seek answers (to iWork questions, anyway), tap the wrench icon in the upper-right corner of Pages, Numbers, or Keynote, and slide your digit down to the Help link. From there, the iPad whisks you into Safari, where you can browse through your selected iWork app's user guide (like the one below).

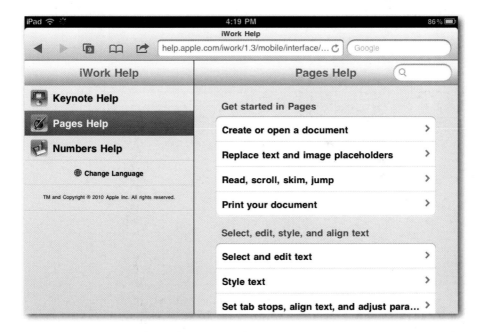

Tip Although it's obviously Apple's favorite solution, iWork isn't the only game in town for iPad users who use Microsoft Office. Other options include DataViz Documents To Go ($10) and Quickoffice Connect Mobile Suite for iPad ($15). Both are available in the App Store and claim to have good compatibility with editing those inevitable Microsoft Office files that turn up on your tablet.

 slide to unlock

Organize and Sync Media Files with iTunes

iTunes is a master of many trades. It's a repository for all the audio, video, book, and podcast files in your media library. It converts compact disc tracks into digital files for iPads, iPhones, and iPods. And it has its own online mall that you can pop into any time of day or night to buy the latest Stephen King audiobook, grab a copy of the new U2 album, or rent a digital download of *The Social Network*.

Another cool feature of iTunes? It syncs any or all of your media to your iPad. You may have already dabbled in a bit of this in Chapter 7 with the iTunes App Store, or in Chapter 8 when you read up on the iBookstore. This chapter focuses on iTunes basics: downloading Store purchases to your computer—and then getting what you want over to your iPad. (For more on mastering the art of iTunes, see Chapter 12.)

So if you're thinking of syncing, flip the page.

The iTunes Window

iTunes is your iPad's best friend. You can do just about everything with your digital media here—convert songs on a CD into iPad-ready music files; buy music, movies, and TV shows; add apps; listen to Internet radio stations; and more. Here's a quick tour of the iTunes window and what all the buttons, controls, and sliders do.

The gray Source panel on the left side of the iTunes window displays all your media libraries—for audio, videos, books, and more.

❶ Click any icon in the Library group—Music, Movies, TV Shows, Podcasts, and so on—to see that library's contents in iTunes' main window. Programs you buy through iTunes (so you can later sync them to your 'Pad) land here under Apps. Want to customize the libraries iTunes lists? Press Ctrl+comma (⌘-comma) to call up iTunes' Preferences menu, and then click the General tab. In the "Show:" area, turn on (or off) the check-boxes for, say, Podcasts or iTunes U, as you see fit.

❷ In the Store section of the Source panel, click the shopping-bag icon to shop for new stuff. Other items you may see here include a Purchased icon that lists what you've bought through iTunes and a Purchased on iPad list. The Downloads icon lists items you're in the process of down-loading or subscription files (like TV episodes) awaiting you or just now arriving in iTunes.

❸ If you have a music CD in your computer's drive, it shows up in the Devices area, as does a connected iPad. Click the gray Eject icon next to the gadget's name to safely pop out a disc or disconnect an iPad.

❹ In the Shared area, browse the media libraries of family members on your Home Sharing network. You can stream files if you see a stacked playlist icon, or copy music and videos between machines. (See page 185 to learn how to share libraries.)

❺ iTunes keeps all your song lists—whether the iTunes Genius automatically generated them or you lovingly handcrafted them—in the Genius and Playlists sections. The iTunes DJ feature, which quickly whips up randomly selected party mixes, lives here, too.

❻ When you click an icon in the Source list—for Music, say—iTunes' main window displays all the items in that category. Three columns sitting above the main song list let you browse your collection by genre, artist, and album. Naturally, this part of the window is called the Column Browser. You see it here in the top position, but you can display it as a series of full-height vertical columns on the left by choosing View→Column Browser→On Left.

The outer edges of the iTunes window are full of buttons and controls:

❼ Play and pause your current song or video—or jump to the next or previous track. The volume slider adjusts the sound.

❽ The center of the upper pane shows you what song is currently playing. To the right of that you have handy buttons to change views in the center part of the iTunes window and a search box to find songs fast.

❾ At the bottom-left corner of the screen you'll see shortcut buttons for (from left to right) creating a new playlist, shuffling or repeating a playlist, and displaying album artwork or videos.

❿ The lower-right corner of the iTunes window has a few buttons of its own. If you have an Apple TV or connected speakers, you see the square AirPlay icon first in line. The iTunes Genius is next—with a song selected, click the ❈ icon to create a Genius-generated playlist based on that tune. And the boxed-arrow icon on the end toggles on iTunes' Sidebar panel to show you music and video you might like based on your library or to display posts on Ping, Apple's social network for music lovers (see page 220). You toggle the sidebar off with this icon, too.

How iTunes Organizes Your Content

As mentioned earlier, iTunes groups your media into libraries in the Source list. Music, videos, applications, and other content you download from the iTunes Store land in their respective Source list libraries—songs in the Music library, *30 Rock* episodes in TV Shows, and so on. That paid-for music and video also lives in the Source panel's Purchased list, a one-click trip to see where all your spare cash went.

But say you add files that *don't* come from the iTunes Store, like videos you download from the Internet Archive (a great source of free public-domain material, including eBooks, old movies, and years' worth of Grateful Dead live concert recordings; go to *www.archive.org*). If one of these files ends up in the wrong part of the iTunes library, you can fix it so that it lands in the proper place—movies in Movies, podcasts in Podcasts, and so on. Click the file you want to reassign in the iTunes window and choose File→Get Info (or press Ctrl-I or ⌘-I) to call up the Info box. Click the Options tab and, next to the label "Media Kind," select the right category from the pop-up menu, and then click OK.

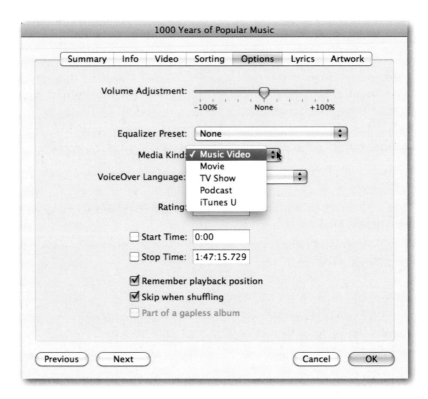

Where iTunes Stores Your Files

Behind its steely silver-framed window, iTunes has a very precise system for storing your music, movies, and everything else you add. Inside its own iTunes folder on your hard drive (which, unless you moved it, is in Music→iTunes [Home→Music→iTunes]), the program keeps all your files and media information. (If you're running Windows 7 or Vista, your iTunes folder is at User→<user name>→Music→iTunes, and Windows XP users can find it at My Documents→My Music→iTunes.)

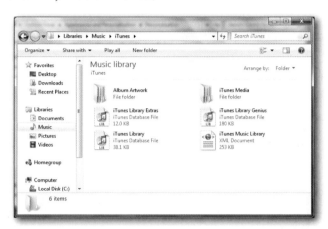

Your iTunes library file, a database that contains the names of all the songs, playlists, videos, and other content you added to iTunes, sits inside the iTunes folder. Be careful not to move or delete this file if you happen to be poking around in the folder. If iTunes can't find it, it gives a little sigh and creates a new one—one that doesn't have a record of all your songs and other media goodies.

If you *do* accidentally delete the library file, your media is still on your computer—even if iTunes doesn't know it. That's because it stores all your media in the iTunes *Music* folder (or *Media* folder, as explained in the Tip below), which is also inside the main iTunes folder. You may lose your custom playlist if your library file goes missing, but you can always add your media files back to iTunes (File→Add to Library) to recreate your library.

 Tip Older versions of iTunes (from back when iTunes managed only music) store your stuff in the iTunes Music folder; newer versions use the iTunes Media folder. If you have a Media folder, iTunes neatly groups things into subfolders like Games, Music, TV Shows, and Movies, making it much easier to find your downloaded episodes of *Mad Men* among all the song files. If you want to reorganize media-style, choose File→Library→Organize Library and choose "Upgrade to iTunes Media organization."

The iTunes Store

Click the iTunes Store icon in the Source panel and you land in iTunes' virtual aisles. The Store is jam-packed with digital merchandise, all neatly filed by category across the top of the main window: Music, Movies, Audiobooks, and so on (but not iBooks; Apple's iBookstore is only available through the iPad's iBooks app). Click a tab to go to a store section. You can also hover over a tab and click the triangle that appears; a pop-up menu lets you jump to a subcategory within the section (Blues, Pop, and so on for Music, for example).

The main part of the iTunes Store window—that big piece of real estate smack in the center of your browser—highlights iTunes' latest audio and video releases and specials. Free song downloads and other offers appear here, too. This window is usually stuffed full of digital goodies, so scroll down the page to see featured movies, TV shows, apps, and freebies.

If you're looking for a specific item, use the search box in the upper-right corner to hunt your quarry; enter titles, artist names, or other searchable info.

Preview songs by double-clicking the track's title. The Buy button is there waiting for your impulse purchase, making it extremely easy to run up your credit-card tab.

If your iPad is in range of a wireless or 3G network connection, you have a third way to get to the Store: over the airwaves, as explained on the next page.

The Wireless iTunes Store

If you have an iPad, you don't even *need* your stodgy old computer to shop the iTunes Store—you can tap your way right into it over a wireless Internet or 3G connection. Many WiFi–enabled Starbucks coffee shops also let you browse and buy in the iTunes Store, including whatever music is currently playing right there at Starbucks.

Now, to buy stuff when you're out and about—and in the mood to shop:

❶ Tap the purple iTunes icon on the iPad's Home screen. Make sure you have a 'Net connection; see Chapter 3 for guidance on making that happen.

❷ The Store appears on-screen. It opens on the Music page the first time out but remembers your last open page if you've been here before. If you want to buy music, tap your way through categories like "New Releases" until you find an album or song you like. (Tap an album to see all its songs.)

❸ Tap a title for a 90-second preview.

❹ For other purchases, tap an icon (Video, TV Shows, and so on) at the bottom of the window, or use the search box at the top to enter keywords. (Want programs? Hit the Home screen's App Store icon.)

❺ To buy and download music, videos, and audiobooks, tap the price, and then tap Buy Now. For free items like podcasts, tap the Free button.

❻ Type in your iTunes Store password and let the download begin. You can check the status of your purchase-in-progress by tapping the Downloads icon, which also lets you pause a download if you need to. (If you don't have an account, tap the Create New Account button on the sign-in screen and follow the steps. You can sign in and out of your account with a link at the bottom of the Store screen.)

Tap the Purchased icon on the iTunes screen to see all the music you've ever bought through your iTunes account—and re-download the songs to your iPad.

To get these fresh iPad-bought songs or videos back into your iTunes library (which, of course, sits on your computer), sync up your iPad when you get home. The tracks appear in a new playlist called "Purchased on PadMan" (or whatever you called your tablet this week).

Check for Downloads

It's bound to happen sometime: You're breathlessly downloading a hot new book or movie and your computer freezes, crashes, or your Internet connection goes on the fritz. Or you and your Wi-Fi iPad were in the middle of snagging an album from the wireless iTunes Store, and the rest of the gang decided it was time to leave the coffee shop.

If this happens, don't worry. Even if your computer crashes or you get knocked offline while you're downloading a purchase, iTunes is designed to pick up where it left off. Just restart the program and reconnect to the Internet.

If, for some reason, iTunes doesn't go back to whatever it was downloading before The Incident, choose Store→Check for Available Downloads to resume your downloading business.

You can also check for available purchases any time you think you might have something waiting, like a new episode from a TV Show Season Pass.

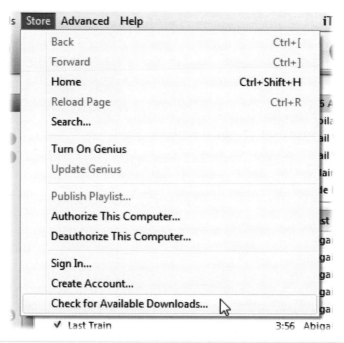

Tip Want an easy way to download *all* your iTunes Store purchases to *all* your devices automatically? Install iTunes 10.3 with its iTunes in the Cloud feature and choose Edit (iTunes)→Preferences→Store. In the Automatic Downloads area, turn on the checkboxes next to Music, Apps, and Books. iTunes stores a copy of your purchases, no matter what Apple device you bought them on. Then, when you next sync any device with iTunes, it sends a copy of those purchases to that device.

Authorize Computers for iTunes and Home Sharing

Apple's usage agreement lets you play Store purchases on up to five computers: PCs, Macs, or any combination thereof. Although iTunes Plus songs (those with liner notes and other extras) and songs sold after April 2009 don't have password-demanding copy restrictions, music tracks purchased before 2009 and most videos still do.

For protected content, you must type in your Apple user name and password on each computer to authorize it to play any songs, videos, or audiobooks purchased with that account. Each computer must have an Internet connection to relay the information back to Store headquarters. (You don't have to authorize each and every purchase; you just authorize the computer itself.)

You authorized your first machine when you initially signed up for an Apple Account. To authorize another computer, choose Store→Authorize Computer.

You can also share media among the computers on your home network, using the Home Sharing feature built into iTunes 9 and later.

❶ In the iTunes Source list, click the Home Sharing icon. On the screen that appears, type in an iTunes account name and password. (If you don't see the cute little house-shaped Home Sharing icon in the Source list, choose Advanced→Turn On Home Sharing. If you get told to authorize the computer for that iTunes account, choose Store→Authorize Computer.)

❷ Click the Create Home Share button.

❸ Repeat these steps for every computer you want to share files with on the network (up to four others).

Once you set up all the computers, each of their iTunes libraries appears in everyone else's Source list. Click the triangle beside the House icon for the library you want to explore. Click on a file to stream it to your own machine over the network. If you must have this file on your computer, select it and click the Import button in the bottom-right corner of the iTunes window. Click the Settings button next to it if you want to automatically copy certain types of files, like Music, among these machines—and your iPad.

Deauthorize Your Computer

Unless you have iTunes Plus tracks, you won't be able to play copy-protected purchased music, books, or videos on a sixth computer if you try to authorize it. Apple's authorization system will see five other computers already on its list and deny your request. That's a drag, but copy protection is copy protection.

To play protected files on Computer Number 6, you have to deauthorize another computer. Choose Store→Deauthorize Computer from the computer about to get the boot, and then type in your Apple Account user name and password. The updated information zips back to Apple.

Are you thinking of putting that older computer up for sale? Before wiping the drive clean and sending it on its way, be sure to deauthorize it, so your new machine will be able to play copy-protected files. Erasing a hard drive, by itself, doesn't de-authorize the computer.

If you forget to deauthorize a machine before getting rid of it, you can still knock it off your List of Five, but you have to reauthorize every machine in your iTunes arsenal all over again. To make it so, in the iTunes window, click the triangle next to your account name and choose Account. Type in your password. On the account information page where it lists the number of computers you authorized, click the Deauthorize All button (you only see this button if you've hit the five-computer limit.) Once you click to deauthorize all your machines, go back to the computers in your Home Sharing network and re-authorize each one.

Automatically Sync the iPad

As with every iPod model that's come before it, the iPad offers the simple and effective *Autosync* feature. Autosyncing automatically puts a copy of every song, video, podcast, and other media in your iTunes library right onto your player. In fact, the first time you connect your iPad to your computer, a Setup Assistant offers to copy all the media files in your iTunes library over to your tablet. If you opt to do that, you automatically turn on autosync. (Change your mind later? Never fear. Page 188 explains how to change sync options.)

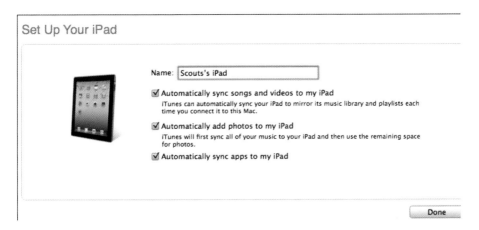

If you added more music to iTunes since that first encounter, the steps for loading the new goods onto your iPad couldn't be easier:

❶ Plug the small end of the USB cable into your Windows PC or Macintosh.

❷ Plug the cable's flat Dock Connector end into the bottom of the iPad.

❸ Sit back and let iTunes leap into action, syncing away and doing all that heavy lifting for you.

You can tell the sync magic is working because iTunes gives you a progress report at the top of its window that says "Syncing iPad…" (or whatever you've named your tablet). When iTunes tells you it's finished updating your 'Pad, you're free to eject it, unplug the cable, and take off.

Autosync is a beautiful thing, but it's not for everyone—especially if you have more than 16, 32, or 64 gigabytes worth of stuff in your iTunes library. (That may sound like a lot of room for music, but once you start adding hefty video files, that space disappears fast.) If that's the case, iTunes fits what it can on the iPad.

If autosync isn't for you, jump over to the next page to read about more selective ways to load up your 'Pad.

Manually Sync to Your iPad

If you opt out of autosyncing your iPad, you now need to go ahead and choose songs or videos for it. Until you do, the iPad just sits there, empty and forlorn in your iTunes window, waiting for you to give it something to play with.

Manual Method #1

❶ Click the iPad icon on the left side of the iTunes window. This opens up a world of syncing preferences for getting stuff on your iPad.

❷ Click the Music tab, then turn on the "Sync Music" checkbox.

❸ Click the button next to "Selected playlists, artists, and genres" and check off the items you want to copy to your iPad. (No playlists yet? See Chapter 12.)

❹ Click the Apply button at the bottom of the iTunes window. (As the rest of the chapter explains, the steps are similar for movies, TV shows, podcasts, and more.)

Manual Method #2

❶ This one's for those into fine-grained picking and choosing: Click the Summary tab and turn on "Manually manage music and videos." Now you can click the songs, albums, or videos you want and drag them to the iPad icon in the iTunes Source pane.

Manual Method #3

❶ Every item in your iTunes library has a checkmark next to its name when you first import it. Clear the checkmark next to whatever you *don't* want on the iPad. (If you have a big library and want just a small subset of your media, hold down the Control [⌘] key while clicking any title; that performs the nifty trick of removing *all* the checkmarks. Then go back and check the stuff you *do* want.)

❷ Click the iPad icon under Devices in the Source list, and then click the Summary tab.

❸ At the bottom of the Summary screen, turn on the checkbox next to "Sync only checked songs and videos" and then click the Sync button.

Sync Music

Once your iPad is connected and showing up in iTunes, you can modify all the settings that control what goes onto (and comes off of) your tablet. Thanks to the long, scrollable screen full of checkboxes and lists in most categories, it's easier than ever to get precisely what you want on your 'Pad.

If you want to sync up all or just some of your music, click the Music tab.

In addition to synchronizing all your songs and playlists by title, you can sync them by artist and genre as well. Just turn on the checkboxes next to the items you want to transfer to the iPad, click the Apply button, and then click the Sync button to move your music.

Chapter 13 has more on playing music on the iPad.

> **Tip** Want to prevent iTunes from trying to sync your iPad every time you connect it— especially if you're connecting it to a computer that's not your own? To bypass the sync just once, hold down the Shift and Control keys on a Windows PC (⌘-Option on a Mac) right after you plug in your tablet's USB cable and wait until the iPad pops up in iTunes. To permanently put the kibosh on iTunes' activity, choose Edit→Preferences→Devices (iTunes→Preferences→Devices) and turn on the checkbox next to "Prevent iPods, iPhones, and iPads from syncing automatically."

Sync Video

In iTunes, videos fall into two main classifications—movies and TV shows—and each collection gets its own tab in iTunes. (Podcasts, which can be either audio or video files, stay together in the Podcasts part of the iTunes Library.)

Full-length movies are huge space hogs and can take up a gigabyte or more of precious drive space—which is a significant chunk of a 16-gigabyte iPad. Serious movie-watchers tend to move films on and off space-limited portable devices. So iTunes gives you the option to load all, selected, or even just unwatched films. To change up what's playing at your portable cineplex, click iTunes' Movies tab when your iPad's connected to your computer and turn on the checkboxes next to your cinema selections.

Since the iTunes Store sells TV shows by season or individual episode, iTunes lets you sync TV shows in several ways: by show, by selected episodes, by the number of unwatched episodes, and so on. Click the TV Shows tab with your iPad connected and make your choices.

Once you decide which movies and TV shows you want to port over to the tablet, click the Apply button and then click Sync. Chapter 14 has more on watching video on the iPad.

Sync Photos

The iPad, in case you haven't noticed, makes a handsome electronic picture frame. To get your pictures on it, you can sync photos from your computer's existing photo-management program, like Adobe Photoshop Elements—or you can copy over a folder of photos. (Chapter 15 has more on displaying photos and making slideshows on the iPad.)

To tell iTunes which pictures you want to take along on your iPad, click the Photos tab. Here, you can select the photo program or folder you want to pull the pictures from, and then turn on checkboxes next to the photos and photo albums you want on the iPad. If you use iPhoto '09 or later on the Mac, you can pull over iPhoto Events, Faces, and Places, iPhoto's way of grouping photos by either what's in them or where you took them. Once you pick your pictures, click Apply and then the Sync button.

 Syncing photos between your iPad and other Apple devices will get a lot easier in the Fall of 2011, when Apple rolls out its iCloud service. Using the service's Photo Stream feature, pics you take or import on one device (or computer) automatically get copied to your iPad, iPhone, or anything else you have connected to iCloud. Apple has details at http://www.apple.com/icloud/features/photo-stream.html.

Sync Info

As you may remember from Chapter 6, the iPad can carry around a copy of the same personal contact list that you keep on your computer. Even just having the email addresses of everyone you know is handy when you're catching up on your email in the backyard hammock. Through iTunes, you can grab contacts from a number of popular programs, including Microsoft Outlook 2003 and later, Windows Address Book, Outlook Express, and Windows Contacts. Macs can tap into contact files stored in the Mac OS X Address Book and Entourage 2004 and later. You can also import addresses from Yahoo and Gmail accounts as long as you have an Internet connection.

To copy contacts over to a connected iPad, click the Info tab and use the pop-up menu to choose the program you keep you contacts in. Scroll down the Info screen to see all the other personal data you can sync up:

- **Calendar appointments.** Put your schedule on the iPad by turning on the check-boxes for your Outlook or iCal calendars.

- **Notes** from Microsoft Outlook or the Mac's Mail program

- **Bookmarks** from Internet Explorer or the desktop version of the Safari web browser get shuttled over to the iPad's copy of Safari.

- **Email account settings** (but not the actual messages) get ported over to save you from having to muck around in the iPad's mail settings.

Make your choices, click the Appy button, and then click Sync to move your life onto the iPad.

 To sync iTunes with Entourage, you need to have it dump your information into iCal first. To make that happen, choose Entourage→Preferences→Sync→Services and turn on the checkboxes for syncing Entourage data with Address Book and iCal.

Sync Podcasts

One of the coolest features of the iTunes Store is the Podcasts section. Podcasts are like radio and TV shows you can download on a regular basis— for free. Every major media outlet has some sort of audio or video podcast available now alongside more low-budget creations. For example, you can get the video from each week's edition of *Meet the Press* from NBC, *Slate* magazine's audio critique of released movies, or your favorite shows from National Public Radio.

To sign up for podcasts, click the Podcasts link on the main iTunes Store page and browse until you find something you like. Then click Subscribe.

Once you subscribe to a show, iTunes automatically deposits the latest episode on your computer as soon as it appears online. Since you may not want to fill up your iPad with tons of podcasts, you can tell iTunes which ones to copy over each time you sync up. With the iPad connected, click the Podcasts tab and turn on the checkboxes for the shows you want to sync regularly. Use the pop-up menus to get the number of episodes you want to carry around at any one time, click Apply and then click Sync.

 Note Electronic textbooks are one way to get an education on the iPad, but you can also download free lectures and tutorials from a huge number of universities around the world. Just click the iTunes U link on the iTunes Store page. To sync the files to the iPad, connect it and click the iTunes U tab to selectively sync up all the content you want to take with you. It's academic!

Sync Books

If you're a big audiobook fan and have been hunting in vain for an Audiobooks tab in iTunes, don't worry, you're not missing it. The controls for syncing audiobooks to the iPad are on the Books tab, shoved way down on the screen, where you may have missed it. Scroll down, turn on the checkbox next to Audiobooks (circled), and sync away. You can sync all or selected audiobooks.

You sync text-based eBooks (iBooks and books in the ePub format) the same way, as you can see below. Chapter 8 has all the details on buying and managing eBooks. Note that, in iTunes, you can only *back up* your iBooks, you can't buy them or *read* them on your computer screen. If you have the iBooks app on your iPhone or iPod Touch, you can sync books back to iTunes as well by plugging in those devices and choosing File→Transfer Purchases from iPhone/iPod.

You can also sync PDF files on and off the iPad (see page 138). Just tap the Collections button in the iBooks app and choose PDFs to see them.

You can listen to audiobooks anywhere, and here's the cool part: When you sync your iTunes-purchased audiobooks back and forth between your iPad and iTunes, they get bookmarked, so you can always pick up listening where you left off on either your iPad or in iTunes.

Sync Apps and Games

It's easy to download apps and games directly on the iPad over its WiFi or 3G connection. You can also buy, download, and install new iPad programs from the big comfortable shopping window of iTunes—and then sync them all over to your connected iPad later. This sort of thing can be helpful if, say, you want a 300-megabyte birdwatching app that can take awhile to download on your iPad—besides, Apple currently limits individual App Store downloads to 20 MB over a 3G connection.

Syncing apps and games through iTunes has several other advantages. First, you get a backup copy of the file on your computer (and even in your computer's backup file) instead of having it just on the iPad until you sync up again. Second, it's easier to rearrange your apps with your iPad connected; iTunes displays all your iPad app screens at once, so you can click and drag the apps around in relation to other apps and screens. When you rearrange app icons on the iPad itself, you have to blindly drag them across each screen.

And third, if you have a bunch of space-hogging apps and an iPad with a small drive, you can sync the apps on and off the tablet as you need them. Turn on the checkboxes next to the apps and games you want to copy over and click Apply or Sync (or Apply and then Sync if you tinkered with the icon layout).

Troubleshoot Syncing Problems

Apple has tried to make the whole getting-stuff-on-your-iPad process as simple and flexible as possible. Every once in awhile, though, minor hardware or software issues may trip up a smooth sync and make you wonder what's making the iPad so unfriendly toward your files. These next couple of pages explain some of the more common problems—and how you fix them.

- **Your iPad doesn't show up in iTunes.** The first step to syncing is getting the iPad to appear in the iTunes Source list. If it's not there, check a few simple things. First, make sure you have the latest version of both iTunes and the iPad firmware installed (page 292). If so, check to see that the USB cable is firmly plugged in on both ends. If that doesn't help, try plugging the smaller end into a different USB 2.0 port on your PC or Mac. Also, make sure your iPad has a decent battery charge. Still no luck? Restart the iPad (page 288) and while you're at it, restart the computer as well. Antivirus software may be hindering the communication between your iPad and iTunes, so check your security settings or temporarily turn off the antivirus program to see if that's the problem. If nothing else works, Apple recommends reinstalling iTunes (page 290).

- **Weird error messages while syncing.** You may see iTunes toss up an alert box saying something like "Error 13019" and suddenly stop syncing. If that happens, try turning off the checkbox for Sync Music, click Apply, and then click Sync. After iTunes gets done syncing, go back to the Music tab and turn on the Sync Music checkbox again. Then try to freshly sync all those tunes again.

If you're syncing contacts, calendars, notes, and other items from the Info tab, you may see a Sync Alert box pop up if, say, you have two different versions of someone's contact file between your computer  and iPad (usually from editing it on both machines between sync sessions), or if more than 5 percent of the information will get changed on the computer during the sync session. Click the Show Details button to see the different versions and pick the one you want to go with. You can also cancel the Info tab sync if you want to check out your files on both computer and iPad but don't have time to deal with it now.

- **Some items didn't sync to the iPad.** The two most common reasons for an incomplete sync are fullness and formats. If the iPad's drive is close to overflowing, you simply can't fit any more content on its bulging drive. And if some of the files you try to sync are in incompatible formats, the iPad won't sync them. (This is often the case with video files—there are many formats around the Web, but the iPad only works with a few of them: .mp4, .m4v, and .mov.) In either case, iTunes probably displayed a message about the situation. The solutions are simple: Delete some other files from the iPad to make room for the new things you want to sync, and convert incompatible files to formats that work on the iPad. (Apple's $30 QuickTime Pro software at *www.apple.com/quicktime* is one of the many software options here.)

Tip A bad or damaged cable may be the reason your syncing is stinking. If you have another Apple USB cable from an iPod or iPhone, try swapping it in. If your cable is noticeably damaged, you can get a replacement for $19 at *store.apple.com*. It's called the Dock Connector to USB Cable and you can find it in the Accessories area.

Use iTunes Home Sharing on Your iPad

As mentioned earlier, you can use iTunes' handy Home Sharing feature to stream media from your computer to your iPad over your home wireless network. Tapping into shared media libraries greatly increases your choice of audio and video files, and sharing's especially useful if you have, say, a combined 500 GB of media across your network devices and only a 16 GB iPad.

To use Home Sharing, you need to turn it on in both iTunes and on your iPad, and you need to do the same on all the participating devices on your home wireless network. You also need an Apple Account ID. Here's how to set it up:

❶ If you haven't already, open iTunes and choose Advanced→Turn On Home Sharing. Type in your Apple Account name and password, and click the Create Home Share button.

❷ On the iPad, tap Home→Settings→iPod. In the Home Sharing area (circled), type in the same Apple Account name and password.

Now it's time to decide what to stream. For music, go to the iPad's Home screen and tap the iPod icon. On the iPod screen, tap the Library icon on the top left side. In the box that pops up (shown here), tap the name of the library you want to sample. All the songs and playlists from that library now appear in iTunes, ready to play on your iPad.

To stream video, tap Home→Videos→Shared. Tap the square gray library icon so see all the TV shows, movies, music videos, and other clips available to watch. Tap a video thumbnail to stream the file to your iPad screen.

You can't stream photos to the iPad with Home Sharing, but iTunes can beam them to a second-gen Apple TV. In iTunes, tap Advanced→"Choose Photos to Share" and turn on the checkboxes next to the photo albums you want to show off. Then use the Apple TV remote and its Photos menu to view them.

> **Tip** Want to keep sharing a Mac's iTunes library, even if that host Mac decides to take a snooze during the movie? On that Mac, choose ⬢→System Preferences→Energy Saver and turn on the checkbox next to "Wake for network access."

Stream iPad Files With AirPlay

The iPad can pull in content from iTunes libraries, but it can also push out its own music, video, compatible apps, and photos to other devices with *AirPlay*, Apple's technology for wirelessly streaming files to AirPlay-compatible speakers, stereos, and gadgets like Apple TV. A music system linked to the network through an Apple AirPort Express base station is also AirPlay-friendly.

Once you have your AirPlay-equipped device set up on your home network, pumping out the music, video, and photos from your iPad is easy. Just start

up the file you want to stream, look for the AirPlay icon [⬛] on the iPad's screen and tap it. On the menu that drops down (shown at right), choose where you want to see or hear your selection, like "Apple TV" or "Basement Stereo." Your song, video, or photo slideshow begins playing on the chosen system.

You control playback from the iPad itself. For audio and video, the standard old playback controls (▶, ❙❙, ❙◀◀, and ▶▶❙) appear on the iPad's screen, letting you pause, play, and jump around in the content stream. As for photos, you simultaneously see your images on an Apple TV-connected television screen and on your iPad. You can swipe through them at your own pace, which makes it a snap to provide impromptu narration for your instant slideshow. If you created automatic slideshows on your iPad (page 262), you can beam those to the big screen through AirPlay as well.

When you're done streaming and beaming, tap the AirPlay icon and tap iPad on the menu to return all your audio and video output to the tablet.

 Note Video streaming is great, but it's a bandwidth hog. To throw your videos up on the HDTV by way of Apple TV, your network router needs to use the 802.11a, 802.11g, or 802.11n standard—the older 802.11b networks are too slow for playback.

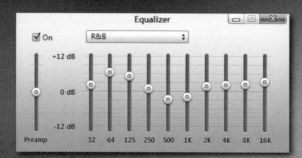

Equalizer

☑ On   R&B ▾

+12 dB

0 dB

-12 dB

Preamp   32   64   125   250   500   1K   2K   4K   8K   16K

 slide to unlock

Master iTunes

As you can tell from the last chapter, iTunes is an important part of your iPad experience, because it brokers the transfer of songs, music, videos, books, personal info, and apps between your tablet and computer. In addition, it keeps a copy of all the digital goodies you buy and helps you organize your growing media collection.

If you've never had an iPod or iPhone before you got your iPad, you may not know what a powerful media jukebox program iTunes is in its own right. As this chapter explains, you can customize iTunes' look, make play-lists in all kinds of ways, change a song's file format, adjust each song's equalizer settings, and even back up your entire iTunes library to a set of discs for safekeeping.

So when it comes time to charge your iPad for a few hours, take a spin through iTunes.

Change the Look of the iTunes Window

Don't be misled by iTunes' stylized brushed-aluminum look. You can push and pull its various window parts like salt-water taffy:

- If you set the column browser to appear above the iTunes window, you can adjust the sizes of the panes by dragging the tiny dot (circled) at the top of the song list window up or down. (By default, the column browser appears on the left but you can change it by choosing View→ Column Browser→On Top.) In either place, press Ctrl+B (⌘-B) to toggle the columns on or off.

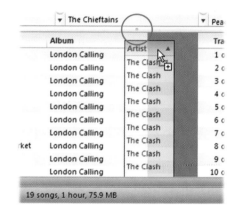

- iTunes divides your main song list into columns that you can sort and re-arrange. Click a column title (like Name or Album) to sort the list alphabetically. Click again to reverse the sort order. Change the order of the columns by dragging them, as shown above.

- To adjust a column's width, drag the right-hand vertical divider line (circled). You may need to grab it in the column title bar.

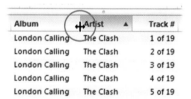

- To resize all the columns so they expand to precisely fit their contents, right-click (Control-click) any column header and choose Auto Size All Columns.

- To add (or delete) columns, right-click (Control-click) any column title. From the pop-up list of column categories (Bit Rate, Date Added, and so on), choose the column name you want to add or remove. Checkmarks indicate currently visible columns.

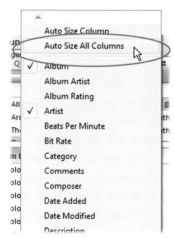

Change the Size of the iTunes Window

Lovely as iTunes is, it takes up a heck of a lot of screen real estate. So when you're working on other things, you can shrink iTunes down to size. In fact, iTunes runs in three sizes: small, medium, and large:

❶ *Large.* This is what you get the first time you open iTunes. (Hate the music hard-sell from the Ping sidebar on the right? Close the panel by clicking the square button in the lower-right corner.)

❷ *Medium.* Switch back and forth between large and medium by pressing Ctrl+M (Shift-⌘-M) or choosing View→"Switch to Mini Player."

❸ *Small.* To really scrunch things down, start with the medium-size window, then drag the resize handle ( ) leftward. To expand the panel, reverse the process.

Tired of losing your mini-iTunes window among the vast stack of open windows on your screen? Make the iTunes mini-player *always* visible on top of other open documents, windows, and assorted screen detritus. Open iTunes' Preferences window (Ctrl+comma [⌘-comma]), click the Advanced tab, and then turn on the checkbox next to "Keep Mini Player on top of all other windows." Now you won't have to click frantically around the screen trying to find iTunes if you get caught listening to your bubblegum-pop playlist.

Change Import Settings for Better Audio Quality

iPads can play back music in several digital audio formats: AAC, MP3, WAV, AIFF, and one called Apple Lossless. If you find your songs' audio quality lacking, you can change the way iTunes encodes, or *converts*, them when it copies tracks from your CDs. iTunes gives you two main options in its import settings box. Go to Edit (iTunes)→Preferences→General, and then click the Import Settings button to get there. Your options are:

- **Audio format (use the drop-down menu beside "Import Using").**
  Some formats tightly compress audio files to save space. The tradeoff: lost sound quality. Highly compressed formats include AAC (iTunes' default setting) and MP3. Formats that use little or no compression include WAV and AIFF, which sound better but take up more space. Apple Lossless splits the difference: It has better sound quality than AAC and MP3 but isn't as hefty as WAV or AIFF.

- **Bit rate (beside "Setting").** The higher the number of bits listed, the greater the amount of information iTunes uses to recreate your song (in other words, your files take up more storage space). The advantage? Better sound quality.

To see a song's format and other technical information, click its title in iTunes, press Ctrl+I (⌘-I), and then click the Summary tab in the Get Info box.

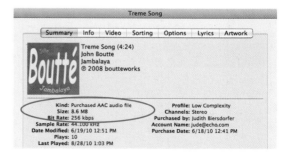

Four Ways to Browse Your Collection

Instead of just presenting you with boring lists, iTunes gives you four options for browsing your media collection—some of them more visual than others. Click the View button at the top of iTunes to switch among them.

- **List View** is iTunes' all-text display; you can see a sample of it on page 203. Press Ctrl+B (⌘-B) to toggle on and off the vertical (or horizontal) panes that group your music by genre, artist, and album. Press Ctrl+Alt+3 (Option-⌘-3) to jump back to List View from another view.

- **Album List View** displays an album cover in iTunes' first column if you have five or more tracks from that album. (Choose View→Always Show Artwork to override the five-track minimum.) Press Ctrl+Alt+4 (Option-⌘-4) to jump to Album List View.

- **Grid View** presents your media collection in a nifty array of album covers and other artwork. Adjust the size of the covers with the slider at the top of the window. Press Ctrl+Alt+5 (Option-⌘-5) to switch to the Grid.

- **Cover Flow** is the view for you if you *really* like album art. Your collection appears as a stream of album covers. (Ctrl+Alt+6 [Option-⌘-6] is the shortcut.) To browse them, press the left- and right-arrow keys on the keyboard or drag the scroll bar underneath the albums. Click the ▣ button by the slider bar to turn your whole screen into Cover View, complete with playback controls.

Search for Songs in iTunes

You can call up a list of all the songs with a specific word in their title, album name, or artist name just by clicking the Source pane's Music icon (🎵 , under "Library") and typing a few letters into the Search box in iTunes' upper-right corner. With each letter you type, iTunes shortens the list of songs it displays, showing you only tracks that match what you type.

For example, typing *train* brings up a list of everything in your music collection that has the word "train" somewhere in the song's information—maybe the song's title ("Boat Train") or the Steve Earle album (*Train A Comin'*). Click the other Library icons, like Movies or Audiobooks, to comb those collections for titles that match a search term.

You can also search for specific titles using the iTunes browser mentioned earlier in this chapter. If you can't see the browser pane, press Ctrl+B (⌘-B) to summon it. The browser reveals your music collection grouped by categories like genre, artist, and album (select the categories at View→Column Browser). Hit the same keys again (Ctrl+B [⌘-B]) to close the browser.

> **Tip** If you're searching for music in general, why not see what your pals are listening to? Ping, Apple's social-networking service in iTunes (page 220), lets you create profile pages, follow your friends' musical tastes, and more; click the Ping icon under "Store" in the Source list or check out *www.apple.com/itunes/ping*.

Change a Song's File Format

Sometimes you've got a song in iTunes whose format you want to change—you might need to convert a big AIFF file before loading it onto your iPad, for example. First, head over to Edit→Preferences (iTunes→Preferences), click the General tab, and then click the Import Settings button. From the Import Using pop-up menu, pick the format you want to convert *to* and then click OK.

Now, in your iTunes library, select the song you want to convert and choose Advanced→Create MP3 Version (or AIFF, or whatever format you just picked).

If you have a whole folder or disk full of potential converts, hold down the Shift (Option) key as you choose Advanced→"Convert to AAC" (or your chosen encoding format). A window pops up so you can navigate to the folder or disk holding the files you want to convert. iTunes won't convert protected media: Audible.com tracks and older tracks from the iTunes Store that still have copy-protection built in. If you bought a song after April 2009, though, odds are you're delightfully free of such restrictions, since that's when Apple stopped copy-protecting music.

iTunes deposits your freshly converted tracks in your library, alongside the songs in their original format.

> **Tip** Although you intentionally created a duplicate of a song here, you may have unintended dupes as a result of home sharing, ripping the same album twice, or other accidental copying. To find these duplicates—and recover a little hard drive space—choose File→Display Duplicates. iTunes dutifully rounds up all the dupes in one window for you to inspect and possibly delete. Just make sure they are true duplicates, not, say, a studio and a live version of the same song. (To search for exact duplicates, hold down the Shift [Option] key and choose File→Display→ Exact Duplicates.) Click the Show All button to return to your full music collection.

Improve Your Tunes with the Graphic Equalizer

If you want to improve the way your songs sound, use iTunes' graphic equalizer (EQ) to adjust the audio for the type of music you play. You might want to boost the bass tones in dance tracks to emphasize the booming rhythm, for example.

To get the equalizer front and center on your screen, choose View→Equalizer (Window→Equalizer) and unleash some of your new EQ powers.

❶ Drag the sliders (bass on the left, treble on the right) to accommodate your listening tastes (or the strengths and weaknesses of your speakers or headphones). You can drag the Preamp slider up or down to compensate for songs that sound too loud or too soft. To create your own presets, click the pop-up menu (circled) and select Make Preset.

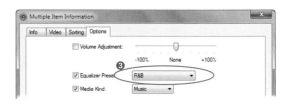

Treble sliders

Bass sliders

❷ Use the pop-up menu to choose one of the canned presets for different types of music (Classical, Dance, Jazz, and so on).

You can apply equalizer settings to an entire album or to individual songs.

❸ To apply settings to a whole album, select the album's name (either in Grid View or in the iTunes browser pane). Then press Ctrl+I (⌘-I) and click "Yes" if iTunes asks whether you're sure you want to edit multiple items. In the box that pops up, click the Options tab and choose your preferred setting from the Equalizer Preset pull-down menu.

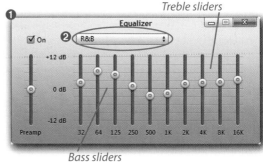

 Note *Equalization* is the art of adjusting the frequency response of an audio signal. An equalizer emphasizes, or boosts, some of the signal's frequencies while lowering others. In the range of audible sound, *bass* frequency is the low rumbly noise; *treble* is at the opposite end of the sound spectrum, with high, even shrill, notes; and *midrange* is, of course, in the middle, and it's the most audible to human ears.

❹ You can apply equalizer presets to individual songs as well. Instead of selecting the album name in the iTunes window, click the song name, and then press Ctrl+I (⌘+I). Click the Options tab and choose a setting from the Equalizer Preset menu.

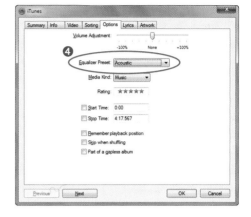

❺ Finally, you can change the EQ settings right from your song lists by adding an Equalizer column. Choose View→View Options and then turn on the Equalizer checkbox. A new column appears in your track lists, where you can select EQ settings.

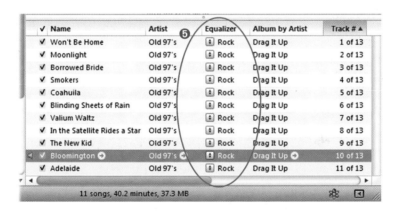

Tip The iPad offers more than 20 equalizer presets you can use on the go. To set your iPad's equalizer to a setting designed for a specific type of music, tap Settings→iPod→EQ. Flick down the list of presets until you find one that matches your music style, and then tap to select it. Your iPad now lists the preset's name next to "EQ" on the Settings menu, and your music, hopefully, sounds better.

Edit Song Information

Tired of seeing so many tunes named *Untitled* in your library? You can change song titles in iTunes—to enter a song's real name, for example, or to fix a typo—a couple of ways.

In the song list, click the text you want to change, wait a moment, and then click again. The title now appears highlighted and you can edit the text—just as you do when you change the name of a Word document on a desktop computer.

Another way to change a song's title, artist name, or other information is to click the song in the iTunes window and press Ctrl+I (⌘-I) to summon the Get Info box. (Choose File→Get Info if you forget the keyboard shortcut.) Click the Info tab and type in the new track information.

Too much work? You can always try Advanced→Get CD Track Names and see what comes up, although the Gracenote database iTunes uses may not know the title if it's something deeply obscure or homemade.

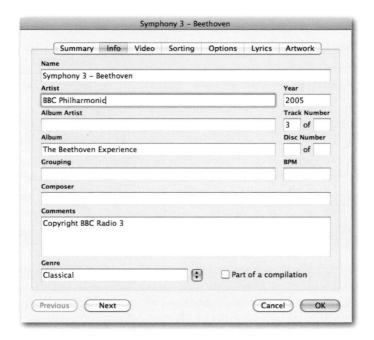

Tip Once you have a song's Get Info box onscreen, use the Previous and Next buttons to navigate to other tracks grouped with it in the iTunes song list window. That way, you can rapidly edit all the track information in the same playlist, on the same album, and so on, without closing and opening boxes the whole time.

Edit Album Information and Song Gaps

You don't have to adjust your track information on a song-by-song basis. You can edit an entire album's worth of tracks by clicking the Album name in the iTunes column browser (or on its cover in Grid View) and pressing Ctrl+I (⌘-I) to bring up the Get Info box.

Ever careful, iTunes flashes an alert box asking if you really want to change the info for a bunch of things all at once. Click Yes.

You can make all sorts of changes to an album in the four-tabbed box that pops up. Here are a few examples:

❶ Fix a typo or mistake in the Album or Artist name boxes.

❷ Manually add an album cover or photo of your choice to the whole album by dragging it into the Artwork box.

❸ Click the Options tab and change the Equalizer preset for all the songs.

❹ Have iTunes skip the album when you shuffle music—great for keeping winter holiday music out of your summer barbecue rotation.

❺ Tell iTunes to play back the album without those two-second gaps between tracks by choosing the "Gapless album" option. (Perfect for opera and *Abbey Road*!)

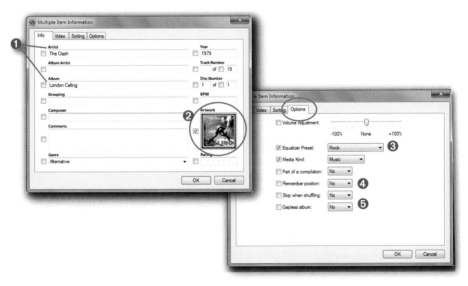

Make a New Playlist in iTunes

To create a playlist, press Ctrl+N (⌘-N). You can also choose File→New Playlist or click the + button at the bottom left of the iTunes window.

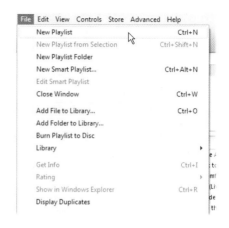

All freshly minted playlists start out with the impersonal name "untitled playlist." Fortunately, iTunes highlights this generic name, ready for editing—just type in a better name: Cardio Workout, Hits of the Highland Lute, or whatever you want. As you add new lists, iTunes alphabetizes them in the Playlists area of the Source list.

Once you create and name a spanking-new playlist, you're ready to add your songs or videos. You can do that in three ways, so choose the one you like best.

Playlist-Making Method #1

❶ If this is your first playlist, double-click the new playlist's icon in the Source list. You get your full music library in one window, and your empty playlist in the other. (iTunes may pop up an intro screen. Ignore it and go to step 2.)

❷ Go back to the main iTunes window and drag the song titles you want from your library over to the new playlist window. (Make sure you click the Music icon [♫] in the Source list to see all your songs.) Drag songs one at a time, or grab a bunch by selecting multiple tracks by Ctrl+clicking (⌘-clicking) each title.

Playlist-Making Method #2

❶ Some folks don't like multiple windows. No problem. You can add songs to a playlist by highlighting them and dragging them to the playlist's icon right from the main iTunes window.

❷ If you've created lots of playlists, scroll down to get to your new one.

Playlist-Making Method #3

❶ You can also pick and choose songs in your library and then create a playlist out of the highlighted tunes. Select tracks by Ctrl+clicking (⌘-clicking) the titles.

❷ Then choose File→New Playlist From Selection, or press Ctrl+Shift+N (⌘+Shift+N). The songs you selected appear in a brand-new playlist. If all of them came from the same album, iTunes names the playlist after the album (but it also highlights the title box so you can rename it).

Don't worry about clogging up your hard drive. When you drag a song title onto a playlist, you don't *copy* the song, you just tell iTunes where it can find the tune. In essence, you're creating a *shortcut* to the track. That means you can have the same song on several playlists but only one copy of it on your computer.

That nice iTunes even gives you some playlists of its own devising, like "Top 25 Most Played" and "Purchased" (a convenient place to find all your iTunes Store goodies listed in one place—and one to *definitely* back up to a CD or DVD; see page 225).

Change or Delete an Existing Playlist

If you change your mind about a playlist's tune order, drag the song titles up or down within the playlist window. Just make sure to sort the playlist by song order first (click the top of the first column, the one with the numbers listed in front of the song titles).

You can always drag more songs into a playlist, and you can delete titles if you your playlist needs pruning. Click the song in the playlist window and then hit Delete or Backspace. When iTunes asks you to confirm your decision, click Yes. Remember, deleting a song from a playlist doesn't delete it from your music library—it just removes the title from that particular playlist. (You can get rid of a song for good only by pressing Delete or Backspace from within the iTunes library; select 🎵 under "Library" to get there.)

You can quickly add a song to an existing playlist right from the main iTunes window, no matter which view you happen to be using: Select the song, right-click (Control-click) it, and then, in the pop-up menu, choose "Add to Playlist." Scroll to the playlist you want to use and then click the mouse button to add the track.

To see how many playlists contain a certain song, select the track, right-click (Control-click) it, and then choose "Show in Playlist" in the pop-up menu.

When it's time to get rid of a playlist once and for all because the party's over, select the playlist icon in iTunes and press the Delete key. You see a message box from iTunes asking you to confirm your decision. If you autosync your iPad, the playlist disappears from there, too.

Make a Genius Playlist in iTunes

Playlists are fun to make, but occasionally you just don't have the time or energy. If that's the case, call in an expert—the iTunes Genius. With the Genius feature, you click any song you're in the mood for and iTunes crafts a playlist of 25 to 100 songs that it thinks go well with the one you picked.

The first time you use it, Genius asks permission to go through your music collection and gather song information, and then it uploads that data anonymously to Apple. Apple's software analyzes your information and then adds it to a big giant database of everybody else's song info (to improve the Genius's suggestions). After that, the Genius is ready for duty. Here's the procedure:

❶ Click a song title in your library.

❷ Click the Genius button (⚛) at the bottom right of iTunes. If you're playing the song, click the Genius icon in the iTunes display window.

❸ iTunes presents you with your new playlist in a flash.

❹ Use the buttons at the top of the Genius window to adjust the number of songs in the playlist, refresh it with new songs if you want a different mix, and—best of all—save the playlist permanently.

The Genius doesn't work if it doesn't have enough information about a song—or if there aren't enough similar songs that match your kick-off song. In that case, pick another tune. If you frequently add new music to your library and want to get it in the mixes, inform the Genius at Store→Update Genius.

And if you have the Genius sidebar open as you listen to music, the Genius cheerfully presents you with a list of complementary songs that you can buy right there to round out your listening experience.

> **Note** If you declined iTunes' initial offer to activate the Genius, you can summon it again by choosing Store→Turn On Genius. And if you're regretting your choice to invite the Genius into your iTunes home, kick him out for good by visiting the same menu and choosing Turn Off Genius.

Genius Mixes in iTunes

Yes, the iTunes Genius feature takes almost all the effort out of making a play-list—all you do is click the Genius button. But if even a one-button click seems like too much effort, iTunes makes hands-off playlist creation even *easier*. Welcome to Genius Mixes.

The Genius Mix feature works like this: iTunes takes it upon itself to search your entire music library and then automatically compose (depending on the size of your library), up to 12 different song collections. Unlike a Genius playlist of tunes calculated to go well together, a Genius Mix is more like a radio sta-tion or cable-TV music channel based on *genre*. Depending on what's in your iTunes library, the Genius could present you with a hip hop mix, a country mix, a classical mix, and so on. In addition, the Genius Mix creates up to 12 playlists at once, all saved and ready to play, unlike the Genius's single mix that you have to save to preserve.

If you don't already see a square purple Genius Mix icon (❄) in your iTunes Source list, choose Store→Update Genius. Once activated, the Genius quietly stirs up its sonic concoctions from your music library.

To play a Genius Mix, click the Genius Mix icon in the Source list. The iTunes window reverts to Grid View and displays the mixes it cre-ated, each represented by a quartet of album covers from tracks in the mix. Pass your mouse pointer over the album squares to see the name of the mix or click the squares to start playing music.

Like most traditional radio stations, you don't get to see a list of what's actually *in* a particular Genius Mix—it's all a surprise. If you don't care for a song the Genius included, hit the forward button or tap the right-arrow key on your computer keyboard to skip to the next track.

Genius Mixes can be another great way to effortlessly toss on some back-ground music at a party, and you may even hear songs you haven't played in forever. Want to take the Genius Mix with you? Sync it to your iPad (page 189).

You're the Critic: Rate Your Music

Although there's no way to give a song two thumbs up in iTunes, you *can* assign an album or each song in your collection a one- to five-star rating. Then you can use the ratings to produce nothing but playlists of the greatest hits on your hard drive.

If you assign an album a single rating, *all* the songs on that album get the same number of stars. If you rate just a few tracks on an album but not all of them, the album rating reflects the average of the *rated* songs—so an album with two five-star songs and a bunch of unrated tracks gets a five-star rating.

❶ To add ratings, first make sure you turn on the Album Rating and/or Rating columns in the iTunes View Options box (Ctrl+J [⌘-J]).

❷ Click the song you want to rate to highlight it. iTunes displays five dots in the Rating column (in iTunes' main window). When you click a dot, iTunes turns it into a star. Now either drag the mouse across the column to create one to five stars, or click one of the dots itself to apply a rating (click the third dot, for example, and iTunes gives the song three stars).

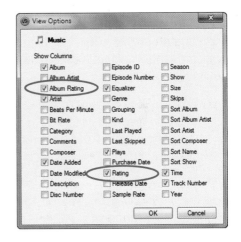

❸ Once you assign ratings, you can sort your song list by star rating (click the Album Rating or Rating column title), create a Smart Playlist (page 218) of only your personal favorites (File→New Smart Playlist; choose Album Rating or Rating from the first drop-down menu), and so on.

You can even rate songs on your iPad, and iTunes records the ratings the next time you sync up.

To rate a song on your iPad, start playing it and tap the small album cover in the Now Playing corner to switch to the full-screen Now Playing window. Tap the screen to get the hidden playback controls to appear, then tap the ▤ icon on the bottom right corner. The album cover spins around to reveal the track listing. Swipe your finger along the row of dots above the song list to transform those empty dots into critical stars for the track that's currently playing.

Smart Playlists: Another Way for iTunes to Assemble Song Sets

As cool as the Genius is, sometimes you want a little more manual control over what goes into your automatically generated music mixes. That's where Smart Playlists rise to the occasion.

Once you give it some guidelines, a *Smart Playlist* goes sniffing through your music library and comes up with custom mixes based on those guidelines. A Smart Playlist even keeps tabs on the music that comes and goes from your library and adjusts itself based on that.

You might tell one Smart Playlist to assemble 45 minutes' worth of songs that you've rated higher than four stars but rarely listen to, and another to play your most-often-played songs from the 1980s. The Smart Playlists you create are limited only by your imagination.

❶ To start a Smart Playlist, press Ctrl+Alt+N (Option-⌘-N) or choose File→New Smart Playlist. A Smart Playlist box opens: It sports a gear-shaped icon (✿) next to its name in the Source list (a regular playlist has a blue icon with a music note icon in it).

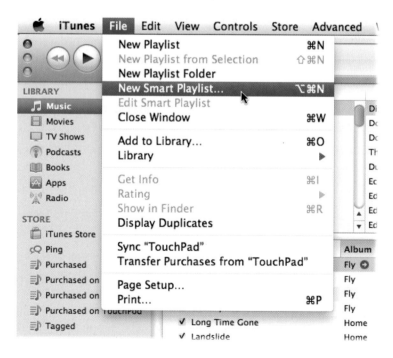

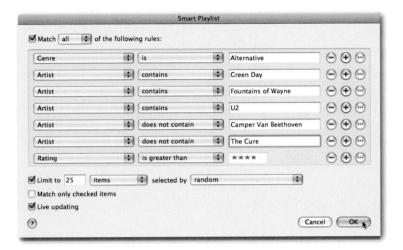

❷ Give iTunes detailed instructions about what you want to hear. You can select a few artists you like and have iTunes leave off the ones you're not in the mood for, pluck songs that only fall within a certain genre or year, and so on. To add multiple, cumulative criteria, click the + button.

❸ Turn on the "Live updating" checkbox. This tells iTunes to keep the playlist updated as your collection, ratings, and play count change. (The play count tells iTunes how many times you play a track, a good indicator of how much you like a song.)

❹ To edit an existing Smart Playlist, right-click (Ctrl-click) the playlist's name and then choose Edit Smart Playlist.

A Smart Playlist is a dialogue between you and iTunes: You tell it what you want in as much detail as you want, and the program whips up a playlist according to your instructions.

You can even instruct a Smart Playlist to pull tracks from your current Genius playlist. Just click the + button to add a preference, choose Playlist as another criteria, and select Genius from the list of available playlists.

> **Tip** When you press Shift (Option), the + button at the bottom of the iTunes window turns into a gear icon (⚙). Click this gear button to quickly launch the Smart Playlist creation box.

Ping Your Way to New Music

Facebook, MySpace, Twitter, Tumblr, Flickr—if there's anything the top social-networking sites have proved, it's that people like to share stuff with their friends. And now there's Ping, Apple's very own social network designed to connect people who have a mutual love of music.

In case you had any doubt about what Ping is supposed to be, Steve Jobs himself described it as "Facebook and Twitter meet iTunes." (While Ping was originally supposed to link with Facebook through the Facebook Connect service so you could easily update your profile with your Ping activities, a case of "unfriending" between Apple and Facebook prevented the partnership. So far, anyway.)

As with any social network, the first thing you have to do is set up your profile page, your own little part of Ping where you can list your favorite bands and artists, keep track of upcoming events, exchange notes with other music-minded pals, and hear samples of what your friends are listening to.

To set up your Ping profile:

❶ **Click the Ping link in the Source list.** Apple doesn't force all iTunes users to join, so you have to click a button that says Turn On Ping and agree to the legal disclaimer about using the service and privacy.

> **Turn On Ping**

❷ **Fill in your personal details.** Like most social-networking sites, you fill in your name, the city where you live, and other information. You can also add a photo to your profile page. Since this is a music-themed service, you can announce your three favorite genres of music on your page, too. You can tell as much or as little about yourself as you want, and even select up to eight iTunes tracks (complete with audio samples) to display on your page. People who follow you can read your info (they see your Ping status updates and iTunes purchases as you make them), and, in return, you can see theirs if you follow them.

❸ **Adjust privacy settings.** As part of your profile setup, Ping asks how public you want to be so other members can find you. You have three choices. You can let everyone else on the service look at and "follow" your profile page—whether you know them or not, which is a good way to find new friends (and sometimes stalkers). You can also make your basic profile visible to others only after you give them permission to see it. And lastly, you can hide your page from everyone and just use it as a personal place to track concert listings.

❹ Find friends. Once you set up your profile page and privacy settings, Ping encourages you to find other media lovers on the service. You can search for the email addresses of people you know and invite them to be your Ping friends. At the same time, your friends—and links to their Ping pages—appear on your own patch of Ping real estate.

When you get Ping set up, it works just like any other social network. You can post your thoughts on the current state of music—and read those of your Ping friends. You can sign up to follow bands and musicians who use Ping—to see what Lady Gaga, Yo-Yo Ma, and others are up to, for example. You can write your own album reviews, comment on friends' pages, browse music news, and check concert listings for your favorite groups. You can click the Like button next to albums or tracks to publicly post your approval.

Items you buy in the iTunes Store get listed on your Ping page, too, so everyone knows what you're into these days. If you'd rather keep your '80s synthpop addiction a secret, hide your purchases by clicking the Remove button next to the item on your Recent Activity feed.

If you use the handy Ping sidebar to see what your pals are listening to, you're not chained to the desktop for updates. On the iPad, tap Home→iTunes→Ping (right) to keep up with Ping things while you're out with your tablet.

Ping isn't for you? If you want to turn it off, click the Account link on the main Store page and log into your iTunes account. On the Account Settings page, click the buttons to either edit your profile (which you can also do from a link on your Ping page itself) or turn off Ping for good.

Set Up Multiple iTunes Libraries

There's Home Sharing and then there's home, sharing. Many families have just one computer. If everyone's using the same copy of iTunes, you soon get the Wiggles bumping up against the Wu-Tang Clan if you have iTunes shuffling the music tracks, or when you autosync multiple iPads. Wouldn't it be great if everyone had a *personal* iTunes library to have and to hold, to sync and to shuffle—separately? Absolutely.

To use multiple iTunes libraries, follow these steps:

❶ Quit iTunes.

❷ Hold down the Shift (Option) key on your PC or Mac keyboard and launch iTunes. In the box that pops up, click Create Library. Give it a name, like "Tiffany's Music" or "Songs My Wife Hates."

❸ iTunes opens up, but with an empty library. If you have a bunch of music in your main library that you want to move over to this one, choose File→"Add to Library."

❹ Navigate to the music you want and add it. If the songs are in your original library, they're probably in Music→iTunes→iTunes Media→Music (Home→Music→iTunes→iTunes Media→Music), in folders sorted by artist name. Choose the files you want to add.

To switch between libraries, hold down the Shift (Option) key when you start iTunes, and you'll get a box that lets you pick the library you want. (If you don't choose a library, iTunes opens the last one used.) Tracks from CDs you copy go into whatever library's open. And now that you have those songs in the new library, you can switch back to the other one and get rid of them.

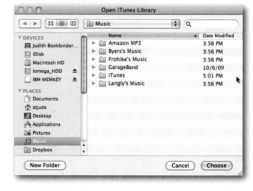

 Tip Multiple libraries can be a real help if you have a huge video collection that you want to store on an external hard drive to save space on your main computer.

See Your iTunes Purchase History and Get iTunes Store Help

Ever notice songs in a playlist or in your iTunes library that you don't remember buying? Good thing that iTunes keeps track of what you buy and when you buy it. If you suspect that one of the kids knows your password and is sneaking in forbidden downloads or maybe that your credit card was wrongly charged, you can contact the Store or check your account's purchase history to see what's been downloaded in your name.

To do the latter, in the iTunes window, click the triangle next to your account name and choose Account from the menu. Type in your password and then click Purchase History. Your latest purchase appears at the top of the page, and you can scroll farther down to see a list of previous acquisitions. Everything billed to your account over the months and years is there, including gift-certificate purchases. If you see something wrong, click the "Report a Problem" link and say something.

If you have other issues with your account or want to submit a specific query or comment, the online help center awaits. From the iTunes Store's main page, click the Support link. Your web browser presents you with the main iTunes service and support page; click the link that best describes what you want to learn or complain about. For billing or credit card issues, check out the iTunes Account and Billing Support link on that same web page.

> **Tip** iTunes 10.3 and later lets you re-download Store purchases made on other devices (like an iPhone) to your computer. Click the Purchased playlist in the iTunes Source list and click the Download Previous Purchases link at the bottom of the window to see a list of all the music, apps, and books you've bought. Click the iCloud icon, type in your iTunes password, and grab those files again.

Move the iTunes Music/Media Folder to an External Drive

Media libraries grow large, and hard drives can seem to shrink, as you add thousands of songs and hundreds of videos to iTunes. You may, in fact, think about using a big external drive for iTunes storage (and more iPad videos). That's just dandy, but you need to make sure that iTunes knows what you intend to do.

If you rudely drag your iTunes Music (or Media) folder to a different place without telling iTunes, it thinks the songs and videos in your collection are gone. The next time you start the program, you'll find a newly created, empty Music folder. (While iTunes remains empty but calm, *you* may be having heart palpitations as you picture your media collection vanishing in a puff of bytes.)

To move the Music folder to a new drive, let iTunes know where you're putting it. Before you start, make sure iTunes has been putting all your songs and videos in the iTunes Music folder by opening the Preferences box (Ctrl+comma [⌘-comma]) and confirming the folder location. Then:

❶ Click the Advanced tab and turn on the checkbox next to "Keep iTunes Music folder organized."

❷ Click the Change button in the iTunes Music folder location area and navigate to the external hard drive.

❸ Click the New Folder button in the window, type in a name for the iTunes library, and then click the Create button.

❹ Back in the Change Music Folder Location box, click the Open button.

❺ Click OK to close the iTunes Preferences box.

❻ Choose File→Library→Organize Library and then check "Consolidate files."

Ignore the ominous warnings (*"This cannot be undone"*) and let iTunes heave a complete copy of your iTunes folder to the external drive. Once you confirm that everything is in the new library, trash your old iTunes Media folder and empty the Trash or Recycle Bin to get all those gigs of space back.

Back Up Your iTunes Files to Disc

If your hard drive dies and takes your whole iTunes folder with it, you lose your music and movies—and your iPad will be lonely. Apple's new iCloud service lets you re-download songs, apps, and iBooks you've purchased, but you may have library items that are unavailable in the iTunes Store (or that you home-ripped) that are gone forever. Luckily, iTunes gives you a super simple way to back up your files onto a CD or DVD.

❶ In iTunes, choose File→Library→"Back Up to Disc."

❷ In the box that pops up, choose what you want to back up—everything, or just items you paid for in the iTunes Store. Later, after you back up the first time, you can turn on a checkbox to back up only the stuff you added since the last backup.

❸ Have a stack of discs ready to feed into your computer's disc drive. Depending on the size of your library, you may need several CDs (which store up to 700 megabytes of data each) or DVDs (which pack in at least 4.7 gigabytes of files per disc). You'll get nagged by iTunes to feed it a new disc once it fills up the current one.

If you ever need to use your backup copies, open iTunes and put in one of those discs to start restoring your files. Remember, there's nothing really exciting about file backups—until you have to use them to save the day.

Play Music and Other Audio

When the first iPad was announced in January 2010, many technology critics dismissed it as "a giant iPod Touch" before going back to complaining about other things they hadn't actually experienced. Although that particular response was snarky, it was also correct. Partly, anyway. Among many other things, the iPad *is* a giant iPod Touch. And what a handsome flat-screen jukebox it is.

Thanks to its larger size, the iPad makes playing music, audiobooks, podcasts, and iTunes U lectures a breeze—it's easy to find the tracks you want to hear, create your own playlists, control your music, and admire full-screen cover art on the bigger screen.

Granted, the iPad is a bit bulky to haul to the gym or schlep along for your morning jog, but it's a great music machine for other situations—like when you have a stack of email to get through and you want to bliss out to a little Yo-Yo Ma.

Whether you're after background music or front-and-center playback controls, this chapter shows you how to get your iPad singing. And if you pony up $5 for Apple's GarageBand app for iPad, you may even find yourself singing along to your *own* songs on the tablet. Play on!

Get Music and Audio for Your iPad

Have absolutely no music or audio files on your computer? Here are a few ways to get them on your iPad. (If you've had an iPod for years and have the music-transfer thing down cold, feel free to skip to the next page to see how the iPad organizes your music once you get it on there.)

Import a CD

You can use iTunes to convert tracks from your existing audio CDs into iPad-ready digital music files. Start up iTunes and stick a CD in your computer's disc drive. The program asks if you want to import the CD into iTunes. (If it doesn't, click the Import CD button at the bottom right of the iTunes window.) If you're connected to 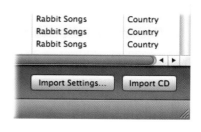 the Internet, iTunes automatically downloads song titles and artist information for the CD. (Yes, strange as it may seem, music managers like iTunes don't get information about an album from the album itself, they search for it in a huge database on the Web.)

Once you tell iTunes to import music, it begins adding the songs to your library. You can bring in all the tracks from a CD or skip unwanted tracks by turning off the checkboxes next to them. Eject the CD when iTunes finishes.

Import Existing Songs into iTunes

If you've had a computer for longer than a few years, odds are you already have some songs in the popular MP3 format on your hard drive. When you start iTunes for the first time, the program asks if you'd like it to search your PC or Mac for music and add it to iTunes. Click "Yes" and iTunes will go fetch. If someone else in the house uses iTunes and you both have Home Sharing turned on (page 185), iTunes searches the shared libraries, too (page 198).

Buy Music in the iTunes Store

Another way to get music is to buy it from the iTunes Store (page 182). Once you have an iTunes account (page 118), you can buy and download audio directly from your iPad (page 183) or via iTunes on your desktop computer. To shop from your computer, click the iTunes Store icon on the left side of the iTunes window and browse away.

When you buy music and audiobooks through iTunes, you need to sync up your 'Pad to transfer those files to the tablet (page 189). If you already have music on your iPad, read on to see how to organize and control it.

Explore the iPod Menu

The iPad has a Photos icon and a Videos icon, so you'd think it would have a Music icon for tunes, because that would make some *sense*. It doesn't; Apple put all the iPad's music functions in its iPod app, so tap the iPod icon on the iPad's Home screen.

The iPad divvies up the iPod screen into four distinct areas:

❶ **Controls & Search bar.** Located at the very top of the screen are all the iPod's audio playback controls, like volume, next/previous buttons to move between songs or audiobook chapters, and a time counter for the track that's playing. The search box in the top-right corner can help you find a tune fast, too.

❷ **Library.** As in iTunes, your music, podcast, audiobook, and iTunes U tracks are all grouped under tappable sub-menus, as are any playlists you made (page 212). The Now Playing pane in the bottom-left corner displays the cover art for the current selection; tap it to get to the giant Now Playing screen (page 232).

❸ **Bottom bar.** The lower edge of the iPod window is further concerned with music organization. Click the **+** icon to create a playlist with the songs you choose. Click the atom-shaped Genius icon to have the iPad *automatically* generate a playlist based on songs like the one currently playing. In the center of the bar, click the appropriate button to display your collection by Songs, Artists, Albums (above), Genres, or Composers.

❹ **Main window.** No matter which media collection you choose—music, podcasts, audiobooks, or playlists—the iPad displays track names in the center of the screen. Most views show cover art in one size or another, except Songs, which shows a text list of tracks, and Genre, which shows themed art depicting "Folk," "R&B," and other music disciplines.

Play Music

To play a song, just tap its title on the screen. If you sort your music collection by album, tap the album cover to spin it around and reveal its list of songs, and then tap a title to hear it play. Use the playback controls at the top of the screen to adjust the volume, to play and pause songs, and to jump between tracks.

To switch to the full-screen version of the album cover along with the Now Playing screen's controls (page 232), tap the artwork in the Now Playing corner.

If you have a playlist on the iPad that you'd like to hear, tap the name of it in the Library list and tap the title of its first song to kick it off. Should the iPad screen go to sleep while you're rocking out, the album cover of the current song appears on your Lock screen when you wake it back up. (Don't have any album art, just a big gray music note? See page 234.)

 Tip The iPad lets you keep playing music even as you move on to other things, like Safari browsing or note-writing. If you need to call up the iPod controls in a hurry while you're on another screen, you can program the iPad to summon them with a double-click of the Home button. Page 9 has instructions.

Play Audiobooks and Podcasts

Spoken-word tracks like audiobooks, podcasts, and iTunes U lectures use some special controls that music tracks don't need. To see them, tap the Now Playing artwork in the corner of the main iPod screen, which enlarges the artwork full-screen. Tap it to see the controls. The usual playback buttons and sliders are at the top of the screen, and you can drag the slider to any point in the recording to jump around within it. But now you can do other things, like:

❶ Tap the envelope icon (✉) to email a link to the podcast to a friend.

❷ Speed up or slow down the narrator's voice. Tap the ⒈ˣ button for normal speed, ⒉ˣ for double-time (if the person is talking too slowly), and ½ˣ for half-speed (in case the person's talking too fast).

❸ Tap the ☰ icon to see other chapters in the audiobook or other episodes in the podcast series.

❹ Tap the ↺ button to replay the last 30 seconds of a recording, in case you spaced out and missed something.

❺ Tap the left-arrow button (◄) in the bottom-left corner to leave the Now Playing screen and go back to the iPod's list of audio files.

Control the Now Playing Screen

To keep the full-size Now Playing album art nice and tidy, the iPad displays its playback controls atop the art. Here's what all the screen iconography means:

- **Volume.** Drag the round 🔊 icon forward or backward on the slider bar to increase or decrease the iPad's volume. (You can also use the Volume rocker on the right side of the iPad.)

- **Play/Pause (▶/❚❚) button.** If you have music playing, the Pause button looks like a pair of upright sticks (❚❚). If you tap ❚❚ to pause a song, it turns into the triangular Play button (▶). Tap ▶ to resume your tune.

- **Previous, Next (◀◀, ▶▶).** These buttons, which evolved from the rewind and fast-forward buttons on tape players, perform the same tasks as they used to—only better. Tap ◀◀ to go to the start of a song (or if you're *at* the start, to jump to the previous song). Tap ▶▶ to skip to the next song.

  Like old tape players, if you hold down one of these buttons instead of just tapping it, you rewind or fast-forward through a song, just like bygone days, when your ancestors wanted to find the good part of a tune. When you press the icon, the track audibly zips by and goes faster if you continue pressing the button.

To see a list of all the tracks on an album, tap the button in the lower-right corner, circled above. The cover spins around to reveal the song list.

Now, those are the obvious controls. Then there are the ones that look like iPad hieroglyphics, numbered here for your illumination.

❶ **Loop button.** Got a particular album, playlist, or song you just can't get enough of? As it plays, tap the Loop button (⊜) to turn it blue (⟳). This tells the iPad to play the music over and over, until you tap Loop again.

❷ **Scroll slider.** Perched at the top of your screen, this slider displays your progress through a track. It also displays, in minutes and seconds, how much of the song you've heard and how much you have left to hear. You can jump around in the progress bar by dragging the little white dot. And you can see where the tune falls in the current playlist or album.

❸ **Shuffle button.** If you don't want to hear songs on an album or in a playlist in their usual order, tap Shuffle (✕) to play the tracks randomly.

❹ **Genius playlist.** Tap the ✴ icon to make a Genius playlist based on the song currently playing. Page 237 has details.

To assign a song a one- to five-star rating, swipe the series of dots below the scroll slider to convert them into stars. Tap the album icon in the bottom-right corner to return to the full-screen album art. Tap the arrow in the bottom-left corner to return to the full list of songs.

Get Album Art in iTunes

Are you plagued with gray music-note icons mixed in with regular album art on your iPad's screen? Do you long for a fully arted album collection? While songs purchased from the iTunes Store include album-cover artwork, tracks you rip from your own CDs don't. But you have options.

Automatically Add Art

You can ask iTunes to head to the Internet and find as many album covers as it can. You need a (free) iTunes Store account to make this work, so if you haven't signed up yet, flip back to page 118. To make iTunes fetch covers, choose Advanced→Get Album Artwork.

Since Apple has to root around in your library to figure out what covers you need, you get an alert box warning you that the company will be getting (and then dumping) personal information from you. Click OK and let iTunes get to work—which may take a while. When iTunes finishes, you should have a healthy dose of album art filling up the iTunes window.

Manually Add Art

Despite its best intentions, sometimes iTunes can't find an album cover (or retrieves the wrong one). If that happens, take matters into your own hands by manually adding your own album artwork—or a photo of your choice. If Pachelbel's *Canon in D* makes you think of puppies, you can have a baby dachshund photo appear every time you play that song.

❶ To add your own art to a song, pick a photo or image—JPEG files are the most common.

❷ If you found the cover on Amazon (*hint*: a great source!), save a copy of it by dragging it off the web page and onto your desktop or by right-clicking (Ctrl-clicking) it and choosing "Save Image" in your browser.

❸ With your image near the iTunes window, select the song and click the Show Artwork button in the bottom-left corner of the iTunes window.

❹ Drag the image into the iTunes Artwork pane to add it to the song file.

No matter which method you choose, the art rides along when you sync the songs over to your iPad.

Add Lyrics in iTunes

You can add lyrics to a song just like you add album art. Select a song in iTunes and press Ctrl+I (⌘-I) to call up the Get Info box. Then click the Lyrics tab.

Here, you can either meticulously type in a song's verses or look them up on one of the hundreds of websites devoted to lyrics. Once you find your words, getting them into iTunes is a mere cut 'n' paste job. If you want to add lyrics to all the songs on an album, or have several sets to add to the same playlist, click the Next button (circled). That advances you to the next song, thereby saving you repeated keystrokes invoking the Get Info command. Now that you've spent all that time grooming your song files, sync them to your iPad to get the fruits of your labor onto the tablet's screen.

When you're listening to a song on the iPad's Now Playing screen, just tap the album cover to see its lyrics.

> **Tip** Don't see lyrics when you tap? Jump to the Home screen and tap Settings→iPod, and then set the button next to "Lyrics & Podcast info" to On.

Make Playlists

You have a few ways to make *playlists*—those personalized song sets made up of tunes you think go great together. You can create them in iTunes and sync them over to your iPad (page 212), you can make them on the iPad itself, or you can have the iPad make them for you.

In iTunes, one way to make a new playlist is to choose File→New Playlist. When the Untitled Playlist icon appears in the iTunes Source list, click once to select it—so you can type in a better name—and then drag songs from your library onto the playlist name. You can also select a bunch of tracks in the library (hold down the Control key while clicking), and choose File→New Playlist From Selection. Then sync the new playlist to the iPad (page 189).

You can make a playlist from tracks in the *iPad's* music collection, too:

❶ On the main iPod screen, tap the **+** button at the bottom of the Library column. In the box that pops up, give the resulting blank playlist a memorable new name and tap Save.

❷ A list of all your iPad-resident songs pops up. Each time you see one worth adding, tap its name (or the ⊕ button). You can also tap one of the icons at the bottom of the screen, like Artists or Albums, to find the stuff you want—or tap the Sources button at the top of the screen.

❸ When you finish, tap Done. Your playlist is ready to play.

To rework a playlist, tap its name and then tap the blue Edit button. You can add tracks to the mix by tapping the Add Songs button.

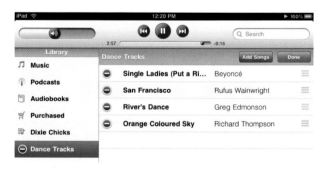

You can reorder the songs in a playlist, too. Note the "grip strip" at the right edge of song titles (≡). With your finger, drag these handles up or down to rearrange the tunes. When you finish, tap Done. To remove a song from a list, tap the universal iPad Delete symbol (⊖), and then tap the Delete confirmation button on the right side. (Remember, while the song's no longer in your playlist, it's still in your library.) Note the ⊖ next to the playlist names in the Library list. Tap one to whack the whole playlist.

Make Genius Playlists on the iPad

Apple's *Genius* feature in iTunes and on the iPad analyzes your music collection and automatically generates Genius Mixes and Genius Playlists for you. These are sets of songs (or in the case of the Mixes, entire music genres) that the Genius thinks sound good together.

Your iPad automatically generates the Genius Mixes. They appear in the Library list when you have enough music to collect into genres; click the Genius Mixes icon to see them. Genius Playlists are a little more personalized, because they require you to choose the first song, which inspires the Genius to select songs that go with it.

❶ Tap the ✳ icon at the bottom of the iPod window. When the Songs list appears, tap the track you want to use as the playlist foundation.

❷ The Genius whips together a song set. If you don't like the resulting mix, tap the Refresh button atop the screen to get new tunes.

❸ If you love the work of the Genius, select or tap the Save option at the top of the screen. Tap New to start over again.

To delete a Genius playlist, select it in the Library list and tap Delete. As in iTunes, Genius playlists are named after the song you chose as the cornerstone of your mix. When you sync the iPad with iTunes, the Genius playlists get copied over to iTunes. You can't delete them from the iPad after you sync them with iTunes; you have to trash them from the iTunes side of the USB cable and resync your tablet to get them off the iPad.

> **Tip** If a currently playing song is totally the vibe you want for a playlist, you can summon the Genius from the Now Playing screen (page 232). Just tap the screen to call up the playback controls, and then tap the atom-shaped Genius icon in the lower-middle part of the screen.

Make Music With GarageBand

So far, this chapter has been all about playing other people's music on your iPad—which can be quite fun, because some people are pretty darn good at making music. But what if you have your own tunes in mind with no place to turn them into real music?

Good news. You can compose songs in an electronic eight-track recording studio that just happens to be thinner than most music-theory textbooks. For a mere $5, you can get a copy of Apple's GarageBand app, which turns your iPad into that studio. Just visit the App Store and search for *GarageBand*.

The GarageBand app is the tapworthy cousin to Apple's desktop GarageBand program, which is part of its iLife suite of creative software for Mac OS X. Over the years, many Mac users have composed their own songs, edited audio files, and generally had a good time noodling around in GarageBand. The iPad app works on both first- and second-generation models, so you don't have to have the latest hardware to start your own one-'Pad band.

The first thing you see after you open the app is the Touch Instrument browser, which displays several screens' worth of digital instruments. You get a selection of guitars, bass guitars, drums, and keyboards to choose from, and you play them right there on the iPad by tapping and swiping. The virtual instruments sound just like their real-life counterparts, but they're much easier to haul around. (Hey, when was the last time you could fit a fully playable grand piano in your backpack?)

Once you get the hang of playing the Touch Instruments, you can record your efforts. And with the iPad's built-in microphone, you can record your own vocal accompaniment.

As you record the different elements of your song and save them to the iPad, you can begin to piece together each part into a unified composition on the track-mixing screen, shown at the top of the next page.

You can layer eight tracks in each song. You can even add some of the 250 professional musical loops included with the app to enhance your song. (If you're new to the music business, *loops* are short audio snippets of percussion and other instruments that automatically repeat, hence the name "loop.")

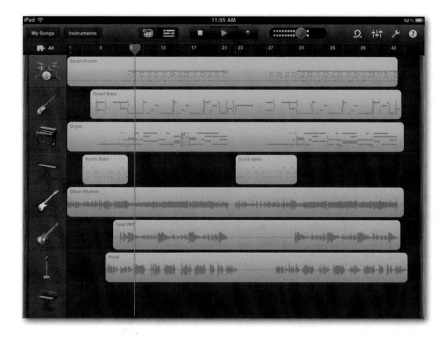

When you finish a song, you can email it as an AAC audio file right from the iPad. You can also export it into iTunes the next time you sync up your tablet. Once the track is in your iTunes library, you can burn it to a CD or add it to a playlist.

With its huge collection of musical instruments, mixing controls, and sound effects, GarageBand may seem a little overwhelming at first. But don't get stressed—the app comes with its own tutorial file. Tap the wrench icon at the top of the screen and then tap Help on the menu. And if you tap the **?** icon in the top-right corner, GarageBand displays helpful yellow tool tips (shown below) on-screen to guide you as you go. And finally, there's a whole manual for the app online at *http://www.apple.com/support/ipad/garageband*.

14

  slide to unlock

Watch and Edit Videos

Apple added video playback powers to its handheld gadgets in 2005, when it introduced the first video iPod. Over the past six years, Apple's device screens have gradually increased in size from 2.5 inches on that ground-breaking 'Pod to 9.7 inches on the iPad's majestic, high-resolution, backlit display. The tablet is perfect for immersing yourself in a movie—or for watching it inflight with your spouse while crammed into a couple of knee-knocking coach seats.

You find video for your iPad in all sorts of places. You can buy, rent, or stream movies, TV shows, music videos, and video podcasts from iTunes; download video-streaming apps from the App Store; watch website streams via Safari; launch the iPad's built-in YouTube app; or even shoot a clip or two yourself with the iPad 2's Camera app (the latter two video-friendly apps are discussed back in Chapter 6).

And if the whole family wants to watch a video, you can connect your iPad to your TV and see it on an even bigger screen.

From getting video onto your tablet to sharing it once it's there, this chapter guides you through one of the most fun parts of the iPad experience.

Get Video Onto Your iPad

Depending on what you want to watch and where you want to watch it, you can get movies moving on your iPad in a variety of ways. Here are the common methods of video acquisition (aside from shooting your own, which is explained back on page 101):

- **The iTunes Store, desktop edition.** You can shop the iTunes Store from your desktop computer, browsing through the hundreds of movies, TV shows, video podcasts, music videos, and iTunes U lectures offered for sale or rent (see page 113 for an overview of shopping the Store). When you buy or rent a video, iTunes downloads the file to your computer. Plug in your iPad and transfer the video with a quick sync (page 190).

- **The iTunes Store, iPad edition.** You can also buy Store videos right from your iPad. Tap the purple iTunes icon on the iPad's Home screen, browse until you find what you want, and click to buy or rent the video. (Video podcasts and iTunes U content are free.) iTunes downloads the file to your iPad, where you can find it by tapping the Videos icon on the Home screen. Videos you buy on the iPad get synced back to the iTunes library the next time you plug in your 'Pad; videos you rent, don't.

- **Video-streaming apps.** With a speedy and steady Internet connection, you can skip bloating up your iPad with space-hogging videos and stream them with programs like the Hulu Plus app (TV shows for $8 a month) or the free PBS app (shown at right). ABC has its own app, where you can watch recent episodes of the network's prime-time shows—with commercials, alas. The App Store also hosts a streaming app from Time Warner cable, plus the iPad version of Netflix. The ubiquitous movie-rental company streams full-length theatrical films to the iPad with a paid monthly membership, which starts at $8 (go to *www.netflix.com*).

- **Video-streaming websites.** While many websites use Flash to play videos and therefore won't work on the iPad, other sites use Apple's QuickTime (page 66) and play back just fine. In addition, sites are slowly switching to a new, more versatile web-page technology called HTML5, which supports video playback out of the gate, so, in time, you'll be able to play virtually all website streams on your 'Pad, too.

Transfer Video from iTunes to iPad

Chapter 11 gives you the lowdown on moving all kinds of files between iTunes and your trusty iPad, but here's a quick summary:

- **Synchronization.** Connect your iPad to your computer and click its icon under Devices in iTunes' Source list. Click the Movies tab and turn on the "Sync movies" checkbox; you can also sync individual movies to your tablet. If you have TV programs in your iTunes library, click the TV Shows tab and adjust your syncing preferences there. Ditto for video podcasts on the Podcasts tab and iTunes U media on the iTunes U tab.

- **Manual management.** Click the appropriate library in iTunes' Source list (Movies, TV Shows, Podcasts, and so on), and then drag the files you want from the main iTunes window onto your connected iPad's icon.

The iTunes Store is chock-full of video choices, but sometimes you want to add your own flicks to your iTunes library. No problem, just drag the file from your desktop and drop it anywhere in iTunes' main window, or choose File→"Add to Library" to locate and import your files. Once you get videos into iTunes, you can play them there or copy them to your iPad.

Another way to add videos to iTunes is to drag them into the "Automatically Add to iTunes" folder. This clever folder analyzes the file and—based on the file's extension—shelves it in the right spot. You  find the auto-folder not through iTunes, but by navigating your system files. In Windows, it's usually at C:/Music→iTunes→iTunes Media→Automatically Add to iTunes (Home→Music→iTunes→iTunes Media→Automatically Add to iTunes). If iTunes can't categorize a file, it dumps it into a Not Added subfolder.

> **Tip** The iPad can play video in high-definition formats, but as members of the AV Club know, the video industry applies the HD label to a few different resolutions. Here's the scoop: The iPad plays back hi-def video at the lowest HD resolution there is, 720p. If you need to convert your clips into different resolutions to get them to play on your hardware, see page 250 for a list of video-conversion programs. If you find all these numbers confusing, see *http://www.geek.com/hdtv-buyers-guide/ resolution/* for more on HDTV screen resolutions.

Find and Play Videos on the iPad

To play a video on the iPad, tap open the Home screen's Videos icon. On the next screen, tap the type of video you want to watch: Movies, TV Shows,  Podcasts, or Music Videos. Then find the item you want to watch and tap the title or the Play button to start the show.

But how do you *run* the show when your gadget has no physical controls? Easy; the playback buttons are *on the screen*.

When you watch video, *anything* else on the screen distracts you, so Apple hides these controls. Tap the screen once to make them appear and again to make them disappear. Here's what they do:

- **Done.** When the video is over (or when *you're* over the *video*), tap the blue Done button in the top-left corner to stop the show and jump back to your video library.

- **Scroll slider.** The bar at the top of the screen shows the time elapsed, as well as the time remaining, in a clip. To jump around during playback, drag the little white dot to the desired point in the video.

- **Widescreen/Full Screen.** See the little ▣ or ▬ button in the top-right corner of the screen? Tap it to adjust the zoom level of the video, as described in "Zoom/Unzoom a Video," below.

- **Play/Pause (▶/II).** Just as they do with music files, these buttons start playback and temporarily pause it when you need a break.

- **Previous, Next (I◀◀, ▶▶I).** If you want to relive the glory days of VHS tapes, hold your finger down on either of these buttons to see the video speed by in reverse or whip ahead in fast-forward motion.

  Many movies from the iTunes Store now contain chapter markers that identify a film's scenes, just like physical DVDs do. (Some video-conversion software also adds chapter markers.) Tap the I◀◀ or ▶▶I buttons to skip to the previous or next chapter in a video.

- **Volume.** To raise or lower a video's playback volume, drag the white knob on the slider below the playback buttons. If you like physical volume controls, you can use the volume rocker on the side of the tablet.

 If you're watching a video that has multiple audio tracks, subtitles, or closed captioning, tap the playback control icon shown at the left to get to the settings for those features.

Zoom/Unzoom a Video

The iPad's beautiful screen is one of its major selling points. At a resolution of 1024 × 768 pixels, it's just this side of HD resolution (1280 × 720). That's okay for old-fashioned TV shows with their squarish 4:3 aspect ratios, but the screen isn't the right dimensions for today's widescreen movies and HDTV shows. To compensate for this proportion contortion, the iPad puts black bars above and below widescreen pictures to make them rectangular; for square-shaped TV shows, it adds bars to the sides.

The appearance of the black bars (called letterboxing) sends some people around the bend. They paid good money to see the *whole* screen filled up. The iPad acknowledges these feelings and has a solution. Simply double-tap the video as it plays. The iPad enlarges the image to fill the entire screen. (If the playback controls are visible, you can also tap ▣ or ▬.)

Truth is, part of the image is now off the screen; you lose the top and bottom of TV scenes, and the left and right edges of movie scenes. If this effect winds up chopping off something important—say on-screen credits—restoring the original letterbox view is just a quick two-tap away.

Play iPad Videos on Your TV

Movies on the iPad are great, but watching them on a bigger screen is often even more gratifying—especially if everyone in the house wants to watch. You *can* put all those movies and videos up on your TV screen— you just need to connect your iPad to your television set. *What* you connect them with depends on the hardware involved.

First of all, if you have a second-generation Apple TV (that's the little black square one), you can use its built-in AirPlay wireless capability to beam your video stream onto the big screen over your WiFi network. Page 199 has the details on getting set up with AirPlay.

But if you don't have an Apple TV, you can use good old-fashioned cables to connect your iPad. Today's TV sets (and those fancy AV receivers that connect all the components in your entertainment center) usually offer a few types of video port for connecting new gear. You can use component, composite, or VGA cables to tether your iPad to a TV or a projector. And you can watch high-definition videos over an HDMI connection with a special adapter.

The easiest place to find *any* of these iPad cables is the Apple Store (*store.apple.com*). Here, you'll see the Apple Composite AV Cable (shown right) for TVs that have older video inputs. You can also find the Apple Component AV Cable, made for high-end TVs and widescreen sets that handle higher-quality video and audio connections. Each type of  cable costs $40, but that includes an integrated AC adapter to power your iPad for a whole-weekend movie marathon.

Apple's Dock Connector-to-VGA adapter sells for $29. And if you want to perch your 'Pad on a stand, the iPad Dock includes a port for these AV cables for $29 as well. Third-party docks and cables are also out there.

 Tip Want your video to remember where you paused or stopped it? Easy. On the iPad, tap the Home screen, and then the Settings icon. On the Settings screen, tap Video and next to Start Playing, select Where Left Off.

If you use HDMI cables to connect high-definition components to your nice, big widescreen HDTV, you can use an HDMI cable to connect your iPad, too, and get HD playback from your tablet—as long as you have Apple's $40 Digital AV Adapter (shown at right). It plugs into the iPad's dock connector on one end and has an HDMI jack, plus a second dock connector, on the other end (in case you need to charge the iPad with its AC adapter while you watch). You don't, however, get another white AC cube, so keep track of the power plug that came with your iPad. And you don't get the HDMI cable that links the adapter to your TV, either.

The AV adapter gives second-generation iPad owners a special bonus, too: screen output at the 1080p resolution (the best there is). You can use the adapter to *mirror* the tablet's own screen, letting you see whatever's on the iPad displayed on your TV. You can use the AV Adapter with a first-generation iPad to show photos and videos, but you don't get the screen-mirror effect—and both iPad generations get video output at the lower-resolution (but still technically high-definition) 720p.

Whatever cable you use, the iPad senses when you connect it to a TV set and automatically pipes its video feed to the big screen, but there are some settings you can adjust at Home→Settings→Video. You can turn on closed captioning for videos that include subtitles. You can also flip the On button next to Widescreen if you don't want your widescreen movies squashed into the 4:3 aspect ratio of older TV sets. And if you travel internationally, pick a

TV Signal. Choose NTSC if you live in the U.S. or Japan, and PAL if you're connecting to a European or Australian TV set.

Once you get the iPad hooked up to play movies, be sure to select the alternate video source on your television set, just as you would to play a DVD or game. Then call up the video from the iPad's library, press the Play button, pop up the corn, and enjoy the show from big screen to bigger screen.

Edit Videos on the iPad

All iPads can play video, and with the right apps, all iPads can edit video clips, too. If, however, you want to *shoot* video—or use Apple's own iMovie app to edit videos—you need to have the second-generation iPad, with its camera and zippy A5 processor inside.

Page 101 explains how to operate the iPad's video camera, so flip back if you need a refresher course in principal photography (or at least to see a still shot of the cat smacking the dog in the head). And remember, whatever you shoot lands in Photos→Camera Roll and not where you'd logically look, namely the Videos menu.

Editing Video on the iPad 2

Once you get the hang of capturing video with the iPad (which, quite frankly, feels like shooting a movie with a ceiling tile until you get comfortable with gripping the 10-inch slab and aiming it at your subject), your clips will begin to pile up in the Camera Roll.

Look through them—do you have a video where all the good action is in the middle? You know, the one where the first 5 minutes consists of absolutely nothing but you coaxing an under-performing baby into demonstrating her agility with Cheerios. Or all those clips where the last 2 minutes show the inside of your tote bag because you forgot to turn off the camera? That stuff is easy to fix on the iPad.

Here's how to trim off the unnecessary parts on either end of a clip (keep in mind you can't edit *within* a clip):

❶ Open the video you want to edit.

❷ Tap the screen to call up the editing controls. The frame-viewer bar at the top of the screen displays scenes from the clip.

❸ Use the frame-viewer to find the frames you want to cut off. Press the outer edge of the bar so it turns yellow (as shown below), and then drag either end of the bar to isolate just the frames you want. Tap the Trim button in the top-right corner of the screen to cut away the detritus and leave the delicious center of your video.

After you tap the Trim button, the iPad offers to trim the original clip (which makes this edit permanent) or save the edited video as a *new* clip—while leaving the original intact.

Video-Editing Apps for the iPad

While the iPad 2's basic video-editing tool lets you trim bad bits from either end of a clip, you may find that's not enough. If you want to stitch different clips together, score background music, put in titles, and add Hollywood-style scene transitions, you need an app for that. And fortunately for you, there are video-editing apps that let you do all these things. When you get to the App Store, search for *video editing*.

Two apps pop up immediately. One is the previously mentioned iMovie for iPad by Apple (shown below), which costs $5 and requires an iPad 2. The other is ReelDirector, a $2 app from Nexvio that works on both-gen iPads.

"Hey," you say, "How do I get video clips on my original iPad if it doesn't have a camera?" Just shoot the clips on whatever camera you use to shoot video, and convert them to iPad-approved video formats (page 250). Then import them into your iTunes-compatible desktop photo program of choice and sync them over to the iPad; just make sure you check the "Include videos" box (page 191 describes the syncing process in detail). Then craft your opus and export it to your favorite video-sharing site so the world can see your hilarious short of the hamster mingling with *Star Wars* action figures.

Video Formats That Work on the iPad

As discussed in Chapter 11, the iTunes Store now sells movies, TV shows, and music videos. You can also import your own home movies, downloaded movie trailers, and other videos into the iPad via iTunes, as long as the files have one of these file extensions at the end of their name: *.mov, .m4v,* or *.mp4.*

Other common video formats, like *.avi* or Windows Media Video (*.wmv*), won't play in iTunes, but you can convert them with Apple's $30 QuickTime Pro software or any of the dozens of video-conversion programs floating around the Web. (If you're unsure whether a file's compatible, it's always worth trying to drag it into iTunes' main window and then choosing Advanced→"Create iPad or Apple TV Version.")

Here are a few popular video-conversion tools:

- **Aneesoft iPad Video Converter**. Aneesoft offers several DVD and video conversion programs for both Windows and Mac OS X systems. Free trial editions are available to download from the site, and full versions cost $35 or less. (*www.aneesoft.com*)

- **Wondershare iPad Video Converter.** Based in China, Wondershare offers two $30 conversion programs for Windows: one for DVDs and one for other types of video files. (*www.wondershare.com*)

- **HandBrake.** Available in versions for Windows and Mac OS X, this easy-to-use bit of freeware converts DVD movies and other files for everything from iPods to the Apple TV. (When converting for the iPad, go for the higher-quality settings for bigger screens—using  the iPod setting may lead to a fuzzy picture when blown up to iPad size.) You can get HandBrake at *http://handbrake.fr.*

> **Tip** Movies and TV shows get their own libraries in the iTunes Source list. If you import a video yourself and it's in the wrong place in the list, you may need to tweak the file's labeling info. Open the file's Get Info box (Ctrl+I [⌘-I]), click the Options tab, and then assign it a video format from the Video Kind drop-down menu: Music Video, Movie, TV Show, Podcast, or iTunes U file.

Delete Videos

Having a personal movie library with you at all times is great, but if there's one thing about high-quality videos, it's that they're *huge*. Sure, TV show and movie rentals from iTunes delete themselves when they expire, but what about your regular collection? A long movie can take almost up to 2 gigabytes of your limited iPad drive space. And if you're traveling with a full iPad and want to download a fresh flick for the plane, what do you do?

Fortunately, you *can* delete videos directly off the tablet—without having to link your iPad to the computer and turn off checkboxes to "unsync" files by way of iTunes. (However, removing the files the iTunes way is another way to regain drive space, with the added advantage that the videos stay safely in your computer's iTunes library, ready for you to sync to your iPad again should you want to watch it again.)

When you're ready to lose a movie or two, go to the iPad's Videos area and tap open the category for the relevant file. Press your finger down on the icon until the ✖ appears on the corner (circled). Tap the ✖ and in the box that pops up, tap Delete (or Cancel, if you have second thoughts). The selected video goes *poof!* off the iPad. If you synced it from your computer through iTunes, a copy is still there and you can sync it back to your 'Pad later if you miss it.

Note Pay attention to what you're deleting. If you accidentally delete an unwatched or unfinished movie-rental download on the iPad, it's gone for good. You have to rent the whole thing all over again to see it. And remember, you can rent movies in iTunes on your computer and transfer them to the iPad, but you can't sync a movie you rented on the iPad back to iTunes.

slide to unlock

View, Edit, and Manage Photos

With its big glossy screen and wide black or white border, you could easily mistake the iPad for one of those digital picture frames designed to sit on your mantle and show an ever-running slideshow of your kids and pets. The iPad is no imposter here—it can serve as a digital photo album whenever you want it to. (You can even *take* those pictures with the latest iPad; flip back to Chapter 6 for photo-snapping instructions.)

Your thin little tablet can replace stacks and stacks of paper-based photo albums. You can overlay your snaps on a map showing where you shot them (opposite page), and you can email your favorites to friends.

With the proper apps, you can touch up your photos on the go, too. And with the right kind of audio-video cable or a second-generation Apple TV, you can play your pictures on the big screen for the whole family—making it the Kodak Carousel of the 21st century.

A picture may be worth a thousand words, but when your friends see what you can do with photos on the iPad, you may hear a few thousand more.

Get Pictures Onto Your iPad

The iPad can display your handsome photographs in most of the file formats digital cameras use, including JPEG, PNG, TIFF, GIF, and even those large, uncompressed RAW files favored by serious photographers who don't want to sacrifice a pixel of precious image data. But to show your pics *off* on the iPad, you have to first get them *onto* the iPad. You do that in several ways.

Transfer Photos with iTunes

If you keep your digital photo collection organized in programs like Adobe Photoshop Elements, iPhoto, or Aperture—or even loosely in a folder on your hard drive—you can sling them onto your iPad with an iTunes syncing session. Chapter 11 has detailed information on syncing iPad content using iTunes, but here's what you need to do for photos:

❶ Connect your iPad to your PC or Mac with the iPad's USB cable.

❷ Once the tablet shows up in iTunes' Source list, click its icon to select it.

❸ In the iTunes tabs for your iPad, click the one for Photos, the last tab over.

❹ Turn on the checkbox next to "Sync photos from," and then choose your photo program or photo-storage folder; that lets iTunes know where to find your pics. You can copy everything over or just the *albums* (sets of pictures) you select. If you don't use any of the programs that the "Sync photos from" menu lists and you just want to copy over a folder of photos from your hard drive, select "Choose folder" from the menu and then navigate to the desired folder.

❺ Click Sync (or Apply, if this is your first time syncing photos) after you make your selections.

Once you start the sync, iTunes "optimizes" your photos. This has nothing to do with your photographic skills and everything to do with storage. If necessary, iTunes down-samples your pics to "TV quality" so they take up less room on your 'Pad but still display in high-res format on your tablet or TV screen.

> **Note** You can only sync photos from one computer to the iPad. If you try to grab photos from another machine, iTunes erases all the pics from the first one.

Transfer Photos from Mail Messages and Web Pages

Do you have a bunch of photos someone sent you as file attachments to an email message? Or do you see a copyright-free image on a web page you want to include in your collection? To add these pictures to your iPad's Photos program, press your finger on the photo. Wait for a box to pop up with a Save Image button. Tap it to store a copy of the picture in the Photos→Saved Photos album, where you can admire it. If you have multiple photos attached to an email message, the iPad asks if you want to save them all.

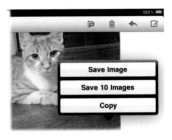

Transfer Photos with the iPad Camera Connection Kit

The iPad can slurp up pictures from your digital camera too, but there's a catch: You first have to plunk down $29 for Apple's iPad Camera Connection Kit at *store.apple.com* or other fine retail establishments.

The kit contains two white adapters for the iPad's Dock Connector port. One has a jack for your camera's USB cable and the other has a slot for Secure Digital memory cards full of pictures—in case you don't have your camera's USB cable. (While Apple's USB adapter *officially* works with cameras only, word is that some USB keyboards and headsets *unofficially* work with it.)

Once you plug an adapter into the iPad and insert a memory card or connect your camera via USB cable, wait for the iPad's Photos app to open, and then:

❶ Tap Import All to grab all the pictures, or tap individual shots to check-mark them before you tap the Import button.

❷ When the iPad asks, decide if you want to *keep* or *delete* the photos on the camera or memory card after you import them.

❸ To see the new arrivals on your iPad, tap Photos→Last Import.

Unplug the iPad camera connector and put it in a safe place. When you get back to your computer, you can sync these pictures back to iPhoto or Adobe Photoshop Elements by connecting the iPad and using your picture program's command to import the new photos.

> **Tip** You can also import photos to your iPad from your iPhone. Connect the iPad to the phone with that familiar USB-to-Dock Connector cable and follow the steps above.

Find Pictures on Your iPad

Now that you've got some pictures onto your iPad, it's time to locate them. Go to the Home screen and tap the Photos icon.

The iPad organizes your picture collection in up to five ways—if you happen to use all the features of iPhoto '09 and later on the Mac. After you open the iPad's Photos app, tap the buttons at the top of the window (circled) to see the ways you can sort your images:

- **Photos.** This view displays thumbnails of all your pictures lumped together in one place. If you didn't group your images into albums before you transferred them, they all show up here.

- **Albums.** If you imported individual albums by ticking off their boxes in iTunes, tap the Albums button to see those pictures grouped under the same album name as they were in your photo program.

- **Events.** Mac folks using recent versions of iPhoto or Aperture can also view photos by Event. These two programs group similar images, like those taken on the same day, into Events. Tap the Events button on the iPad to see any of these sets synced from your Mac.

- **Faces.** Apple introduced a face-recognition feature in iPhoto '09 and later that automatically groups photos based on the people in them. If you use this feature on the Mac, iTunes gives you the option to sync entire albums of just one person. Then you can find your Cate or Zachary photo sets when you tap the Faces button on the iPad.

- **Places.** If you geo-tag your photos—by shooting them with a GPS-enabled camera or by manually placing them on a map with tools in iPhoto '09 or later—the iPad groups them based on their geographic coordinates. Tap Places to see your photo sets stuck to a world map with virtual red push-pins.

In album form, your picture sets look like a stack of loose photographs clumped together in a sloppy pile. Tap one of the piles with a fingertip and the photos disperse and snap into a grid where you can see each one as a small thumbnail. If you're not quite sure what photo is in which album pile, pinch and spread your fingers over a pile to see a quick animated preview of its contents without opening the album all the way.

Tip Want to take a screenshot of some cool thing on your iPad? Hold down the Home button and press the Sleep/Wake button as though it were a camera shutter. The resulting snap lands in Photos→Camera Roll (or Saved Photos on first-gen iPads). You can transfer the pic back to your computer the next time you sync. If your computer has a program that senses when you connect a digital camera, it will likely leap up and offer to pull in the iPad's screenshots for you.

View Pictures on Your iPad

To see the pictures you synced over from your computer, tap the Photos icon on the iPad's Home screen. Then tap the Photos button at the top of the screen to see your pictures in a grid of thumbnails. If you chose to copy over specific photo albums, tap the name of an album. Mac syncers can also tap the Events, Faces, or Places button to see photos sorted by those categories, as page 254 explains.

On the thumbnails screen, you can do several things:

- Tap a thumbnail to see the photo full-size on the iPad screen.

- Double-tap an open photo to magnify it.

- Spread and pinch your fingers on-screen (those fancy moves described in Chapter 2) to zoom in and out of a photo. Drag your finger around on-screen to pan through a zoomed-in photo.

- Flick your finger horizontally across the screen in either direction to scroll through your pictures at high speed. You can show off your vacation photos really fast this way (your friends will thank you).

- Rotate the iPad to have horizontal photos fill the width of the screen or to have vertical photos fill its height.

- With a photo open, tap the iPad's glass to display a strip of itsy-bitsy thumbnails of all the photos in the current album at the bottom of the screen. Tap or slide to a thumbnail to jump to a particular picture.

Tap the 📤 icon in the menu bar to email a picture (page 259), send it to MobileMe (page 272), assign it to your iPad's Contact's program (page 96), set it as wallpaper (page 266), print it (page 32), or copy it.

To get back to your library, tap the Photos or album-name button at the top of the screen.

Email and Print Photos

To share your photos, you can email or print one or a bunch of pics right from the iPad's Photos app:

- **One photo.** To email or print the photo currently on-screen, tap the iPad's glass to make the photo controls appear, and then tap the ![icon] icon in the upper-right corner. Tap Email Photo to have the iPad's mail program attach the photo to a new message, ready for you to address. Tap Print for a paper copy (as long as you have your iPad configured for printing; see page 32).

- **Multiple photos.** To email a bunch of pictures at once, tap open the album containing the photos. Tap the ![icon] icon in the top-right corner, and then tap the pictures you want to send; blue checkmarks appear in the corner of each thumbnail you select. Tap the Email button to attach them to a new message. If you have a draft message in progress, tap the Copy button, then switch to the mail program, open your message, and hold down your finger until the Paste button appears. Tap it to paste in the pictures. Tap Print for paper copies of the checked photos.

Delete Photos

You can delete photos from your iPad in two ways. If you synced photo albums over from iTunes, connect the iPad to your computer, open iTunes, hit the Photos tab, and turn off the checkboxes by those albums. Click Apply and then Sync to "unsync," or remove, those pics from the iPad's gallery.

If you have pictures in your Camera Roll or Saved Photos album you want to ditch, you can delete a currently open picture by tapping the ![icon] icon and then tapping Delete Photo. To delete multiple pictures from the Camera Roll/Saved Photos thumbnail view, tap the ![icon] icon, then tap the unwanted pictures to assign the Blue Checkmarks of Selection. Tap the small red Delete button on the menu bar (circled), and then tap Delete Selected Photos. There's a blue Cancel button on the other side of the menu bar if you change your mind.

Edit Photos on the iPad

In the dark, badly cropped days before there were apps, you couldn't do much besides *view* the digital pictures you snapped, downloaded, or received on your mobile gadget. It was a "look, don't retouch" approach to photos. Thankfully, things have changed.

Need to chop out that goofy guy off to the side in your Mount Rushmore photo? Want to lighten the exposure of that party shot so you can see the birthday girl's face? With the growing collection of photo-editing programs in the App Store, you can improve your photos, right there on your iPad.

And best of all, once you're done, you can share them online, send them to other people by email, or (if you have a second-generation Apple TV) proudly beam the fruits of your labor right onto your TV with AirPlay.

If you think you'd like to do some photo-editing on your iPad, jump into the App Store and search for *photography* or *photo editing*.

Companies add apps to the Store every week, but two that were designed for editing photos are Adobe Photoshop Express for iPad (free, shown below) and Ghostbird Software's PhotoForge for iPad ($4, shown on the opposite page). Of the two apps, Adobe Photoshop Express is probably easier to learn and hey, you have to admit, the price is right. PhotoForge, on the other hand, aims to be a full-on digital darkroom packed with enough tools, filters, and controls to rival some desktop photo-editing programs.

With either program, you can make these adjustments in your photos:

- **Crop.** Need to tighten the focus or remove background clutter around your subject? Use the crop tool to chop out the unwanted elements.

- **Straighten.** If your picture was unintentionally shot at an angle or simply looks too crooked for your taste, tilt it a few degrees.

- **Rotate.** Spin a vertical photo sideways or a horizontal pic into portrait mode. This can be helpful for emailed images that come to you in the wrong orientation.

- **Contrast.** Bumping up the contrast can perk up photos that seem flat and muddy.

- **Exposure.** When a photo looks too light or too dark, fiddling with the exposure controls might help.

- **Saturation.** Not all digital cameras have accurate sensors, so if the green, green grass of the ballpark looks pale or brown, increasing the color saturation can liven up the shot.

Both Adobe Photoshop Express and PhotoForge can convert color shots to moody black-and-white images. You can also apply filters and special effects to your shots. Adobe's app even offers extra filters and tools as in-app purchases you can buy to enhance the original free program. And when you get done improving your photos, save them back to the iPad's Photos library, where you can easily email them or upload them to the Web right from your tablet, no desktop or laptop computer required.

> **Tip** As you may have guessed, Adobe Photoshop Express for the iPad is a member of Adobe's large family of photo-editing software. Other members of the clan include Adobe Photoshop Express for iPhone and iPod Touch, Adobe Photoshop Elements for home users with Mac and Windows systems, and the mighty Adobe Photoshop for Mac and Windows, the industry standard for professional image-editing. Adobe also runs Photoshop.com, an online gallery and editing site. In fact, if you sign up for a free account at Photoshop.com, you get 2 free gigabytes of space on Adobe's servers to show off your uploaded photos, whether you spruced them up on the iPad or not.

Play Slideshows on Your iPad

A photo slideshow takes all the photo tap-and-drag work out of your hands, freeing you up to sit back and admire your pictures without distraction. To run a slideshow on your iPad, you need to set up a few things, like how long each photo appears on-screen and what music accompanies your photo parade.

The iPad keeps its slideshow settings in two different places. All of the timing and order-of-pic options are in the iPad's Settings area. To get there, tap Settings→Photos. Here, you can choose:

- **Play Each Slide For...** Pick the amount of time you want a picture to stay on-screen. You can choose 2, 3, 5, 10, or 20 seconds (for those photography buffs with really long attention spans).

- **Repeat.** Tap this setting to On if you want the slideshow to keep looping, starting over again after it plays through the first time.

- **Shuffle.** To randomly mix up the order of the pictures in an album, tap the On button next to "Shuffle."

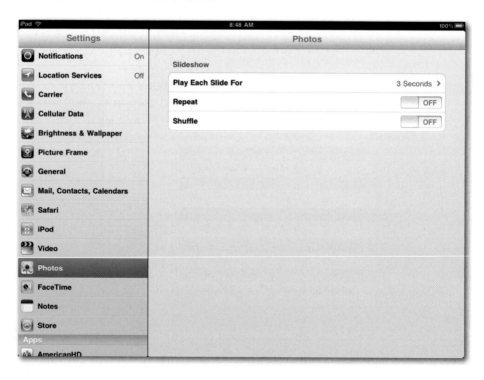

 Note Looking for info on the iPad's native photo-related apps like Camera, Photo Booth, and FaceTime? Just flip back to Chapter 6—they're all there.

Now that you have these matters worked out, go back to the Photos app and tap open the album you want to present as a slideshow. On the upper-right side of the menu bar, tap the Slideshow button. As you can see from the image above, the Slideshow Options box unfolds. Here, you can choose:

- **The transition effect between photos.** Dissolves, wipes, and all the usual razzle-dazzle styles are here.

- **Music.** If you want to set your show to music, tap the On button next to Play Music. Next, tap Music and in the box that appears, select a song from any of the tunes you synced over to your iPad.

Once you make all your selections, you're ready for showtime. Tap the Start Slideshow button. To stop the show, tap the iPad screen.

> **Tip** If you plan to do a lot of slideshows, consider getting an iPad dock or a folding case that lets you prop up your iPad at a nice hands-free viewing angle.

Play Slideshows on Your TV

You have a couple ways to get your photos flipping across a TV screen. For one, you can wirelessly stream them with AirPlay to a connected second-generation Apple TV box (page 199). The other way is to connect the tablet to the TV with a cable (flip back to page 246 for help connecting your iPad to a television set).

Once you make the iPad-TV link, you're almost ready to start the show. You need to adjust a few more things on the iPad.

❶ Tap Settings→Video. When you connect an Apple-approved AV cable to the iPad, your slideshow automatically appears on your TV set instead of on your tablet. In the TV Out section here, you can toggle Widescreen On or Off, depending on the type of TV screen you have.

❷ In the TV Signal area, select your local television broadcast standard. If you're in North America or Japan, choose NTSC. If you're in Europe or Australia, choose PAL.

Tip If you wrangle your picture collection in iPhoto '09 or later on the Mac, you can export your intricately crafted and scored iPhoto slideshows as little movies sized up just for the iPad—and put them right into iTunes. Select a slideshow in iPhoto and click the Export button. In the "Export your slideshow" box that appears, turn on the checkbox for Medium or Large (the preferred settings for iPad viewing) and make sure you turn on the checkbox next to "Automatically send slideshow to iTunes." Click the Export button. To actually complete the transfer, connect your iPad to your computer and click the Movies tab on the iPad preferences screen in iTunes. Select the slideshow and sync away.

❸ Turn on your TV and select the iPad as your video input source. You do that the same way you tell your TV to display the signal from a DVD player or videogame console: Typically, you press the Input or Display button on your TV's remote to switch from the live TV signal to a new video source.

❹ On the iPad, navigate to the album you want. Press the Slideshow button in the menu bar at the top of the screen, tap the Start Slideshow button, and the show begins.

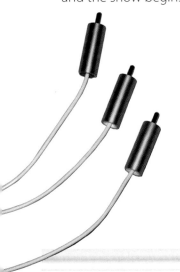

Tip Apple sells its own AV cables (shown at left) for either component or composite video connections between the iPad and the input jacks on your TV or AV receiver. The cables are $49. If you want to hook up the iPad to a TV, computer monitor, or projector that uses a VGA connection, you can get the $29 Dock Connector to VGA Adapter. And if you have a high-definition TV and want to pipe in *whatever* happens to be on the iPad screen at the time over an HDMI cable, Apple's $39 Digital AV Adapter will do the trick—they're all conveniently available in Apple's stores or online at *store.apple.com*.

Change the iPad's Wallpaper

The iPad comes pre-stocked with several gorgeous high-resolution photos—mostly of nature scenes and textured patterns intended as background images for both the Lock and Home screens. (In case you're wondering what the difference is, the Lock screen is the one you see when you first turn on the iPad, and the Home screen has all your app icons scattered about.)

If you want to change these background images to spice things up, you can assign new photos in two ways.

The first is to go to the Home screen and tap Settings→Brightness & Wallpaper. Tap the Wallpaper icon (circled). On the next screen, choose a photo from any of your photo albums, or tap Wallpaper to pick an Apple stock shot. Tap the photo you want to use. You can drag the image around and finger-pinch and spread to shrink or enlarge the parts of the picture you want to display.

When you're done, tap the appropriate button at the top of the screen. You have your choice of Set Lock Screen, Set Home Screen, or Set Both. You can also bail out with a Cancel button in the left corner.

The second way to wallpaper your 'Pad is to pick a picture out of one of the iPad's photo albums and tap the ⬆ icon at the top of the screen, then tap the "Use as Wallpaper" option. Here, you can size and save the photo as mentioned above. No matter which way you choose to change it, there's nothing like fresh new wallpaper to personalize your iPad—and show off your own photography.

Turn the iPad into a Picture Frame

As mentioned at the beginning of this chapter, the iPad resembles a digital picture frame. And if you *want* one of those, you can turn the iPad's Lock screen into a 10-inch window that displays your photo collection, a pleasant diversion as the iPad recharges from a wall outlet.

❶ Go to the Home screen and tap Settings→Picture Frame.

❷ Pick the type of transition between photos you want to use—either the traditional Hollywood-style "Dissolve" or Apple's new foldy-paper "Origami" animation. You can also set the amount of time each photo stays on-screen, whether the iPad zooms in on photos, and whether the pics appear in random order.

❸ At the bottom of the Settings screen, choose the album of images you want to use—or let the iPad grab all the photos you added to it.

 To test out your framed slideshow, press the Sleep/Wake button to turn off the iPad screen and press it again to get back to the Lock screen. Tap the small flower icon next to the lock slider to start the slideshow. If you want to pause the pictures, tap the iPad's screen. You can either tap the flower icon again to resume the show, or swipe the slider to unlock the iPad and get back to work.

 If you're a Mac user with at least iPhoto '09 and you used the Faces feature to ID and tag the kissers in your pictures, the Picture Frame app will zoom in to show off those faces in close-up shots. It only works with the "Dissolve" transition, though.

16

  slide to unlock

Sync Up with MobileMe

E ven though your iPad is a cool personal media center, under the hood, it's a computer (a sleek one, yes, but a computer nonetheless). Odds are, you have another one or two computers in your life—at work, at home, or both. You may have an iPhone, too. Each of these devices can send and receive email, store contact information, keep track of your appointments, and save website bookmarks. Wouldn't it be great if they could all share all this information so that all your gadgets were always in sync and always up-to-date?

That's where Apple's MobileMe service *used* to come in. In early June of 2011, Apple announced it would phase out MobileMe in favor of a new online service called iCloud. Scheduled to arrive in Fall 2011, iCloud will handle all your info-synching needs between computers and devices. The service gives you 5 gigabytes of free online storage so you can sync, share, and back up contacts, calendars, mail, documents, music, and more between Macs, PCs, iPads, iPhones, and iPod Touches.

If you already have a MobileMe account, this chapter tells you how to use it until iCloud blows in. While you can no longer sign up for a new MobileMe account, existing MobileMe-ers can still use the service to keep your contacts, calendars, and more in sync across your computer and your Apple devices. MobileMe itself will be active until June 30, 2012, giving you plenty of time to transition your stuff to the new iCloud service. But if you can't wait to gaze up into iCloud, read about it at *http://www.apple.com/icloud*.

Sign Up for MobileMe

MobileMe isn't an Internet service provider that gets you on the Web—you still have to pay your cable or DSL company for that. Instead, it's an Internet *service* that syncs your email, contacts, calendars, and bookmarks—all the programs you use to manage mail and personal information, in other words—across your devices.

On the PC side, MobileMe works with Outlook 2007 and 2010 and Windows Mail, and you can sync bookmarks from Internet Explorer and Safari. (Outlook 2011 owners can sync contacts, but not calendars.) On the Mac side, you can sync data from the Mac OS X Address Book, iCal, and Safari.

When you sign up for MobileMe, you get an @*me.com* email address. MobileMe keeps all your me.com mailboxes current across your gadgets, whether you read messages in your dedicated mail program or on the Web. (MobileMe can receive mail from other POP-based mail services, too, and deposit them in their own folder on your iPad so you know which account they came from, but it doesn't synchronize the mail from these accounts across your devices.)

You also get an online photo and video gallery, and a chunk of space on Apple's servers called an iDisk, where you can back up or share large files. iDisk comes with 20 gigabytes of storage, but Apple will gladly sell you more—40 gigabytes costs another $49 a year, for example.

So how do you get started with MobileMe? Easy. Connect your iPad to your computer and click the Info tab in iTunes. In the MobileMe area, click Learn More.

iTunes whisks you away to MobileMe's sign-up area, where you supply your credit-card number, pick out a user name and password, and download any necessary software, like the MobileMe control panel for Windows. (Alternatively, you can road-test MobileMe for 60 days for free at *www.apple. com/mobileme*).

Once you're all signed up and have that software installed, it's time to set up your computer and then your iPad. The next page explains how.

Sync Using MobileMe

While MobileMe will seamlessly sync up your machines, you have to tell it *what* to sync.

❶ In Windows, choose Start→Control Panel→Network and Internet→ MobileMe. On a Mac, choose →System Preferences→MobileMe.

❷ Click the Account tab and sign in with your user name and password.

❸ Click the Sync tab. Turn on "Sync with MobileMe" and choose how often you want MobileMe to push data out to your iPad (and any other device you use with the service). Most people choose "Automatically," which syncs your info whenever you connect to the Web, and then once an hour if you stay online.

❹ Next, choose the info on your computer, like email accounts, contacts, appointments, and bookmarks, that you want to sync to your iPad and other devices.

❺ Click the Sync Now button to upload the info on your computer to Apple's servers. Then click OK to close the box.

All right, that part's done. Now you need to set up your iPad to accept the data MobileMe sends.

Set Up MobileMe on Your iPad

❶ On your iPad, choose Settings→Mail, Contacts, Calendars.

❷ Tap Fetch New Data. On the next screen, set the Push option to On.

❸ In the line above Fetch New Data, tap Add Account, choose MobileMe, and fill in your user name and password.

❹ Turn on Mail, Contacts, Calendars, and Bookmarks. You can even activate Find My iPad—which maps the location of a lost or stolen tablet on *www.me.com* if it's within range of a 3G or known Wi-Fi network.

Use the MobileMe Gallery

MobileMe's life-synchronization function is just one of its features. You also get an elegantly designed online gallery where you can post your favorite snaps and videos for all to see. That way, your relatives don't have to download huge email attachments, saving them tons of time and hard drive space. (And if these are personal family photos, you can even password-protect them.)

Creating an album in the MobileMe gallery and filling it with images is easy, thanks to the service's built-in tools. Here's what you do:

❶ Find some photos or videos on your computer you'd like to share.

❷ Log into your MobileMe account at *www.me.com*.

❸ Click the Cloud icon in the upper-left corner, and, when the MobileMe icon bar appears (shown right), click the gallery icon (it looks like a framed sailboat photo).

❹ When the gallery page appears, click the little + button at the bottom left (circled) to add a new photo album. The Album Settings screen appears, asking you to name the album and set up permissions for what viewers can do there, like download your photos or upload theirs (which is useful when everybody at the family reunion brought their own camera).

❺ Click the Create button to add the new album to your gallery.

❻ On the next screen, click the green arrow. In the box that pops up, click the Choose button, navigate to the photos on your computer, and then click the names of the photos you want to add to your newly created album. Hold down the Ctrl (or ⌘) key to grab multiple files as you click.

❼ Click the Select button to start the upload. You can upload images in the JPEG, GIF, or PNG formats and video in the MOV format, but nothing bigger than 1 GB in size. MobileMe resizes images larger than 6 megapixels for onscreen display, but this doesn't affect the originals.

Besides photo and clip sharing, putting your media files on MobileMe gives you another advantage: You can view your file on your iPad over its Internet connection, which is especially handy if you have a lot of photos and, say, a 16 GB iPad. Why devote some of that precious space to photos and videos when you can store them online and look at them *there*, through the iPad's Web connection? You'll end up with more room on your iPad for music, movies, and apps.

Speaking of apps, you can download a free MobileMe Gallery app from the App Store to make it easy to see your pictures and videos when you're on the go. Rather than fire up Safari and jump to your MobileMe page through the Web all the time, use the gallery app to view and share your media.

To get the gallery app, tap the App Store icon on the iPad's Home screen. Then tap the Search button and look for *Gallery*. When the app appears, tap it, then tap the Free button, and then tap the Install button.

Once you install it, tap open the app and type in your MobileMe account name and password. You'll see all your uploaded albums and videos listed, and samples from your collection will crawl across the screen.

You can share gallery items with friends by tapping the envelope icon in the top right of the My Gallery screen. A Mail message opens with an embedded link to your gallery or a particular album, ready for your pals' email addresses.

Use iDisk

In addition to photo and video sharing, MobileMe gives you some personal Internet-based storage space called an iDisk, where you can store files online. Need to back up some Microsoft Word files but don't have a flash drive handy? Want to make sure you can always get to a set of important PDF documents, whether you're at home or in a London hotel room? iDisk lets you retrieve files from any Web-connected computer.

From your desktop computer, you can tap into iDisk a couple of ways:

- Open your browser and log in to *www.me.com*, and then click the blue iDisk icon in the MobileMe toolbar.

- On a Mac, double-click the iDisk icon in the Finder sidebar.

- In Windows, add the iDisk as a network drive. For Windows XP, choose Start→Network→My Network Places and choose "Add a network place" in the next box. As the Add a Network Place wizard opens, go with "Choose another network connection." When asked for a URL, type in *http://idisk.me.com/YourAccount/*, and then enter your MobileMe name and password.

  For Windows 7 and Vista, choose Start→Computer→Map a Network Drive. In the next box, pick a drive letter, and in the Folder field, type in *http://idisk.me.com/YourAccount*. Turn on the checkbox for "Connect using different credentials/user name." Click Finish and type in your MobileMe user name and password when prompted.

No matter how you get to iDisk, you'll find a series of folders with names like Documents, Pictures, and Public. To upload files to one of these folders, click the upward-pointing arrow in the MobileMe toolbar. To download files, use the downward-pointing arrow.

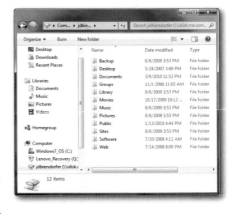

If you have an iDisk icon in Windows Explorer or the Mac Finder, you can just drag files on and off the icon. To share files too huge to email with relatives, friends, and colleagues, use iDisk's Public folder. Add your files to it, click the Share File button, and then send a clickable link to your friends so they can download the files.

The iDisk App on Your iPad

So yeah, MobileMe is great for your desktop computer and all, but just what does it do for you on the iPad? Just as you can get a native iPad app for the MobileMe gallery, so you can get a free iDisk app from the App Store. It gives you access to all the files you stored online. Need to double-check something in an Excel spreadsheet or refer to a PDF manual? Tap the iDisk icon on the iPad's Home screen and browse your way through your MobileMe drive. iDisk is especially helpful if you need to view a Microsoft Office file and don't have iWork (Chapter 10) installed on your iPad—the app renders a read-only version of the file onscreen.

Away from your main computer but need to send that giant Word document to a colleague? The iDisk app, like its desktop counterpart, lets you share files. Open the file you want to send and tap the Share Files icon at the bottom of the screen (.ℕ). The iPad's Mail program opens with a link to the file embedded in the body of the message, ready for your recipient's address.

To stop sharing a file after you've sent out links, open the shared folder, tap the green Share icon on the right side, and then choose Stop Sharing from the menu that slides up.

 Note MobileMe's upcoming conversion to iCloud isn't the only change scheduled for Fall 2011. Apple plans to roll out iOS 5, which brings 200 new features to the iPad, including a new messaging service, a virtual newsstand for digital publications, Twitter integration, and much more. For a preview of the changes to come, stroll over to *http://www.apple.com/ios/ios5*.

A

Set Passcode Cancel

Enter a passcode

| ● | ● | | |

1	2 ABC	3 DEF
4 GHI	5 JKL	6 MNO
7 PQRS	8 TUV	9 WXYZ
	0	⌫

 slide to unlock

iPad Settings

Despite its slim good looks, the iPad is, at its core, a computer. And like most computers, you can customize its settings to suit your needs. Need to tone down the screen brightness, turn on Bluetooth capability, sign up for a month of Verizon 3G service, or add a new email account? You do it all right in the iPad's Settings area. In fact, unless you go in there and poke around for a bit, you may have no idea how much of the iPad you can actually fiddle with—and that's what this chapter is for.

In addition to letting you tweak the way your iPad works, the Settings area also has *re*setting options you can use when your iPad isn't working so great (Appendix B has more on troubleshooting, by the way). So if you want to see where to find the controls to adjust the iPad's date and time, turn off Location Services, or power down the cellular chip in your Wi-Fi + 3G 'Pad when the flight attendant tells you to, turn the page to start the Settings tour.

Tour the iPad's Settings

To adjust the options on your iPad, tap the Settings icon on the Home screen. The list on the left identifies the features you can change, under headings like Safari and Brightness & Wallpaper.

Tap an item in the list to see all its settings on the right side of the screen. Then tap the relevant button, link, or label to get to the setting you want to change. To return to the main Settings area, tap the arrow button underneath the iPad's on-screen clock (circled).

Airplane Mode

Anybody who's flown commercially in the past 10 years knows the drill: Just before the plane takes off, the cabin crew asks you to turn off your cellphone and electronic devices to avoid interfering with the plane's own instruments. Once the captain says you can use your gadgets again, turn on your iPad and choose Settings→Airplane Mode→On. Why? Airplane Mode (signified by a tiny plane icon at the top of the iPad's screen) conforms to federal regulations that prohibit wireless devices because their signals may interfere with the plane's own instruments.

So switching Airplane Mode to On turns *off* your iPad's link to the Internet and the 'Pad's GPS functions. However, you can still use the device to read downloaded iBooks, listen to music, type up Notes and documents, and do other non-Net activities.

"But wait," you say, "many flights now have WiFi available on-board. What about that??" If the plane offers WiFi from Gogo Inflight (which has its own iPad app, by the way) or a similar service, go back to Settings→Wi-Fi and select On so you can override Airplane Mode's WiFi blackout and join the plane's wireless network; your iPad's *3G* network (the one that sends signals along cellphone towers) remains off via Airplane Mode. When the aircraft lands and you're free to move about the cabin and off the plane, don't forget to choose Settings→Airplane Mode→Off.

 Note The settings for 3G iPads can differ slightly from WiFi-only 'Pads. If you see a setting listed here that you don't see on your iPad, odds are you have the type of iPad (whether it's 3G or Wi-Fi + 3G) that doesn't offer the feature, or an iPad system software update has changed things.

WiFi

Tap Wi-Fi on the Settings screen to turn the iPad's wireless networking chip on or off. If you're outside a WiFi zone, turning WiFi off preserves battery life. If you're in a WiFi zone with WiFi set to On, the iPad sniffs around for your usual set of airwaves. If it can't find them, it lists any hot spots it does find and asks if you want to join one. Tap the name of a network to join it, or tap ⦾ to see the network's settings—or click "Forget this Network" to permanently remove it from your list of available networks. To turn off the message bugging you to join a new network, choose Settings→Wi-Fi→Ask to Join Networks→Off.

Notifications

Certain applications, mainly social-networking programs, can *push* notifications to your iPad, even when you're not actively using the program. This basically means that they flag you with a sound or text alert when someone does something like post a comment on your Facebook wall. You might also see a *badge* alert notification—a number in a little red circle on an app's icon.

Push notifications can help keep you up-to-date, but all that notifying can run down your iPad's battery—the slab has to constantly sniff the airways for notices. The notifications you get depend on the app, but to trigger them, tap Settings→Notifications→On, then tap the name of the application, and then choose how you want it to notify you, usually by Sound, Alert, or Badge.

Location Services

Tap Location Services to On if you want the iPad to pinpoint your position on a map or supply information about where you are to certain location-aware applications (like restaurant finders). Tap it to Off if you don't want to be found—or want to save some battery power (Location Services communicates with GPS satellites, cell towers, and WiFi hotspots).

Cellular Data (Wi-Fi + 3G iPads Only)

With a Wi-Fi + 3G iPad, you can get on the Internet using a wireless network (WiFi), just as WiFi iPad owners can. But you can also tap into the Web via Verizon or AT&T's 3G data network. Which one you use depends on which iPad you bought—a Verizon or AT&T model.

New owners of AT&T 3G iPads can choose from two plans. The cheapest one provides 250 megabytes of data for $15 a month. The other plan offers 2 gigabytes for $25 a month. (If you're an original 3G iPad owner, you can still hang on to your original unlimited-data-for-$30-a-month plan.) Verizon has four monthly allowances: 1GB for $20, 3GB for $35, 5GB for $50, or 10GB for $80.

You can find other options at Settings→Cellular, too. You can turn the 3G network off to save battery life. To see how much data you've used, upgrade your plan, add an international plan, or edit your payment information, tap the View Account button. If you're on a foreign trip, you can turn off Data Roaming so your iPad's not grabbing data over pricey international networks. AT&T iPad owners can add a PIN code to lock down the tablet's micro-SIM card so others can't use your tablet; just tap SIM PIN and pick a number. (Verizon iPads don't use SIM cards, so they lack this feature.)

Brightness & Wallpaper

You really get no surprises here. Tapping Settings→Brightness & Wallpaper takes you to where you can a.) use a virtual slider to make the screen dimmer or brighter so it's more comfortable on your eyes, and b.) select a new image to appear as the background wallpaper for both your iPad's Lock Screen (the one you see when you wake the iPad from sleep but before you swipe the Unlock slider) and its Home screen (the screen where all your apps live).

Tap the Wallpaper label here to select new background images from either Apple's stock shots or from a photo collection you added to the tablet (see Chapter 15 to learn how to do that). Tap a thumbnail photo to preview it, and then tap the button of your choice: Set Lock Screen, Set Home Screen, Set Both, or Cancel.

Picture Frame

The iPad's built-in Picture Frame feature (page 267) lets you show off your photo collection when you're not using the tablet for other things. Tap Settings→Picture Frame to tell the iPad how to play the slideshow. You can choose the type of transition between images (the standard Dissolve or the fancier, animated Origami), whether you want the Picture Frame to zoom in on people's faces, and if you want the iPad to shuffle your photos (randomly display them). Finally, you can pick which photos you want to appear. (Hint: It might be a good idea to leave those Las Vegas bachelorette party photos out if you know your mother is coming over for tea this afternoon.) To set up a regular photo-album slideshow, see page 262.

General

The collection of settings under "General" mostly affects the way the iPad itself works. When you tap Settings→General, you see a whole screen full of menus that change the way the iPad behaves. These include:

- **About.** Tap here to see your iPad's vital statistics: its total drive capacity, amount of storage available, system software version, model number, WiFi and Bluetooth network addresses, and serial number. You can also see how many songs, videos, photos, and apps live on your iPad. And as a special bonus for the extremely bored or insomnia-afflicted, you can read Apple's legal and regulatory information, too.

- **Usage.** Check here to see how much of the battery you've drained—or how much of your monthly 3G data plan you've gobbled up so far.

- **Sounds.** Tap Sounds to adjust the iPad's audio level with a volume slider. You can also turn Off (or On) alert sounds for new mail, sent mail, calendar events, lock sounds, and the tap-tap-tappy keyboard click.

- **Network.** This is where you tap to see what WiFi network you're currently connected to—or to pick a new one. If your office has given you a connection to its *virtual private network* (VPN) for a more safe and secure link to the Internet, tap VPN. Here, you can turn on the iPad's VPN function and configure your connection based on information you get from the corporate IT folks.

- **Bluetooth.** To pair up a Bluetooth keyboard (page 31) or headset (page 5), tap Bluetooth to On. Then follow the instructions that came with the keyboard or headset to wirelessly connect it to the iPad.

- **Spotlight Search.** Choose what types of files show up—contacts, apps, music, mail, and so on—when you use your iPad's uber search engine, Spotlight (page 30). Use the grip strip (≡) to reorder the categories so the most important ones show up first in the search results.

- **Auto-Lock.** Tap this setting to adjust how long your iPad screen stays on before it turns itself off (and displays the Lock Screen when you wake it up). You can choose 2, 5, 10, or 15 minutes—or Never.

- **Passcode Lock.** If you have sensitive information on your iPad (or just want to keep the kids out), tap Passcode Lock. On the next screen, tap Turn Passcode On. Think up a four-digit number and verify it. To get by the iPad's Lock Screen now, you must type in this code. If you have really sensitive data on your iPad, tap Settings→ General→Passcode Lock→Erase Data to completely wipe all the information off of the iPad's drive if someone incorrectly enters the passcode more than 10 times. Just make sure you have that top secret info securely tucked away on another computer in a full set of back-up files, since it won't be on the iPad anymore.

- **iPad Cover Lock/Unlock**. If you have one of Apple's fancy Smart Covers (page 296) for your iPad 2, you can flip this switch to On and have the tablet automatically lock up and go to sleep when you close the cover.

- **Restrictions.** Speaking of the kids, tap Settings→General→Restrictions→ Enable Restrictions to set up usage rules for the iPad; you need to set up a Passcode Lock for this feature. Once you do, you can block the kiddies from using iTunes, Safari, and YouTube. (The iPad removes the screen icons for these apps until the passcode is entered.) You can also set limits on installing apps or mapping the kids' whereabouts via Location Services. And you can restrict the type of content they can play on the iPad—like, say, *no* music with Explicit lyrics.

- **Use Side Switch.** Assign your preferred function to the iPad's side switch here: either make it a mute button or use it to quickly lock the tablet's screen orientation so it doesn't spin all over the place when you move.

- **Date & Time.** Tap here to switch between the 12-hour (AM/PM) clock or the military-style 24-hour clock. Frequent travelers can also pick a time zone and manually set the iPad's date and time.

- **Keyboard.** Within the Keyboard settings area, you can turn on (or off) the Auto-Correction and Auto-Capitalization features that fix your typing, activate the spell-checker, and turn on the Enable Caps Lock feature. You also go here to turn on the so-called *". " shortcut* that sticks a period at the end of a sentence, adds a space, and then capitalizes the next letter when you double-tap the keyboard's space bar. Speaking of keyboards, tap International keyboards here to select and add an alternate keyboard in another language, like French or German.

- **International.** World travelers can easily set the language the iPad uses for its menus and commands by tapping Settings→General→International→Language. Tap Settings→General→International to turn on international keyboards (see "Keyboard" above) and format dates, times, and phone numbers based on the standards of a particular country.

- **Accessibility.** Apple builds a number of features into the iPad that make it easier to use for those with visual impairments. Choose Settings→General→Accessibility, to turn on the VoiceOver feature that announces menu names and titles out loud. (VoiceOver requires a bit of setup and offers many special gestures that you can use to operate the iPad; for more

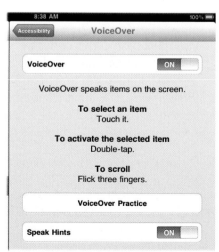

information, tap Home→Safari and go to *help.apple.com/ipad/mobile/ interface* , and then tap Accessibility for in-depth instruction on using this extensive feature.)

The iPad's built-in accessibility settings also include Zoom, for major magnification by double-tapping with three fingers (although, according to Apple, you can't use it at the same time as the VoiceOver function). For easier reading, tap the high-contrast White on Black function that reverses the screen colors. You can also switch the iPad's audio output from stereo to Mono Audio to let those with hearing impairments hear the entire sound signal at once instead of split into two channels. If you want the iPad's auto-correction function to shout out the typos it's fixing while you're busy looking at the keyboard, choose Settings→General→ Accessibility→Speak Auto-Text→On. And you can set the Home button to toggle on or off VoiceOver or the white-on-black screen with a triple-click.

- **Reset.** Tap here to get to all the buttons for blanking out the iPad's memory. You can reset all its settings or just the network settings, reset the dictionary that corrects your typing, revert to the Home screen's original layout, and resume getting those little warnings about using your location settings after you've given programs like Maps permission to use them. If you want to erase everything off the iPad, choose Settings→General→Reset→"Erase All Content and Settings." But remember, you're nuking *everything*—info, music, videos, photos, and iBooks.

Mail, Contacts, Calendars

Settings for the Mail app hog much of the screen when you tap Settings→Mail, Contacts, Calendars. Still, you're probably going to adjust your mail settings more often than your contacts or calendar settings.

For example, you come here to add new email accounts (or delete them), tell your iPad how often to fetch new messages, and change the look of the mail program in general. You can choose the number of messages from your accounts you want to see in the iPad's Inbox (25 to 200 recent messages at a time) and have the inbox preview more or less of a message (one to five lines, or none at all).

You can change the font size to squint less, choose a default mail account if you have more than one, and change your Signature file—the standard bit of text that gets attached to the end of every outgoing message. You can also make the iPad ask you each time you want to delete messages, show (or hide) images in email, and show the To/Cc label to see if a message was addressed directly to you. Want to send a secret copy of a message to yourself? Turn on the Always Bcc Myself setting.

In the Contacts area, specify which way you want the iPad to sort and display people's names—last name *first* and first name *last*, or the first name and then the last name. In the Calendars area, turn on your New Invitation Alert to have your iPad pipe up when someone sends you a meeting invitation, and also select a time zone for your calendar (useful if you live in New York but telecommute to the main office in San Francisco). Finally, you can pick a default calendar for your appointments if you have multiple calendars synced to the iPad.

Safari

The Settings area for the iPad's Safari browser has many helpful buttons. Here, you can choose if you want your search results to come from Google, Bing, or Yahoo, and opt to have the Autofill feature fill in information automatically in web forms. Want to see your Bookmarks Bar at all times in the Safari window? Tap Settings→Safari→Always Show Bookmarks Bar→On to make it so. In the Security area of the Safari settings, you can help protect yourself when web surfing by turning on the Fraud Warning (which spots certain phishing sites out to rip off your personal information),

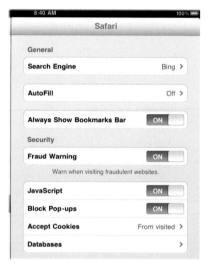

enabling or disabling the JavaScript-powered interactive features some websites use (if you're worried about security), blocking pop-up ads, and rejecting cookies from sites you don't personally visit.

Tap Databases to see content Safari stores locally on your iPad (like files from Apple's online iPad help guide). If Safari is acting sluggish or you want to erase your tracks, tap the buttons to clear the browser's history, cookies, and cache files. Are you a web developer who wants to know why your web page is acting wiggy on iPad Safari? Tap Settings→Safari→Developer→Debug Console→On to get some help deciphering those page errors.

iPod

The iPod settings on the iPad include just four options. You can turn on the Sound Check feature, which smooths out the variable song volumes in a playlist into one fairly consistent sound level. Tap EQ to pick a preferred equalizer preset to make your music sound better. If you worry about hearing loss or damage from headphones full of loud music, tap Volume Limit to On and set a maximum audio level. And if you don't want to see song lyrics or podcast info on-screen when listening to the iPad's iPod, choose Settings→iPod→Lyrics & Podcast Info→Off. And you can turn the Home Sharing feature (page 198) on or off here, too.

Video

In the Video settings, you can opt to have the iPad bookmark the spot in a movie or TV show where you stop it so you can pick right up again when you come back to it. Just tap Settings→Videos→Start Playing→Where Left Off; you can also choose From Beginning if you want to always start the whole thing over again. If you have videos with Closed Captioning text descriptions embedded in the files, you can flip the Closed Captioning control On or Off. And when you're funneling movies and TV shows off the iPad and onto the TV screen (page 246), you can flip the Widescreen button On to make sure the picture retains its original aspect ratio. Using the iPad with a TV in another country? Choose the TV Signal standard here: NTSC or PAL (page 247).

Photos

The iPad keeps a few settings for photo slideshows at Settings→Photos. You can choose the amount of time each picture stays on-screen, Repeat the slide-show over and over again automatically, and decide if you want to Shuffle the pictures into a different order from how they appear in your photo album.

FaceTime

Flip the On switch here to enable your iPad to make and take FaceTime video calls. You can also set up your preferred email address for use with FaceTime.

Notes

Hate the font the Notes app uses? Change between Noteworthy, Helvetica, and Marker Felt. You can also choose an email account to sync with Notes.

Store

Tap the Store icon in the Settings list, then tap the View Account button if you need to see your address and billing information for the iTunes Store or App Store. You can also sign out of your account by tapping the Sign Out button.

App Preferences

Different apps may have application-specific settings as well. The iPad lists the ones that do under Apps in the Settings column. For example, you can change what the iBooks app does when you tap the left margin of the screen—you can go to the previous page or onward to the next page. Each app has differ-ent settings—and some don't have any settings at all—but it's worth a tap of the Settings icon to see what you can adjust.

iPad Troubleshooting and Care

Like most electronic gadgets, the iPad always works perfectly fine—until it doesn't. Many iPad woes are common and pretty easy to fix—the battery ran all the way down and needs to charge up a bit before iTunes will recognize your iPad, or the rotation lock is still on and that's why the screen won't reorient itself. Less obvious glitches in the iPad's behavior can be solved by adjusting something in the Settings area, as explained in Appendix A.

But the iPad is a little mini-computer in its own right, and it can exhibit bigger problems that require more than flipping a setting—and may even need the help of a technical expert. Figuring out what your iPad is trying to tell you when it's sick is the first step in getting it back to good health. This chapter explains what to do if your iPad starts acting weird—and where to go if you need more information or can't fix it yourself.

Apple's iPad Troubleshooting Pages

You can find many solutions to iPad issues through the Web, but if you can't put this book down to go running off to search the Web, here are some common tricks to try if your iPad starts acting up. (For in-depth advice on a variety of iPad ailments, Apple offers a detailed set of troubleshooting documents at *www.apple.com/support/ipad*. This support site also addresses issues with iTunes and syncing content to and from your iPad.)

- **Restart the iPad.** Like a computer that's behaving badly, sometimes restarting your iPad clears up a cranky or stalled system. To restart the tablet, hold down the Sleep/Wake (On/Off) button on the top of the slab until the red "Slide to Power Off" bar appears. Swipe your finger to shut things down. Then press the Sleep/Wake button again until the Apple logo appears on-screen and the iPad starts up again.

- **Force quit a frozen app.** Apps are programs, too, and sometimes software gets stuck (just ask anyone who's used a computer for more than a month). To make a cranky app shut down without having to restart the whole iPad, press and hold the Sleep/Wake button until you see the red "power-off" slider—but don't slide this time. Instead, press and hold the Home button down until the app quits and you find yourself back on the Home screen.

- **Reset an app's settings.** Sometimes an app's custom settings get scrambled, so tap the Settings icon on the iPad's Home screen and check to see if the app has its own entry; tap whatever button is there to reset the app's settings. Page 128 has more on troubleshooting apps.

- **Reset the iPad.** A reset is a bit more abrupt than a restart, but it can free up a completely frozen tablet. The next page tells you how to execute one (a reset, not a frozen tablet).

- **Reset the iPad's settings.** If you're having problems even after you fiddle with an app's settings, you can reset the iPad's settings (not the iPad itself; that's covered next). Choose Settings→General→Reset. The Reset screen lets you wipe your custom configurations (like your network info) and take the iPad back to its factory settings.

- **Check the battery level.** If it's in the red, plug in the iPad to recharge it. iTunes won't download files (like bug fixes) if your iPad is low on batteries.

Reset Your iPad

Restarting your iPad (turning it completely off and back on again) can solve many problems, but what do you do if the iPad doesn't respond to your gentle touch? If you can't even restart your 'Pad, you can physically *reset* it without losing your files. (Resetting is the troubleshooting step Apple recommends if restarting doesn't work; it reboots the tablet if it's too flummoxed to respond to a normal restart.)

To give your iPad the old reset move, follow the steps below:

❶ Plug the iPad into its wall charger if you suspect its battery is running low.

❷ Simultaneously press and hold down the Sleep/Wake button on top and the Home button on the front. Let go when you see the Apple logo. You can hold it up or lay it flat on the table to reset it, as long as you hit the buttons properly.

If the technology gods are smiling on you, your iPad will go through its little start-up sequence and then return you to the main menu.

Download and Reinstall iTunes and iTunes Updates

If iTunes is acting up, you may need to download and install a fresh version of the program. The latest version is always waiting at *www.apple.com/itunes/download*. Your iTunes program itself may also alert you to a new version—or you can make sure it does so in the future:

- If you use iTunes for Windows and installed the Apple Software Update utility when you added iTunes, an alert box appears telling you Apple updated iTunes and offering to install it for you. If you skipped installing the utility, choose Edit→Preferences→General and turn on "Check for updates automatically." If you prefer to check manually, choose Help→"Check for Updates." In either case, you're prompted to snag an update if one's available.

- On the Mac, a built-in Software Update program is designed to alert you, via a pop-up dialog box, about new updates for iTunes. If you turned Software Update off (in System Preferences), you can run it manually by choosing Software Update from the Apple menu ().

Note If you tried reinstalling iTunes to no avail, fully uninstall the old copy first to clear up any lingering problems. One way to do this on a PC is to choose Start→Control Panel→Add/Remove Programs (or choose Start→Control Panel and select "Uninstall a program"). Find iTunes in the list and click the button to uninstall it.

On a Mac OS X system, choose Go→Applications and drag the iTunes application icon to the Trash. Then choose Go→Utilities→Activity Monitor (or go to the Mac's Applications folder and open the Utilities folder to find the Activity Monitor). Find iTunes Helper in the list and click the big red Quit Process button at the top of the window. Finally, choose →System Preferences→Accounts→Login Items. Select iTunes Helper in the list and click the minus button (-) to remove it. Then restart the Mac. Apple has more detailed instructions at *support.apple.com/kb/ht1224*.

As with any software update, once you download the file, double-click the installer file's icon and follow along as the program takes you through several screens of upgrade excitement. If the version of iTunes you're installing is newer than the one you've got, you get "Upgrade" as a button option when you run the installer—and upgrading usually takes less time than uninstalling and reinstalling the media manager.

If you're installing the *same* version of iTunes, the installer may politely ask if you want to *Repair* or even *Remove* the software. Choosing Repair can often fix damaged files that iTunes needs to run properly. It can also be a quicker fix than fully removing the program and reinstalling it again. (See the Note on the opposite page for another uninstall method.)

Reinstalling iTunes doesn't erase all of your music, movies, books, or other items out of your iTunes library. It just gives you a new and hopefully better-working version of the iTunes software.

If you open the reinstalled iTunes to an empty library, don't panic. Quit iTunes and go find the iTunes folder, usually in My Documents→My Music→iTunes or Music→iTunes. Drag the iTunes library file from the iTunes folder onto the computer's desktop. Then go back to the iTunes folder, open the Previous iTunes libraries folder and find the iTunes library file stamped with the date you updated the program. Drag this file out into the main iTunes folder and rename it to just iTunes Library without the date in the file name. Now start up iTunes again and see if everything is all better. If not, take a trip to *www.apple. com/support/itunes* for further help.

Update the iPad's Software

Updating the iPad's internal software—which Apple occasionally does to fix bugs and add features—is much easier than it used to be, thanks to iTunes. No matter which iPad, iPhone, or iPod model you have, iTunes 9 and later handles all software updating chores for you. (Updating gets easier in the Fall of 2011, when the new iOS 5 software lets you wirelessly update your iPad—no computer necessary.)

To make sure you have the latest version of the iPad software, follow these steps:

❶ Connect your iPad to the computer and select it in the Source list.

❷ On the Summary tab, click the "Check for Update" button in the Version area (circled below). If your iPad is up to date, iTunes tells you so.

❸ If iTunes finds new iPad software, it prompts you to download it. Click the Downloading icon in the Source pane to monitor your download progress. Sometimes iTunes will have already downloaded the new iPad software. In that case, just click the Update button in iTunes' main window.

❹ Follow the instructions on-screen.

You mainly just have to sit there while iTunes handles everything. The iPad usually hangs out quietly, displaying a progress bar and an Apple logo on its screen while it's getting its new system software. Once all that goes away, your iPad screen returns to normal and iTunes displays a message letting you know the update is complete.

 Thinking about passing off your old iPad to a relative after you bought a new one, or selling your tablet so you can put the money toward buying the latest and greatest model? Before you send that old model on its way, you may want to make sure the software is fully updated so your recipient has the latest version. You should also wipe all your content off the old iPad, for personal safety's sake more than anything. While restoring the software (page 294) removes your data from view, it may still be lurking deep down, so tap Home→Settings→General→Reset→"Erase All Content and Settings" on the iPad to be sure.

Use iPad Backup Files

You may not notice it at the time, but iTunes creates backup files of your iPad's settings and other system information when you sync the tablet to the computer. It also creates backups when you do more serious stuff, like update or restore the iPad's system software (page 294). Now, you may be thinking, "Cool! I don't have to worry if I accidentally destroy my iPad because I can copy all its content onto a replacement!" This, however, is not the case.

That's because iTunes only backs up data from apps, system settings, and that sort of stuff—not your entire music and video collection, nor your contacts and calendars, nor your actual photos, nor your apps. Apple assumes you have all those files on your computer, from syncing the iPad with iTunes to copy files and programs back and forth.

When you restore an iPad from its backup file, though, it remembers your syncing *settings*, so you just have to let iTunes resync all the content to your iPad during the process. That also means you should connect the iPad to iTunes every once in a while so it can sync up and have a record (back-up) of what you currently have on your iPad.

To restore an iPad from its backup file:

❶ Connect the iPad to the computer you usually sync it with and right-click (Control-click) its icon in the iTunes source list.

❷ From the pop-up menu, choose "Restore from Backup." In the box that appears, choose the backup file you want to use (if you sync more than one iPad to this computer; iTunes sorts the backups by date and device name).

❸ Click the Restore button and let iTunes do its thing.

When iTunes is done, your iPad should look pretty much like it did the last time you backed it up.

> **Tip** If you're worried about security, you can encrypt your iPad backups with a password. Click the iPad's icon in iTunes, click the Summary tab, and then turn on the checkbox next to "Encrypt iPad backup." Enter a password—the same password you'll need to complete step 3 above.

Start Over: Restore Your iPad's Software

Just as an operating system runs your desktop computer, so your iPad has its own software that controls everything it does. *Restoring* the iPad software isn't the same thing as updating it. Restoring is a much more drastic procedure, like reformatting the hard drive on your PC or Mac. For one thing, restoring *erases everything on your iPad*, including your operating system.

So, restore with caution, and do so only if you try all the other troubleshooting measures in this chapter. If you decide to take the plunge, first make sure you have the most recent version of iTunes (flip back to page 290 for information on that), then proceed as follows:

❶ Start iTunes, and connect your iPad to your computer with its cable.

❷ When the iPad appears in the iTunes Source list, click its icon to see the Summary information (in the main area of the iTunes window).

❸ In the Summary area, click the Restore button.

 Note Now, just because you've sucked the life out of your iPad doesn't mean that all your songs, videos, and so on are gone from iTunes. That's the beauty of the iPad-iTunes partnership: By storing everything in iTunes, you can always re-load it onto your iPad, as described on the next page.

❹ As mentioned back on page 293, iTunes backs up your iPad's settings—things like your preferences for contacts and calendar syncing, along with other personalized data. This means much less work getting your iPad all re-personalized after you reinstall its software.

But if you want to wipe every trace of your existence from the iPad, skip the backup.

❺ Because restoring erases everything on your iPad, you get a warning message. If you're sure you want to continue, click Restore again.

❻ If you use a Mac, enter an administrator password; a progress bar appears on your iPad's screen. Leave the iPad connected to your computer to complete the restoration process. You may also see an Apple logo appear on-screen.

After iTunes finishes the restore process, its Setup Assistant window appears asking you to name your iPad and choose your syncing preferences—just like it did when you connected your iPad for the first time. Let the iPad automatically update your files, or add your songs, photos, and videos back manually, and then see if this little procedure fixed the tablet's predicament.

Protect Your iPad

The iPad was meant to be held—held up for others to see, held on your lap, held under your arm as you walk down the hall, and so on. But with *holding* sometimes comes *dropping* (and with *that,* cursing), so protecting your iPad with a case or cover might help cushion its fall. Cases and covers also protect the surface of the tablet, (especially that glossy screen) when it's riding around in a purse or backpack.

In addition to protecting the iPad, adding a case, from a hot-pink zippered number to a stately leather portfolio, shows off a bit of your own personality. Here are a few of the many places to find the latest in geek chic for your iPad:

- **Apple Store.** The company that makes the iPad also makes sure you have plenty of other stuff to buy to go with it, including cases, covers, docks, keyboards, headphones, and more. One iPad protector that Apple is particularly proud of is the Smart Cover for the second generation iPad (shown below), which magnetically clamps to the tablet's edge, can serve as a easel for upright viewing, and even turns the iPad on or off when you open or close the flap. If there's no brick-and-mortar Apple Store in your town, visit the online emporium at *store.apple.com*.

- **Belkin.** After years of making computer and mobile accessories, Belkin has added about a dozen different iPad cases to its product line. Prices range from $30 to $60; the $60 Leather Folio case is shown here. (*www.belkin.com*)

- **Griffin Technology.** A long-time maker of iPod and iPhone accessories, Griffin has jumped right in with iPad gear as well. Several iPad case styles are available here (prices range from $30 to $50) as is the $25 Screen Care Kit for iPad, which includes a low-glare stick-on screen protector and a cleaning cloth. (*www.griffintechnology.com*)

Find a Lost iPad

It can be your worst iPad-related nightmare: Your beloved tablet goes missing. Lost and stolen gadgets are a problem, but Apple offers a handy tracking app that just may help you get your tablet back—by revealing its location on a map. Although the app is called Find My iPhone, it works to pinpoint the location of all iOS devices, iPads and iPod Touches included.

If you skipped installing the Find My iPhone app when you set up your new iPad, here's how to find your iPad using iOS 4.2 and later:

❶ Download the Find My iPhone app from the App Store (page 116).

❷ Create a free MobileMe account. On the iPad's Home screen, tap Settings→Mail, Contacts, Calenders. Under the Add Accounts area, tap Add Account and on the next screen, tap MobileMe. Type in your Apple ID user name and password to create the MobileMe account. Apple sends a message to the email account linked to your Apple ID to verify your request. If you already have a MobileMe account, just tap Settings→Mail, Contacts, Calenders→MobileMe to get to the settings box; Find My iPad is down toward the bottom.

❸ After you verify your account, go back to Settings→Mail, Contacts, Calenders and tap on your new MobileMe account. Next to Find My iPad, tap the button to On. In the permission box that appears, tap Allow.

❹ Tap Home→Settings→General→Location Services→On. This lets the app pinpoint your iPad's whereabouts on a map.

❺ To find your iPad, log into MobileMe (*www.me.com*) with your Apple ID and click the Find My iPhone link. In addition to a map, a box pops up with the option to send a message to display on the iPad's screen while it makes an alarm sound, like a request for its return and your phone number. If you have sensitive information on the tablet, you can also lock it remotely—or wipe its contents entirely. But hopefully, it won't come to that and your lost iPad will come home safely.

Find an iPad Repair Shop

Under its thin, glossy exterior, the iPad is a still a computer, and computers have been known to have technical difficulties. If your iPad begins to have problems—screen fritzing, battery failure, or other unexplained hardware woes, you have some options:

- If you live near an Apple Store (there are 300 of them worldwide; find them at *http://www.apple.com/retail*), call it up and make an appointment at the Genius Bar to have your iPad looked at by an Apple pro. If the iPad is still under warranty, the fix is usually free.

- If there's no Apple Store around, look for a nearby Apple-approved repair shop by searching *http://www.apple.com/buy/locator/service*.

- If there's no reliable repair shop physically nearby, you can try one of the various mail-order repair companies that specialize in Apple products. A quick web search brings up a list of possibilities, but be sure to read the reviews and do some background research on the company to make sure it does good, legitimate work. Sites like iResQ (*www.iresq.com*) and Milliamp (*www.ipadrepair.com*) are two of the better-known online shops. While you may have to wait longer for the fix, the out-of-warranty repair bill often tends to be cheaper.

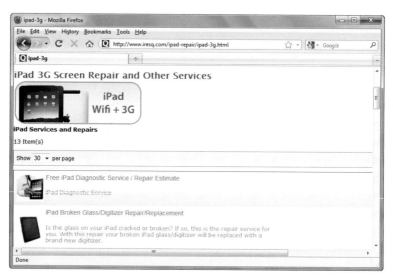

 Tip If your old out-of-warranty iPad needs basic help, like a battery replacement, you might even be able to do it yourself for much less than what a repair shop would charge. Check out iFixit (*www.ifixit.com*), a cheerful site dedicated to DIY gadget repair, for illustrated instructions on a variety of iPad issues.

AppleCare—What It Is and Whether You Need It

You probably have an insurance policy on your house and car, so why not get one for your iPad? That's the logic behind getting the AppleCare Protection Plan for your iPad. The price for this peace of mind? Why, that'd be $79.

When you buy a brand-new iPad, you automatically get free telephone support to fix one problem within your first 90 days of iPad ownership, plus a year-long warranty on the hardware. If your iPad starts acting weird or stops working altogether during this time, Apple will fix it for free or send you a replacement tablet.

If you buy the AppleCare Protection Plan (available in many places where you buy iPads or at *www.apple.com/support/products/ipad.html*), you get:

- Two full years of free telephone support from the date of your iPad purchase

- Two full years of hardware protection from the date of your iPad purchase.

If you need a repair or replacement, your iPad is covered, and so are your tablet's battery and cables. Paying an extra $80 to get the extended warranty may not appeal to everyone, but if you want a little peace of mind with your new iPad, it's a small price to pay, especially if you want to just relax and have fun with your tablet.

> **Tip** Have more questions about the AppleCare plan? Apple has a Frequently Asked Questions page on the topic at *www.apple.com/support/products/faqs.html*. As noted above, you get a full year of limited warranty on the iPad's hardware in case anything goes wrong with it—aside from user-inflicted damage. You can buy AppleCare any time within a year of your iPad purchase date to extend the warranty. So if you don't feel like popping that extra $80 when you buy your iPad, wait and pony up for AppleCare toward the end of the first year—perhaps after you've paid off the credit card with the original iPad charge on it.

Index

Y

Z